Sick as a Parrot

The Inside Story of the Spurs Fiasco

Chris Horrie

To my parents

First published in Great Britain in 1992 by
Virgin Books
an imprint of Virgin Publishing Ltd
338 Ladbroke Grove
London W10 5AH

A catalogue record for this title is available from the
British Library

ISBN 0 86369 620 1

Typeset by Type Out, Streatham, SW16 1LB

Printed and bound in Great Britain by Cox & Wyman Ltd,
Reading, Berks.

CONTENTS

ACKNOWLEDGEMENTS

During my research for this book I sought to interview the current board and management of Tottenham Hotspur PLC and the associated football club. I was directed by the club to a public relations company used by both Mr Alan Sugar and the PLC. After a meeting with an executive of the company I was denied any further official assistance from anyone associated with the club.

This reaction was not entirely surprising. As part of the money-grubbing atmosphere that now surrounds every aspect of British football, the repeated question was: 'What's in it for us?' The logic, expressed to me more than once, was that the club could not see any immediate profit in the venture. The idea that thousands of Tottenham fans, the people who support Spurs financially to an extra-ordinary extent, had a right to the fullest explanation of the events that brought their club to the brink of extinction, was met with blank incomprehension.

Thanks are due to the many people associated with the club, both now and in the past, and several other journalists, who agreed to speak to me on a strictly non-attributable basis.

I would also like to thank Morris 'Mo' Keston, Jeff Randall, Harry Harris, Tristan Cork, Paul Springthorpe, Bart Milner, Paul Charman, Alex Sutherland, Roy Ackerman, Bernie Kingsley, Steve Davies and Stuart Mutler, editor of *The Spur* fanzine. Paul Lindsell did much of the basic research. My thanks also go to my agent Mark Lucas and editor Guy Lloyd for their encouragement and guidance, and to my wife Clare for her patience and support.

PREFACE

In the dilapidated world of English soccer, the bargain basement of Europe, Tottenham Hotspur was the club that had everything. Already a national institution, in the 1980s the club was the first to get a Stock Exchange listing, bringing it millions in extra finance; it redeveloped its stadium into a shining monument of plate glass and steel; and was the first to sell tickets over the phone by credit card. With the help of Saatchi and Saatchi, it became the first to advertise for supporters on TV.

By the middle of the decade Tottenham had a healthy bank balance and Terry 'El Tel' Venables, hyped as 'Europe's biggest soccer brain', as team manager. Spurs then acquired Waddle, Lineker and Gazza, for many the three greatest English soccer talents of their generation, and were poised to win every trophy going. But just a few short years later 'Tottering Hotspur' was the laughing stock of European soccer. The club was effectively bankrupt and lived from day to day.

The Midland Bank, at one point owed more than £10 million, could have closed the club down at a moment's notice. Few doubt this is what would have happened if the Listening Bank, which had its own financial problems, had not feared the PR consequences of closing down a much-loved national institution. People said it would have been easier to close down the Republic of Mexico, which also owed the Midland rather a lot of money, than to pull the plug on the Lillywhites.

At the same time, board members were at each other's throats. Their dreams of huge new profits from merchandising and corporate entertainment had evaporated. The trophy cupboard was empty; Waddle and Gascoigne were quickly sold and Lineker was soon to follow.

In 1991 Tottenham won the FA Cup. But in the following season the lads finished fifteenth in the League – the worst performance since rejoining Division One fifteen years previously. How could it have happened?

The fans, outraged and bewildered by these events, organised demonstrations and an attempted shareholders' revolt, based on a simple demand to know what was going on. They did much to prevent the club falling into the clutches of Robert Maxwell and into the problems created by the collapse of his financial empire a few months later. Instead, they delivered it into the hands of an improbable alliance of financiers led by Venables and Alan Sugar. A huge new injection of cash eased the immediate problems, but the future still looked far from certain.

In the course of writing this book I was constantly surprised by the way in which this small company, with a turnover of less than £30 million, had been placed at the centre of a whirlwind where billions were at stake. All the financial fads of the roaring 1980s swirled around the club: property and share dealing, aggressive mergers and acquisitions, debt financing, public relations, merchandising, tabloid circulation wars, the leisure and heritage industries, boardroom wrangling, satellite TV and £300 million television rights deals.

The more I looked into the story, the more I found myself at the centre of an extraordinary web of events. One thread led into the collapse of the Blue Arrow empire which, in turn, was on the fringes of the series of financial scandals that did so much damage to the City in the 1980s. Another turn led to the story of Robert Maxwell, bizarre enough in its own right; yet another to the bitter fight between TV stations for viewers and advertisers.

Outside the world of business I naturally found Tottenham Hotspur was a highly emotive subject for everyone directly involved, from fans and ex-players to members of the board. Many of the people I met were genuinely hurt by the scandals. It was as though there had been a personal assault on a member of the family. To some the idea that their beloved Spurs might have ceased to exist was absolutely unimaginable, a fate worse than death. It is partly a tribute to these people's loyalty that this did not happen. And it is for them that I wrote this book.

Chris Horrie
London, April 1992

PART
ONE

1: THE CURSE OF THE LEMON-COLOURED FOOTBALL BOOT

According to legend the story of Tottenham Hotspur began when a group of teenage boys met on a north London street one cold winter's evening in 1882. The lads were members of a grammar school cricket team, keen to try their luck at association football, the new and more proletarian sports craze which was sweeping the country.

From the start the club gained a reputation for stinginess. To save on the cost of hiring a room, the club committee met under a gas lamp in Tottenham High Street. The team made their own goal posts, erected on the swampy Hackney Marshes, and in an early example of the arguments with the football authorities that were to play such an important part in the club's story a century later, the committee complained when it was forced to use approved footballs instead of making its own.

The move to White Hart Lane, originally called Gilpin Park, was typically tight-fisted. The club hired the ground, which had no stands or facilities, from a brewery for a peppercorn rent. In return the club guaranteed to attract at least a thousand spectators every week, to provide custom for the nearby White Hart Inn. The pub, where Jimmy Greaves nearly drank himself to death in the late 1960s, still stands near the entrance to the Spurs' modern stadium. Gate receipts for the first match played at White Hart Lane, a friendly match against Notts County, were £155.

Tottenham joined the second division of the national Football League seventeen years later, and were promoted to the first division at the first attempt. Tottenham,

1

playing in the famous white shirts and dark blue shorts, and by now known as the Spurs or the Lillywhites, were thus nicely placed to ride the rising tide of football's popularity. Apart from Orient (soon to be sidelined as denizens of the lower divisions) Spurs dominated the market for League football in the sprawling suburbs of north and east London.

In the years leading up to the First World War Tottenham's average gate shot up by as much as 10,000 per season. The weekly sea of Edwardian flat caps and handlebar moustaches made the club highly profitable, allowing it to lash out on the transfer market. Frederick 'Fanny' Walden, a winger, was bought from Northampton Town for the record fee of £1,700.

The first real financial challenge for Tottenham came in 1913 when Woolwich Arsenal, backed by rich patrons, moved from the obscurity of south London to a new ground at Highbury, three miles to the west of Tottenham. Served by its own station on the new tube-train network, it was correctly calculated that Arsenal would break Tottenham's monopoly and attract the new generation of supporters.

After the war there was another blow when the League was reorganised by its Management Committee. Tottenham were relegated to Divison Two and Arsenal took their place in the first. The whole episode seemed to be marked by fate and an apocryphal story grew up that a pet parrot, given to the club during a tour of Brazil in 1909, became ill and died soon afterwards.

The Tottenham management and players had every right to feel as sick as their parrot. Arsenal had elbowed them out of the way by using naked political influence and, it was said, straightforward bribery. Although Tottenham were promoted back into the first division after one season, the north London monopoly which would have made them potentially the best-supported club in the country was broken for good. After that, Spurs were destined to live in the shadow of Arsenal, their richer and better-supported neighbour.

2

Arsenal's success was built on lavish investment by the club's board of directors who not only bought players but built a huge new stadium at the same time. The brains behind the operation was Herbert Chapman, the team manager lured from Huddersfield. Chapman had started off as a Tottenham player, where he was chiefly remembered for wearing luminous lemon-coloured football boots, the first of his many innovations, before moving into management.

The boots did not catch on at the time, but Chapman was a visionary always well ahead of his time; his other sartorial invention, putting numbers on football shirts, was much more successful and caught on at once. Chapman also guided the redevelopment of Highbury into the best football stadium in Europe at the time. Two huge stands facing each other on the east and west sides of the ground were built by Claude Waterlow Ferrier, the architect. The east stand was particularly splendid, complete with a vast, echoing marble entrance hall for the directors, with offices and flats served by the modern wonder of an electric lift. But he had to wait twenty years before the authorities accepted his idea of floodlit football, first demonstrated at Arsenal in 1932. Like the boots, Chapman's idea of putting a movable roof over the pitch, creating an indoor arena, had yet to come to pass.

The success Chapman had brought on the field, and the ground he had built to lure spectators, as they were then called, away from Tottenham soon paid off. Arsenal regularly attracted a highly profitable 60,000 or more to every home match. When Chapman died in 1934 the grateful directors erected a gleaming bronze bust in the marble entrance hall.

Tottenham could only look on with envy. Compared with Arsenal's success, all they had to show since joining the League was one FA Cup win in 1921, and one Division Two championship win. The team attracted only half the number of Arsenal's spectators and White Hart Lane was an embarrassment in comparison with the ostentatious grandeur of Highbury.

3

Two rudimentary stands had been built at facing ends of the ground in 1922, using the money from the Cup run in the previous year. These had been adequate at the time, but now that Highbury had been redeveloped Tottenham were again lagging far behind. To stay in the race the Tottenham board was forced to build a new stand on the uncovered east side of the ground. The cost was £60,000, only half of what Arsenal had spent on its main stand, but it would have been enough to bankrupt the club had Barclays Bank not agreed to finance the project on favourable terms.

But they were still the underdogs, like many of their supporters, who were drawn mainly from the poorer parts of the East End and included many Jews. Ethnic allegiance has always been important in British football. Teams like Celtic, Everton, Manchester United and Arsenal itself originally drew upon Irish or Catholic support. Rangers, Liverpool and Manchester City, their respective rivals, were supported by Protestants and Unionists. Years later, when sectarian rivalry was mainly confined to Glasgow, the old prejudices became part of the mythology of each club, fitting in with the tribalism and blind partisanship that forms such a big part of the game's attraction.

The Jews of the East End might have been natural supporters of West Ham United or Millwall, the clubs nearest to strongly Jewish areas such as Whitechapel. But these clubs had always been tinged with the anti-Semitism of the 1930s. Arsenal has plenty of Jewish supporters, but it was Tottenham, the underdogs, with whom they seemed most to identify. Helped by the fact that the club was owned by consecutive dynasties of Jewish businessmen, Spurs picked up an additional, unofficial nickname: the Yids. After the war the name was proudly adopted by a new generation of fans, Jewish or not, who did not automatically associate the word with persecution.

The effects of war on football evened out some of the differences between Tottenham and Arsenal. The League

4

had been suspended for five years and as a result Arsenal had lost a lot of the momentum of the Chapman years. In 1950 Tottenham were promoted from Division Two and in the next season won the championship in front of crowds averaging 45,000. One crucial match against Manchester United, who came second that year, was watched by 70,000. Arsenal could manage only fifth place, the first time since 1925 they had finished lower than Tottenham in the League. Tottenham were beginning to emerge from the shadows. And in the 1960s Spurs pushed Arsenal firmly into the background as the team won everything in sight under Tottenham's answer to Herbert Chapman: Bill 'Old Nick' Nicholson.

In 1959–60, Nicholson's first full season as manager, the Spurs finished third in the League. There followed a clear-out of players, making way for new faces for an assault on the League championship in the next season. One of them was Terry Dyson, the son of a Yorkshire jockey, who had joined Tottenham Hotspur in 1955 for a signing-on fee of £10, but who had remained in the reserves for several years until Nicholson arrived. Dyson was a fast, hard-working forward who was skilful enough, but handicapped by the family trait of being extremely short. At 5' 3" it was obvious that he could never be a great header of the ball, and so he settled for playing on the wing. And yet, in best *Roy of the Rovers* fashion, it was the goal he headed past the great Gordon Banks that won the 1961 Cup final for Tottenham. The League championship had already been won that season and so the team had 'done the Double', becoming the first team this century to win both major football trophies in the same season. Dyson may have scored the winning goal, but he soon sank back into obscurity. All the credit was given to Nicholson.

Old Nick was the original tight-lipped, ashen-faced soccer manager, his forehead apparently flattened by the effect of heading heavy old-fashioned leather footballs as a full back in the pre-war Spurs team. During the war he had served as a PT instructor in the army before returning to the post-war team as a centre half, playing for a few seasons before retiring and becoming the team coach. This meant working with Arthur Rowe, the strange tortured-looking manager who had steered the club out of Division Two in 1950, and who had resigned in 1954 after rows with the club's directors led to a nervous breakdown. But the two men were able to work together for a few crucial years, building up what became the Double-winning team.

Rowe and Nicholson were soccer managers of a new type, deeply influenced by developments in European soccer. Before their arrival soccer was something players did not think about too much, but just did. Despite the pioneering activities of Chapman, the role of the manager in English football was strictly limited. He picked the team, organised the booking of the charabanc for away matches and prowled the local schools, docks or collieries looking for strapping centre forwards and beefy defenders to sign up.

Pep-talks, delivered at half time, were limited to the ubiquitous advice to 'get stuck in' as cups of tea, bread and dripping (or, if it was a rich club like Arsenal, the new luxury of sliced-up oranges) were dispensed. Tactical considerations had not changed much since the turn of the century when B.O. Corbett of Corinthians FC, probably the greatest full back ever to pull on long-johns, explained: 'All finesse which entails loss of time or ground must give way as far as possible to forging ahead.'

By the end of the 1950s Corbett's approach had been elaborated into the 'scientific kick and rush' style pioneered by Wolves under their manager Stan Cullis. In kick-and-rush soccer the ball was not played on the ground or into the middle of the field, which was where the opposing defenders were concentrated. This was partly a tactic, and partly a practical response to the state of most English football pitches which, by October, had usually degenerated to muddy, rutted, ploughed fields. Old-fashioned footballs soaked up water and were virtually impossible to propel through the mud, so it was natural enough to kick them high in the air. But outside Britain, in South America and southern Europe, a new, much more ground-based style of play was beginning to evolve independently of the game's British origins. The English soccer establishment was airily dismissive of these developments which were seen as faintly comical attempts by foreigners, trapped in their benighted mudless and fly-blown countries, incapable of playing the game properly. English soccer was so sure of its automatic supremacy that the Football Association had at first refused to field an England team in the World Cup, writing it off as a foreign gimmick. Games by the national team were based on 'home internationals' against Scotland, Wales and Northern Ireland, and the Commonwealth Cup which England always won by a mile, on one occasion tonking some clueless Ozzies 17−0 in the 1951 final.

The first major crack in English supremacy came in 1953 when the Hungarian national team inflicted a humiliating defeat on England, avenging a series of friendly matches in 1908, which England won 29−2 on aggregate, and becoming the first foreigners ever to win at Wembley. The Hungarians ignored the traditional English set positions such as centre forward and wingers and swarmed all over the pitch, running rings round the England players. They won 6−3. After the game the Hungarian captain Ferenc Puskas explained: 'We improved the English tactic of "kick and run" to "pass the ball accurately and run into a good position" ', adding charitably: 'Perhaps England, once the masters, can now learn from the pupils.'

Few people in the insular world of English soccer listened, but the new Hungarian masters, or 'soccer Svengalis' as they became known, found willing pupils in Italy and Spain where Puskas became team manager of Real Madrid, deploying the new secret weapon of 'possession football'. Abandoning the traditional managerial orange-slicing responsibilities, Puskas instead sat his players in front of a blackboard and worked out tactics for each game, designing detailed set-piece man-oeuvres. The results made the English kick-and-rush

7

teams look like lumbering Neanderthals.

The general reaction of British soccer was the same as British industry's attitude to European competition at the time. British was best, European meant cheap rubbish, and that was an end to the discussion. European soccer was a cheap imitation of the English original, just as the risible Volkswagens and Fiats that people were starting to buy were inferior versions of the solid British Rover, Austin and Morris ranges. People would soon tire of tacky foreign novelty and return to solid British quality. With the advent of the European Cup, at first dominated by Puskas's Real Madrid, it was recognised that while the Europeans could now beat the English, it was typical of the sneaky foreigners to come up with 'possession football', with tactics practised off the pitch in advance, something which was usually seen as a form of cheating.

Training footballers to peak physical fitness, at a time when English players would cheerfully tuck into egg and chips and milk stout on Saturday lunchtime, was not the sporting behaviour of gentlemen. Even worse was the repulsive European habit of theatrically running about the pitch waving arms, kissing and cuddling like a bunch of nancy boys whenever their team scored a goal. Bob Lord, chairman of Burnley (League champions in 1960) and a leading football worthy at the time, summed up the general establishment feeling. 'We taught them how to play football,' he sniffed, 'but they have manufactured unsporting actions of their own.'

Rowe and Nicholson did not see things that way. Before the war Rowe had worked as a trainer in Hungary. Returning to Spurs he put what he had seen into action, placing a maximum 30-yard limit on passes, training players to think for themselves and to run into space to receive passes from others. 'Any clown can play with the ball when he's got it,' Rowe later wrote in the official *Encyclopedia of Association Football*. 'It's the good fellows who get into position to receive.'

This thinking did not appeal to Tottenham's directors. The board was now dominated by the traditionalist Wale family, owners of a local nut- and bolt-manufacturing company, Brown's of Tottenham. The board was used to compliant managers who maintained tradition and were hired and fired with startling frequency. Despite Tottenham's much better performance under Rowe, the board lost patience with him when the results began to falter and started interfering directly in the selection of the team.

The final straw was a series of gripes printed in match programmes criticising the imported European style, demanding a return to the more traditional method of booting the ball up the field. These had been inspired by club chairman Fred Wale, a traditionalist to the core and a close associate of Bob Lord. Rowe could not stand the criticism, which pushed him to the brink of madness, and retired early to be replaced by Jimmy Anderson, very much a stand-in, before Nicholson took over. Evidently made of sterner stuff, Old Nick stood up to the directors and pushed ahead with the European approach.

After doing the Double, Nicholson's position was unassailable, for a few years at least. He used the time to build up his team of 'Glory, Glory boys' with players such as Danny Blanchflower and Dave Mackay at its core. After his moment of glory at Wembley, Dyson was sidelined and replaced by additional expensive signings. Jimmy Greaves was bought from AC Milan in November 1961 for the magic figure of £99,999 after Nicholson had met him in a toilet during a football function.

Greaves almost helped Nicholson to his second consecutive Double, scoring one of the winning goals in the 1962 final against Burnley. But the team faltered in the League and came only third, five points behind the winners, Ipswich. The success continued in next season when the Glory, Glory boys became the first English team to win a major European competition, beating Atletico Madrid 5 – 1 in the European Cup Winners' Cup final in Rotterdam.

Following Nicholson's example, the whole continental bill of goods – blackboards, tactics, Svengalis and all –

was bought by the top English clubs while Bob Lord's once mighty Burnley, still clinging to the past with rules banning post-goal-scoring kisses, long hair and moustaches, began a relentless slide down the League towards Division Four.

As other European-minded managers began to copy Nicholson's approach, Spurs' edge was eroded; five or six years is, in any case, the natural life of a football team. By 1965 the Glory, Glory days were effectively over. Nicholson rebuilt the team and Tottenham came close to doing the Double again in 1967 when they beat Chelsea at Wembley to win the FA Cup and came third in the League. But things were never really the same again. And after a decade of outshining Arsenal, the old enemy was starting to reorganise.

2: OH NO! ARSENAL ARE ON THE TELLY AGAIN!

Success in football, like in any sport, depends largely on an element of luck. And where luck is a factor superstition is bound to follow. The date of Tottenham's Double win confirmed a peculiar numerological belief about years that end with the number 1.

Spurs had won the FA Cup in 1901 and 1921, and in 1951 the team won the League for the first time. The Double had been completed in 1961 and the magic seemed to be working again a decade later when Tottenham carried off the League Cup. But 1971 was a portentous year for another reason: Arsenal did the Double, removing Spurs' unique claim to fame.

In 1961 Arsenal had finished eleventh in the first division and the team had trailed behind Tottenham in the League for the rest of the decade. As Spurs became a part of the national myth about the swinging sixties, Arsenal won nothing at all. In 1966, with Tottenham still near the peak of their powers, the Gunners recorded their lowest League finishing position for 30 years.

Tottenham's supremacy did not last into the next decade. In 1972 Spurs won the UEFA Cup, a competition for runners-up in European leagues, and the year after won the League Cup again. But in the main events of the first division championship and the FA Cup, Spurs were nowhere, relentlessly dropping down the table every season and finishing lower than Arsenal every year.

The last splutter of the Glory, Glory years came in May 1974 when Tottenham made it through to another UEFA Cup final. The team was led in attack by Martin Chivers,

11

bought from Southampton for a new record fee of £125,000. He was joined by Ralph Coates, a lacklustre striker signed from Burnley and now chiefly remembered for his Bobby Charlton-style single-strand, wrap-over hairstyle. The two frontmen were supported by another expensive signing: Martin Peters, the ageing star of England's 1966 World Cup victory.

This time the team lost the final 2 – 0 to the Dutch side Feyenoord in Rotterdam. Some Tottenham supporters, normally immune to the hooliganism that was beginning to be a major problem in English football, rioted and ripped up the seats in the stadium. Nicholson, his morale already slipping because of failures in the League, was sickened to the core. Steve Perryman, the long-serving Spurs captain, described the riot as the end of an era. The resulting ban on Spurs playing in Europe, he later said, removed a prop of superficial European success and caused the team to fall apart.

The next season began with four straight defeats. The team could not manage to score even a single goal in its first three matches, and crowds slumped to 20,000, barely a third of gates recorded during the Double-winning season. Nicholson resigned, which was a hard move to take. He was 55 and Spurs had been everything to him. Becoming manager had been the greatest day of his life. Apart from a six-month stint working at a laundry, and his time as an army PT instructor, he had devoted his life to the club. He had worked at the manager's job round the clock, scouting or sizing up the opposition whenever he was not actually coaching the players.

Martin Peters organised a players' petition, pleading with him to stay. But not all the squad signed; Perryman refused, believing he would have a better chance of success with a new and younger manager. The relationship between Nicholson and his players had been badly affected by the new emphasis on money and bonus payments, and the manager had been disillusioned by a long and acrimonious campaign by Chivers aimed at getting more money.

Nicholson announced that he would leave the club at the end of the season, giving the board time to find an appropriate successor. 'There has been less respect from the players,' he explained, 'and no manager can work without that.' It was a telling remark. Nicholson had started his management career in an age when football supporters wore mufflers and flat caps, carried thermos flasks full of Bovril and directed toothless grins into the Movietone newsreel cameras as they waved their wooden rattles. Thrift was a way of life for supporters, players and managers alike. Nicholson used to inspect the club's supply of practice footballs on a regular basis, making sure they were fully worn out before they were thrown away.

When he had taken the manager's job, players had been virtual serfs, unable to renegotiate contracts and subject to a legally binding maximum wage of £20 a week. Most Division One players earned no more than a gas fitter and all of them tried to learn a trade to fall back on when their inevitably short sporting careers ended. Nicholson himself had earned £2 a week as a player just after the war. When he became the manager this went up to an annual salary of £1,500; appropriately elevating him above the players to the financial status of a bank manager (complete with a Rover and a neat semi-detached house in suburban Enfield, near Tottenham). Any transfer fee over £10,000 drew gasps of amazement, and the record had stood at £20,000.

The changes began in 1961 when the maximum wage was abolished. After that players in demand expected to be paid thousands every week. Transfer fees, ten per cent of which normally went to the player, had increased a hundredfold in a decade. In the year Nicholson left Spurs, a new transfer record of £350,000 was set by Birmingham City's sale of Bob Latchford to Everton. This marked the start of a mad inflation; a decade later million-pound transfer fees became almost commonplace, and the attitude of players had changed as a result. They became

13

fickle and moved between clubs in order to make the most money in the shortest possible time. At the same time the European-style tactical revolution that Nicholson and Rowe had helped introduce to British soccer had been fully adopted by others and had taken a cynical turn. Possession football became machine football, and teams such as Leeds United were seen as physical extensions of the will of their managers.

The result was often grindingly dull and slow, with players bitterly determined not to lose rather than sportingly keen to win. Exciting, individualist attackers such as Jimmy Greaves, or his Manchester United contemporary George Best, were disappearing, squeezed out of the system by the new conformity, unable to shine in teams of over-drilled automatons where the premium was on defence.

The growing cult of the manager in Britain coincided with the start of televised *Match of the Day* football in 1964; and the two phenomena worked together to produce a new wave of British soccer Svengalis who were often more entertaining than the defender-laden teams they put on the pitch. Analytical but ultimately unilluminating post-match interviews with car-coated commentators such as ITV's Brian 'Well, Brian' Moore became part of the telly package.

Don Revie of Leeds United emerged as the agonised *eminence grise* of post-match analysis, exuding *gravitas* far beyond the depth of his thinking, darkly owning up to the use of blackboards and muttering into the *Match of the Day* cameras about 'total football', 'offside traps' and 'off-the-ball channels'. This was fine when the team won, but less able managers were often reduced to explaining losses by forlornly sighing 'Well, Brian' to the cameras, following up with the well-worn soliloquy: 'That's soccer for you. Every game is different. We just take each one as it comes.' The airwaves and tabloid newspapers, which increasingly followed everything on TV as news, were soon crackling with Zen-like offerings from venerated footie philosophers.

Bill 'Shanks' Shankly of Liverpool famously snapped in his granite Scots accent that 'soccer is not a matter of life and death: it is more important than that': wisdom worthy of a medieval Persian Sufi master, and later included in the Archbishop of Canterbury's enthronement service. More catchy stuff came from younger managers such as Malcolm 'Big Bad Mal' Allison, Tommy 'The Doc' Docherty and Brian 'Big Head' Clough.

Another TV twist was given by increasing reliance on the instant video re-runs of goals and controversial incidents such as spectacularly blatant fouls, penalties and dodgy offside decisions. Jimmy 'Just-take-us-through-that-one-again-will-you-Jimmy' Hill became the king of the replay, or 'action replay' as it was known, analysing goals frame by frame, sagely stroking his Acker Bilk beard (which subtly camouflaged a gigantic protruding chin) and flaunting a deep tactical understanding of 'the game as it is now played'.

Nicholson had never invited or liked attention from the press or TV and, anyway, was completely unsuited to join the media circus even if he wanted to. In his last few seasons Nicholson had begun to look as anachronistic as White Hart Lane's old-fashioned 1920s and 1930s stands, built to hold crowds of up to 70,000 but rarely more than half full. He and the club's directors seemed to be trying to preserve a world that had long since disappeared. They had never really been happy with having TV cameras in the ground and Tottenham was one of the last clubs in the country to give in to the two most obvious trappings of televised soccer: pitchside advertising and sponsors' messages on the players' shirts.

Out of the same sense of tradition, some board members begged Nicholson to stay at the club, even though the team was heading for relegation to Division Two. When he refused, the choice of replacement surprised everyone. All previous Tottenham managers had been insiders – either former players like Nicholson, or members of the training staff. Nicholson himself had wanted Danny Blanchflower, the captain of the Glory,

15

Glory team, to take over. But in a rare break with the past the board appointed not only an outsider, but a former Arsenal captain, Terry Neill, to the position.

Neill's appointment was unpopular with the fans because of his connection with Arsenal, the club for which he had played for ten years and with which he was completely identified. The comparison with Nicholson, who had never made any bones about being a Spurs man through and through, was stark, and the glow of the Glory, Glory years still surrounded him and got rosier and rosier as the memory of the actual event began to fade into mythology. Neill, in contrast, was seen as an opportunist biding his time before taking the manager's chair at Arsenal.

Neill at once announced that his aim was to 'put the joy back into Tottenham's football'. This platitude brought a stinging reply from Nicholson's former assistant, Eddie Baily. 'What's he going to do,' Baily asked, 'give them all banjos?' Neill's appointment was unpopular with the majority of players, who naturally feared that the new brush might sweep them away. Others simply did not like his coaching style, and there was another problem – Neill's thick Ulster accent, which some players, including Perryman, had difficulty at first in understanding.

Neill was quickly plunged into the drama of avoiding relegation to Division Two, a struggle that went on all season, right through to the last game against Leeds United. Tottenham needed to win the game to avoid relegation to Division Two, and that did not seem very likely. Leeds were the reigning League champions and were through to the final of the European Cup. Like the previous home match against Chelsea, the Leeds match was played in front of 50,000 people at White Hart Lane, and there was a Cup final atmosphere. Tottenham won 4–2 and the man of the hour was Cyril 'Nice One Cyril' Knowles, the popular full back. After scoring only thirteen goals in some 400 games, he got the two winning

goals. White Hart Lane rang to the sound of the fans'
favourite chant:

> Nice one Cyril,
> Nice one, son;
> Nice one, Sirrrilll;
> Let's aver-naver-one.

The Leeds match proved to be the highlight of Neill's
short stay at Tottenham. After eighteen months he left
for Arsenal as predicted, leaving quantities of egg on the
board's face and bringing it a new wave of criticism for
the way it had heartlessly cast Nicholson off into the
wilderness. Old Nick was working as an adviser to West
Ham United who were involved in European competitions, but his friends knew that he longed to go back to
White Hart Lane. The board got its chance to make
amends by inviting him back as a consultant and adviser
to their next choice of manager – Keith Burkinshaw, a
former Scunthorpe Town supremo who was brought
down from Newcastle United where he had been the
coach.

Burkinshaw attacked the joy problem, not with banjos,
but with a new and more relaxed approach that included
the hiring of a club psychologist to deal with stress,
depression and concentration problems, which he knew
all about from his own days as a player. After starting
life as a coal-miner in Yorkshire, Burkinshaw signed on
as a professional with Liverpool only to spend seven years
in the reserves. During his whole time at the club, he
played only one match in the first team.

Despite the more friendly approach and the arrival in
the senior team of Glenn Hoddle, a promising local lad
later to be hyped as the most skilled English player of
his generation, Burkinshaw could not stop the rot and
in 1977 Tottenham finished at the bottom of Division One.
The club had come full circle after the Glory, Glory years
and were firmly back in the underdog camp.

It was vital that Spurs got back into Division One at
the first attempt; otherwise they would risk being locked

out of TV coverage for years and lose the chance of gaining new and younger supporters. Arsenal were doing well in the League and seemed to be permanently installed on *Match of the Day*. Much to the chagrin of Tottenham supporters, the former Arsenal goalie, Bob 'Butterfingers' Wilson, was well established as a leading pundit. The rescue mission was accomplished, but only just. The team made it back by the narrowest of margins, promoted on goal difference in third place behind Bolton Wanderers and Southampton. After scraping back into Division One, the board decided to invest both in new players and ground improvement on a scale not seen since the 1930s.

Burkinshaw got rid of eight players from the squad, most of them dating back to the Nicholson era, and replaced them with ten new ones. And in July 1978 he pulled off an astoundingly original and expensive transfer deal, exploiting the end of the players' union ban on foreigners playing for British clubs and bringing Ricardo 'Ricky' Villa and Osvaldo 'Ossie' Ardiles to White Hart Lane.

The midfield pair had been the stars of Argentina's victory on home territory in the World Cup just a month previously, and Burkinshaw lured them with the gigantic joint transfer fee of £700,000. This was almost double the transfer record sum of £400,000 established earlier in the year when Graeme Souness, a former Spurs player whose talent had been overlooked by Nicholson, was bought from Middlesbrough by Liverpool.

Ardiles and Villa (the latter sporting long hair, a Jason King-style Zapata moustache and sideburns luxurious enough to send Bob Lord and Fred Wale into a tailspin) were included in the team for the opening of the 1978–79 season, which immediately turned into a disaster. Tottenham won only two of their first eight matches and were beaten 7–0 by Liverpool, Burkinshaw's old club where ex-Spurs player Souness had been installed as midfield general. It was the biggest defeat in the history of the club.

But the Argie pair, especially Ardiles, quickly became popular with the fans as the team limped through the season, finishing in eleventh place. Undeterred by the lack of success, the board decided to continue to spend money, this time on a grandiose plan to rebuild White Hart Lane's dilapidated West Stand. The creaking structure was older and had even fewer facilities than the East Stand that had been built in the 1930s to prevent total eclipse by Arsenal's Highbury stadium. The problem was that most of Spurs' available cash had already been spent on rebuilding the team after the drop into Division Two.

Normally it was a matter of choosing between spending money on the team or on the ground. This time the board took the fateful decision to spend on both. The old West Stand was an embarrassment in an age of European competition; it was like a huge bus shelter, built to keep the rain off the dense crowds standing on the original banked terrace. It had no toilets and people were often reduced to pissing where they stood in the crowd, using a rolled up copy of the match programme to preserve modesty and direct the stream. There had been some minor improvements but when they abandoned their thrifty thermos flasks, up to 12,000 people had to queue at one tea stall. The stand would have to be rebuilt eventually and the time to act was now.

In the 1920s both clubs had competed to build stadiums that would attract the first generation of football fans. With planning restrictions preventing the installation of executive entertainment boxes lifted at Highbury, Spurs were in competition to corner the corporate entertainment market. Arsenal had won the first battle, and the Tottenham board were determined that they would not be the losers again. It was a huge gamble, but if it paid off, it would provide the board with the satisfaction of beating the old rivals off the pitch, even though they were, for the time being, lagging far behind on it. The estimated building cost was three million pounds, an enormous sum for a club with an annual turnover of £2.8 million. The centrepiece of the stand was to be a set of

72 executive boxes that would be leased at £30,000 each for three years, bringing in £2 million. The rest was to be paid for by a special appeal, with a thousand wealthy supporters asked to contribute £1,000 each. The profit would come from higher ticket prices for the 6,500 new seats in the stand, and from lease renewals after three years.

Tradition-bound as ever, the board planned for the stand to be opened in 1982, the club's centenary year and the perfect time to engineer the eclipse of Arsenal. And just as the memory of Herbert Chapman was enshrined at Highbury, the new stand would be an eternal monument to Bill Nicholson, the man they had been unfairly accused of dishonouring.

3: DECLINE AND FALL OF THE GREAT WASTE-PAPER MOGUL

Tottenham Hotspur Football and Athletics Club Ltd had never been a proper commercial business, and it was not run like one. The club had been incorporated in 1898 with assets valued at £500,000. Nobody had ever bothered to update the figure or find out its market value, for the simple reason that it was seen as priceless.

The Tottenham board was entirely amateur, as were all club boards in the country until 1982, when a League ban on paid directors was finally lifted. Football boards had always been seen as the preserve of local worthies and retired businessmen who used them as a mildly exciting alternative to, or extension of, the Rotary Club. A seat on the Tottenham Hotspur board was a status symbol like a local version of a Wimbledon debenture or a season ticket at the Royal Opera House, but there was an important difference: a seat on the Spurs board could not be bought, and membership was by invitation only.

After a minor scuffle over ownership in the 1930s, the club had become the personal fief of Fred Wale and his family, the nut-and-bolt kings of north London. In 1936 the Wales had legally enshrined their control of the club by changing the company's articles of association. The new Article 14 gave the existing board the right to refuse to recognise the voting rights of anyone who had bought shares from the people who held them at the time of the original share offer. The effect was to freeze share dealing and prevent anyone building up a block that could be used at an AGM to vote out the existing board.

As a legal precedent, Tottenham's Article 14 is waved

optimistically under the noses of judges in takeover battles to this day; it's a great favourite with directors of all manner of small and badly managed companies resisting takeover by brisker regimes. This extraordinary, and apparently impregnable, arrangement had been inherited by Wale's son Sydney, who became chairman in 1969, and the company's share register had been left to accumulate dust. The boardroom exuded an air of solid and secure upper-middle-class formality based on the old-fashioned concept of respect, the quality that Bill Nicholson had found so sadly missing in the latest generation of Spurs players and supporters. The Wales, both Fred and Sydney, had always insisted on being called Mr Wale, even by Mr Nicholson, Mr Rowe and Mr Blanchflower. Article 14 made sure that no Mr Tom, Mr Dick or Mr Harry would ever get near the boardroom.

The board had been shaken up slightly in 1961, the year of the Double, when Fred Wale was in his seventies. Young blood had been injected in the form of Charles Cox, a used-car salesman, aged only 63. He was joined by Arthur Richardson, the managing director of a north London waste-paper company, and a mere stripling, aged 56 when he joined the board.

When Fred Wale died eight years later, his son Sydney took over as chairman, but the power passed to Richardson who, although not exactly dynamic, was the more effective businessman. By the time the decision was taken to rebuild the West Stand Richardson was firmly established as chairman, supported by the inclusion of his son Geoffrey on the board, and the redevelopment plan was very much his own brain child.

But Richardson was as much a dinosaur as the stand he planned to demolish. In a world where old-fashioned manufacturing was disappearing, he was like a fossilised version of a patriarchal 1930s factory owner, complete with slicked-back hair, stiff and condescending manner, and tweed suit. As a pillar of the local community he did a lot of work for charity and was a Freemason, Rotarian and Conservative councillor.

22

The players found the chairman, and all the board members, very aloof. Richardson rarely spoke to them and never went into the changing rooms, even when the team had won a Cup final. For Richardson it appeared that the actual football was secondary to the social side of running the club, and the two activities rarely coincided. The board met fortnightly, before each home game, in the stuffy atmosphere of the Directors' Box overlooking the ground. The manager usually gave a short report on the progress of the team, and this was followed by any other business. The agenda then moved on to the main event of a four-course lunch with the directors of the visiting club and local worthies such as the mayor, followed by brandy and cigars.

Richardson did nothing for the fans: some said he saw them as a fickle bunch and a necessary evil. This attitude was based on thinking which had not changed since the 1930s, when apart from the pictures on a Saturday night there was no other form of entertainment for the sort of people who toiled away, bundling up discarded brown paper in his factory. He believed that supporters would always turn up, no matter what. The new West Stand was designed, not for them, but for the greater glory of Arthur Richardson and the Tottenham tradition. It was to be his contribution to posterity.

Others on the board were not so sure. Sydney Wale was worried about the break with his father's maxim that the club could spend on players or on the ground, but not on both at the same time. The fate of Chelsea, who had tried to do the same thing a few years earlier and almost dropped through Division Two into Division Three, provided ample evidence of what could go wrong.

The Chelsea crowds had dwindled to a hardcore, with a fully hooliganised minority who compensated for the team's lack of success by kicking each other and any rival fans who fancied their chances. Egged on by the tabloids, the SCUM, as they were proud to be known, organised their own breakaway hooligan SuperLeague, with a series of pitched battles to determine who were the most

23

violently demented. The dire antics of the team on the pitch almost became an ignored side-issue for them, taking place in the background while the real activity and excitement was 'steaming in' against opposition supporters.

The predictable cycle of clubs winning trophies, prompting proud directors to build ruinously expensive stadiums fit for heroes to play in, had at various times gripped once-great clubs such as Sheffield Wednesday, Aston Villa and Wolves. But in 1981 it was known as the Chelsea Syndrome because of the added menace of violence. Talk about the Chelsea Syndrome made little impression on Richardson. As far as he was concerned Chelsea were an upstart team who had only been in the League since 1905. Spurs were much more like Arsenal who had enjoyed their greatest-ever period of success in the 1930s after building not just a new stand but an entirely new stadium.

People were bound to grumble when money was being spent on the ground. The doom-merchants had predicted catastrophe when the East Stand had been built with borrowed money forty years previously, Richardson remembered. Barclays Bank had been happy to shoulder the debt for such a bankable name as Tottenham Hotspur, and they would do it again. Contacts, reputation and prestige would always pull the club through. The fact that Sir John Quinton, the chairman of Barclays, was a keen Tottenham supporter and season-ticket holder would doubtless help.

Richardson wrote to wealthy fans and invited them to a sales meeting at White Hart Lane. One of those who turned up was Irving Scholar, a 33-year-old multi-million-aire property developer, and a dedicated fan. At first Scholar approached the club simply as a punter interested in buying one of the new boxes. As both a supporter and a businessman he approved of the boxes plan in theory; he was certain that the club could make profits from proper redevelopment of White Hart Lane, if it was handled properly, and by branching out into corporate entertaining and related leisure activities. The strategy was, if anything, too conservative. Scholar offered himself as an adviser, willing to put his development expertise at the disposal of the board, free of charge. As he found out more about Richardson's development plans, what began to worry him was not the strategy but the detail and the existing management's ability to deliver. But Richardson was not interested, interpreting Scholar's approach as yet another backdoor attempt by a nobody to enter the inner sanctum of the boardroom. There had been many Irving Scholars over the years, keen to attach themselves to the club without having established themselves in the community first. Besides, Scholar was only 33, and a callow youth. What could he offer a man like himself, now in his seventies with fifty years of business experience and his all-important contacts?

Richardson's patronising style and lack of expertise in the risky world of property grated on Scholar, who had learned every aspect of the business the hard way. Born in Hendon and educated at Marylebone Grammar School, Scholar left school at sixteen and started work with estate agents Lewis and Tucker for £5 4s 4d a week. He discovered a natural talent for making money in the property game and by the time he met Richardson he was working for the property wing of European Ferries in Monte Carlo where, for tax reasons, he was also nominally resident. He commuted between his Monaco apartment and his house near Regent's Park so he could watch Tottenham. His proudest boast was that most seasons he went to every game, home and away.

Scholar and two business partners had just sold their stake in Townsend Thoresen to his employers for £11 million. He now had plenty of time and money on his hands and was sniffing around London for new challenges and opportunities – and what better than Tottenham, his main interest in life?

Scholar's main worry was that the rebuilding budget of £3 million was an underestimate, and that possible cost over-runs had not been budgeted for. As he knew all too well, major building projects rarely came at their quoted price. All kinds of unexpected extra costs tended to crop up, especially on a site like White Hart Lane, which rests on boggy ground. If building contractors were not tightly managed the threat of non-completion provided tremendous pressures for all kinds of extra spending to get the work done. They too believed in striking while the iron was hot. There was nothing in Richardson's background, it seemed to Scholar, which prepared him to manage a major development like the West Stand.

Scholar's fears were confirmed when Richardson sniffily turned down his offer to act, free of charge, as a management consultant responsible for holding down costs and meeting deadlines. He talked to other business-men who supported Spurs and found, as he later put it, a general feeling that there was 'something very wrong' with the way Richardson was going about things. Apart from the danger of cost over-runs it seemed likely that Richardson had overestimated the demand for boxes. The basic idea was sound, but the whole package was being launched at the start of the biggest recession since the 1930s, and there had been riots on streets in the area around White Hart Lane. Not many companies were going to pay £30,000 for a novelty location in which to sign the big contract or clinch the big deal at a time when there were no big deals or contracts to be had.

After final plans for the new stand were printed in the London *Evening Standard* in December 1981, Scholar was called by Paul Bobroff, another young Spurs-supporting property developer. 'Have you seen it?' Bobroff asked excitedly. 'There's no way that's going to cost £3 million.' Scholar agreed. The cost over-run was going to be huge.

But Richardson was steaming ahead, buoyed up by the revival of Tottenham's fortunes on the pitch. Burkin-shaw's new squad had begun to settle. Ossie Ardiles and Ricky Villa, the two Argentinians, were at the core in mid-field and Hoddle was well established and starting to show his class. League performances were still patchy, but in 1981 the team won the FA Cup, beating Manchester

City 3–2 in a replay after a 1–1 draw. Both matches had taken place at Wembley.

The 1980–81 Cup run, including profitable replays in earlier stages of the competition, had brought a lot of extra cash into the club. Another spin-off, benefiting the players more than the club, was the traditional tacky souvenir novelty pop record performed by Chas 'n' Dave (inventors of Rockney) with the team providing the chorus. A classic of the genre, it contained the rhyme:

> Ossie garna Wemb-lee
> 'Is legs 'ave gorn all tremb-lee.

But success had not come cheap. Burkinshaw had splashed out another £1.7 million on four new players, including strikers Steve Archibald and Garth Crooks. Sydney Wale, alarmed by the direction the club was taking, fell out with Richardson and resigned. This was Scholar and Bobroff's chance to get more involved in the club. They offered to buy Wale's fourteen per cent block of shares that, in normal circumstances, would have given them a seat on the board as holders of the single largest block of shares. Richardson himself had only a few hundred of the 5,000 original shares issued in the club, and all the remaining members of the board had no more than ten per cent between them.

Standing in the way was Article 14, the rule that gave Richardson the right to refuse to recognise any share transfer; this was why he and the rest of the board had not even bothered to build up a majority shareholding, the normal way of ensuring control of any company.

By 1982 all the original shareholders had died off, leaving their yellowing certificates to younger members of their families, which was how both Wale and Richardson had got their respective stakes. Since the company hardly ever paid dividends, and since Article 14 denied shareholders any effective role in the company, the share certificates were only so much scrap paper. If not for their sentimental significance, they might have

27

ended up being reprocessed in Richardson's factory.

The position, as Wale explained it, seemed hopeless. But as property developers, Scholar and Bobroff had been in tighter corners than this. Applying the sort of enterprising legal stealth commonplace in the property world, they quickly found a chink in Richardson's armour.

The trick was to gain a majority holding without placing their names on the share register and thus alerting the board. It was to be done by buying the right to use existing shareholders' proxy votes, leaving the actual shares in their orginal owners' names. Once a controlling stake had been secretly built up in this way, Scholar and Bobroff would be able to get rid of Richardson before Article 14 could be used against them.

With this legal plan of attack in place the two men turned Richardson's main gun against him. The deadening effect of Article 14, together with the board's inept financial record, meant that the shares were widely viewed as worthless. They could therefore be bought very cheaply. Many belonged to widows or elderly daughters of the original shareholders, and this was more good news: even in the non-sexist 1980s, under a ferocious female Prime Minister, women could be relied upon to have little interest in financial matters such as shareholding, and even less in soccer. They might therefore part with their proxies easily, preserving the all-important secrecy. This was especially true, Bobroff found in at least one case, if he could convince them they were honouring the memory of their departed husbands by 'helping him to help Spurs'. He had an early success obtaining a substantial block of proxy votes belonging to the family of the late F.J. Bearman, who had been chairman before the Wales took over and who had little love for Richardson.

Scholar, meanwhile, set out to sweep up smaller shareholdings. He sent out an extraordinary 300 letters to the most promising female names on the share register. Suddenly little old ladies up and down the country started to get letters offering cash up front in return for their proxy shareholders' votes. One delighted widow in the Midlands was offered £34,000 for her 136 shares, previously assumed to be valueless. There was a fantastic reaction. It was like a postal version of *Antiques Roadshow*, the smash hit TV programme based on the ecstasy experienced by the punters when told that old junk fished out of the loft or behind the mantelpiece clock is worth thousands. Most leapt at the offer, assuming Scholar to be some sort of madman or eccentric fan with more money than sense. Some wrote back at once, before he had the chance to change his mind, demanding to know when their cheque, however small, would arrive.

In nine months Scholar and Bobroff bought a controlling 51 per cent stake in the club for just £600,000. They worked at it non-stop through the summer with mounting excitement, boosted by events on the pitch at White Hart Lane. Spurs made it to a Wembley FA Cup final for the second year running, where they drew 1 – 1 with Queen's Park Rangers and then won the replay, also at Wembley, 1 – 0. The win was Spurs' fourth visit to Wembley during the season. In August they had drawn 2-2 with Aston Villa in the Charity Shield, and in March they had played Liverpool in the League Cup final, losing 3 – 1. At the rate Scholar and Bobroff were accumulating shares, they were well on course to be in the Royal Box as directors if the club kept up the momentum and went to Wembley again next season.

Most importantly, the secrecy of the share-buying operation had been maintained. Richardson knew nothing about the plot until Scholar revealed that he was the new effective owner at a meeting in November 1982. The encounter was a tense but relatively brief affair and Richardson bowed out with about as much dignity as he could muster. Scholar and Bobroff formed the new board, maintaining some continuity by placing Douglas Alexiou, Sydney Wale's 40-year-old son-in-law, in the chair. Frank Sinclair, yet another property developer and managing director of Mountview Estates, also joined the board. Scholar, as the biggest single shareholder and architect of the takeover, was to wield most of the power on the new board, working closely with Bobroff. But as a tax exile officially resident in Monte Carlo, he was not allowed to be the chairman of a British company.

On paper Scholar and Bobroff had pulled off a highly lucrative deal, even by the standards of the London property market. Stripped of debt and with a trading profit of £200,000 in 1981–82, the club might have been worth ten times the £600,000 they had paid to get control of it. But the partners had always realised they were buying something of a pig in a poke. In a normal takeover bid the buyers would have demanded to look over the target company's books to see what they were getting. Because of Article 14 and the need for absolute secrecy, this had been impossible. Scholar and Bobroff's accountants now had access to the information they needed to begin to plan a profitable transformation of the club. They knew the company was likely to be carrying heavy debts that might wipe out any immediate profit from the sales of assets. But they had been able to hazard only a rough guess at the scale of the problem.

On the downside, the new owners expected to find a huge debt caused by building the new West Stand, the original spur for their takeover and rescue activities. Some of these likely losses, they hoped, might have been offset by the team's footballing success in recent years. This included a series of good Cup runs and seven Wembley appearances in eighteen months, including Charity Shield matches. According to the hand-to-mouth rules of soccer finance, the windfall profits from the extra Cup matches ought to have provided plenty of positive cash flow, even if the capital account was in the red.

And so the accountants began poking about in the smouldering remains of the Richardson regime, optimistically searching for traces of Wembley gold. The club's finance staff were politely but firmly probed to discover just what the true position was. That was the problem, they replied. Nobody knew for sure.

4: THERE'S ONLY TWO
TOTTENHAM HOTSPURS...

Irving Scholar cut a strange figure in the traditional and insular world of English soccer. For a start he was only 34, which was half the age of most football directors. In contrast to the members of the Richardson board, who were stiffly dignified and turned up at the ground in chauffeur-driven Rovers, Scholar zoomed around in an aggressive Range Rover with the personalised number plate FA HIT. Also, unlike the old board, Scholar was a football fan. Directors, at Tottenham and elsewhere, were naturally loyal to their clubs. But Scholar had watched Tottenham from the terraces, home and away, almost every Saturday since his teens. His rise from the Shelf, Tottenham's version of Liverpool's Kop where the hardcore fans stood, to the boardroom would have been unthinkable just a few years previously and was greeted with enormous suspicion throughout the soccer establishment. The immediate fear, fanned by propaganda from the remains of the Richardson camp, was that he and Bobroff would damage the team and the club. The picture painted was a fan's nightmare. They might sell off star players such as Glenn Hoddle and Steve Archibald to make a quick profit on the transfer market. They might even bulldoze White Hart Lane and the club's training ground, located in a stretch of prime development land in leafy Cheshunt, Hertfordshire. With planning permission they might sell the site to builders and make millions.

The media obligingly trotted out Scholar's standardised and entirely positive biography: how he had fallen in love with Spurs at age five when he had watched the team from his uncle's shoulders, and how as a grammar schoolboy he had run away from home to go to away matches. The favourite legend was his snap decision to rescue the club on his way to an away match against Leeds United, a suitably fearful and portentous occasion for any soccer fan. Scholar told the fans that he was one of them and was aiming for the top trophy available to any English club side: the European Cup. Nothing less would do. But to qualify for the European Cup, Spurs would have to win the League championship, a feat the team had not achieved for 21 years.

Burkinshaw had done well enough. But a commercial transformation was needed to bring in the cash to buy a new Glory, Glory team. Nobody could doubt that Scholar was a man who knew how to make serious money in unpromising circumstances. But if asset-stripping was his game, he said, he would have gone for a club sitting on more promising territory. In grotty, crime-ridden Tottenham, property prices were held down, to use the local estate agents' euphemism, by the area's 'vibrant multi-racial character'. As Scholar pointed out, there was no shortage of other tempting development targets in London at the time.

The financial casualty list included such famous names as Charlton Athletic, Millwall, Fulham and Chelsea, which was still in the grip of the Syndrome. Chelsea was effectively bankrupt, but was sitting on millionaire residential land in the Royal Borough of Kensington and Chelsea. Fulham, after a catastrophic descent from Division One to Division Three, were still hanging on to picturesque Craven Cottage, a stadium possessing the property speculator's Holy Grail of a riverside location in an 'improving' area being steadily annexed by militant estate agents and professional gentrifiers. The Cottage had a capacity of 25,000 but the club could count itself lucky if a fifth of that turned up to an average Saturday League game for the vicarious thrill of watching their team being thrashed, for example, by Wigan Athletic.

Scholar at least had the endorsement of a group of Spurs-supporting self-made Jewish businessmen of his own generation. The old 'Yids' connection was now a matter of myth, but it was a potent one, and the club was an important totem for many in the Jewish community. At an informal level the club acted as a focus for people such as Charlie Saatchi, founder of the advertising agency, Michael Green of Carlton Communications, and Gerald Ratner, the mass-market jewellery man. Anti-Semitism was still a factor in British business life, and acceptance on the normal business scene was sometimes difficult. Instead they tended to gravitate towards Tottenham, where support for the club provided a useful, but unofficial and informal, version of Richardson's Rotary Club and Masonic circuit. All of them had the same sort of background as Scholar; their families tended to know each other and they were said to drive each other on. Spurs pulled them together and they would meet at each other's houses after home matches to discuss business, talk about Tottenham's chances and play poker.

Scholar was also friendly with an older generation of rich Spurs fans who had always been shut out of the finances of the club by the old board. The most famous was Maurice 'Mo' Keston, who had made his money in the East End rag trade. In 1963 Keston hit the headlines as the fan who loved Tottenham Hotspur so much that he changed his religion for them.

The story was based on a friendly match played by the Glory, Glory team in Egypt, when Keston deliberately said he was Christian instead of Jewish on his visa so that he could get into the country to watch the match. Having bamboozled President Nasser, Keston spent most of the tour hiring taxis to take the players to see the Pyramids. He claimed not to have missed a single Tottenham game in thirty years. But he had got into the old board's bad books by throwing a party to celebrate the 1967 FA Cup win that drew some of the players away from the official function, upsetting the assembled local worthies.

Keston first met Scholar when he was a teenager, one

of dozens who used to pester him for the Cup tickets that he was always able to get because of his connections with the players. Scholar had not changed much and still had a boyish enthusiasm for Tottenham. Now he owned the club, he was like a child who had been given the keys to a sweetshop.

Soon after the takeover Scholar spotted Keston milling around the offices and grabbed him by the arm. 'Hey, come here Mo,' he said, 'I'll show you something.' Keston was taken on to the roof of the old East Stand, weaving dangerously through the girders to perch on top of the gable next to the famous Tottenham Hotspur cockerel. 'What about this view?' he asked with a sweep of his arm. 'What say we watch the game from up here this Saturday?' Keston, overweight, wobbled unsteadily and worried about falling off. Scholar then dreamily explained how he wanted to develop the ground, pointing out where the new stands and hi-tech scoreboards would be located with more perilous sweeps of his arm.

Scholar was just as matey with the players and the more humble fans. There was no more 'Mr Richardson'; he was Irving, one of the lads. The old board had maintained a strict rule of never talking to the players, but Scholar was forever at the training ground, joining the small clutch of autograph hunters on the touchline. Fans might see him meandering about the ground and shout something like: 'Ossie played good last Saturday'; he would march up with a gleam in his eye and debate tactics for hours. He was a bottomless repository of soccer trivia, which he tested against Keston to prove who was really the club's Number One supporter. ' 'Ere, I've got one for you,' he would say and out would come a question about who was the first Tottenham player to score more than one hat trick in the FA Cup, or something equally arcane.

Scholar spoke to everyone – fans, players, fellow directors and merchant bankers – in the same way, with a flat, classless north London accent and an intense style usually described as gushing. It was hard for people to get a word in edgeways unless they waited for him to take a deep drag on the endless chain of fags he smoked. His favourite saying was 'Shhh, now listen to me'.

Social events in his house in Chester Square in posh Regent's Park, where the perfectly proportioned Georgian rooms were cluttered up with mountains of tacky Spurs memorabilia, were a nightmare for anyone not interested in football. Conversation would quickly be pulled around to Spurs and out would come treasured souvenirs such as old match programmes, signed photos or the new invention of videoed collections of great goals.

Most of his attention was lavished on the players. One of his first acts as owner was to pull on a real first team shirt and join in a practice match at Cheshunt. The exercise was not repeated. He tore his Achilles tendon during the match, and was hospitalised. But he turned up at White Hart Lane as cheerful as ever, getting the players to sign his plaster cast.

Beneath all the PR and general irrepressible approach, Scholar was horrified by the slack financial management of the club. Both he and Bobroff were genuinely hurt by the way Richardson had risked all the dangers of the Chelsea Syndrome, threatening to destroy any chance of winning the League with debts which were soon reckoned to be the biggest in English football.

It was not just the mismanagement of the stand. Simple matters such as the VAT records had not been kept up to date, and one of the new board's first tasks had been to fend off a court summons for non-payment. Rummaging around White Hart Lane they found great wads of banknotes lying about in the ticket office, and listened with horror to the story of how a huge pile of fivers handed over at the turnstiles had once spilled on to the floor and had to be swept up by the cleaners.

The only firm indicator of the club's financial position was the raw bank balance, which was so bad that the local bank manager had to give express permission for any spending other than petty cash. When Burkinshaw, who had been kept as much in the dark about money as everyone else, wanted to buy new players, board members had been required personally to guarantee the necessary overdraft extension.

Unpaid bills, IOUs and other financial skeletons kept tumbling out of the closets for months before the new board decided that the club owed at least £5 million. Overspending on the new West Stand was revealed as only part of the problem. As Scholar and Bobroff had predicted it had come in at over £4.5 million, which was a million over budget, making it by far the most expensive stand ever built in Britain.

No provision for overspending on this scale had been made by the old board and not even the lower estimated cost had been fully covered. One third of the 72 £30,000 executive boxes remained unsold and a sponsorship package that was supposed to cover part of the cost had not materialised. Worse still, it soon emerged that the £5 million debt was not merely the result of various one-off errors such as the faulty West Stand estimate and the VAT horror; these could be written off as never to be repeated. The figures revealed that the financial fundamentals were all wrong. Income from gate receipts could not possibly cover the club's fixed costs in a normal year, let alone pay off the debts. Scholar worked out that if he relied on footballing income alone Spurs would have to win the FA Cup every year for a decade just to pay off the debts and break even.

The idea of selling off players to meet the bills was not even an option as far as Scholar was concerned. Not only did it represent a step in the direction of the Chelsea Syndrome, it simply wasn't worth it. With so many clubs in the red there was a glut of players for sale. The transfer market had collapsed after reaching a giddy high-water mark with West Bromwich Albion's sale of Bryan Robson and Remi Moses to Manchester United for £1.5 million in 1981; and the fees on offer had at least halved since then.

Tottenham's purchase of Martin Peters from West Ham for £200,000 in 1970 had caused general astonishment, but by the end of the decade million-pound transfer fees had become commonplace. Now, in the recession of 1982, top players were fetching only a fraction of that price, if they could be sold at all. Fees over £300,000 were rare, even for England internationals.

Typically, the Richardson regime had bought players from the top of the market and Scholar was stuck with the high wages and bonuses which always form part of big transfer deals. The club had spent £1.4 million on two good players, Steve Archibald and Garth Crooks, in the summer of 1980. Although Archibald was later sold to Barcelona at a profit, in 1982 Scholar could be certain that their asset value had halved in a little over a year. Only the big Italian and Spanish clubs had the money to buy British players during the 1980s.

With no chance of profitably selling players, and with the gulf between rising costs and falling income set to get worse as the recession continued, Scholar and Bobroff decided to buy time with a £1.3 million rights issue of shares. The new money would plug the immediate gap and would also dilute the holding and voting power of the Richardson camp. Scholar and Bobroff ended up with a 90 per cent holding in the club which, under Section 209 of the Finance Act, made them outright joint owners.

At the end of the 1982–83 season, six months after the Scholar-Bobroff coup, Tottenham finished fourth in the League, a few points behind Manchester United and Watford, but far behind Liverpool who were League champions for the sixth time in eight seasons. During the close season Scholar began preparing the plan that he and Bobroff believed could wipe out the debts and allow them to spend the kind of money on players needed to replace Liverpool at the top of the tree.

What they had in mind was nothing less than the complete commercial transformation of Spurs into a ramified 'leisure' group that would be floated on the Stock Exchange. The aim was to raise enough new capital through the sale of shares to wipe out the debts and start again. This was a bold move that had never been tried before. It would run close to breaking the various rules about the way clubs were owned, imposed as a condition of playing in the Football League by the League's Management Committee.

The League rules limited the size of dividends that could be paid to shareholders, with the further condition that if the club were ever wound up shareholders would get only their original stake back. Any remaining assets would go to the Football League. These restrictions would have been utterly unacceptable to the Stock Market and at first appeared to make flotation an impossibility. But after long sessions with their lawyers and resorting to the same sort of guile that had enabled them to run rings round the old fogeys on Richardson's board, Scholar and Bobroff found a way to skirt the rules.

The idea was to leave the actual Tottenham Hotspur Football and Athletic Club alone, but to make it a wholly-owned subsidiary of a new 'shell' holding company, Tottenham Hotspur PLC which would be floated on the Stock Market. The football club would continue to abide by the League's rules and pay only restricted dividends to its owner, the new PLC. This would not worry the Stock Exchange because, according to plan, the football club would either contribute a small profit or would act as a loss leader for the new operating divisions that would be set up and run for maximum profit in related areas of leisure. The fans might still chant 'There's only one Tottenham Hotspur' from the terraces, but in reality there would be two: the club and the PLC.

It had always been Scholar and Bobroff's intention to split football off from other commercial activities, partly because they believed there was not much profit to be made in soccer, in the short term anyway. Looked at in this way, the League restrictions were an advantage because they would force the new PLC to diversify quickly into highly profitable new areas to achieve a reasonable overall result. Scholar in particular was already looking forward to the day when soccer would contribute only half of the new PLC's income, and money from new commercial operations would subsidise the team just as they did at the successful 'superclubs' on the continent.

Scholar had always been very European-minded. Living part of the time in Monte Carlo, he would fly off to watch European superclubs such as AC Milan Juventus and Barcelona, who played in gigantic hi-tech stadiums. Profits from associated leisure businesses were used to buy the best players in the world. The 1982 World Cup had just upped the stakes in the international transfer market with Diego Maradona, the Argentinian, being transferred to Barcelona for £4.8 million just as Scholar and Bobroff were putting the finishing touches to their takeover plan for Spurs in the summer of 1982.

The new dual structure would allow Tottenham to become the first English club to follow the European example. The requirement to give most of the assets to the Football League in the event of a wind-up would apply only to the club and not to the new PLC. Anyway, this restriction hardly applied as Scholar, a genuine fan, would rather cut off his right arm than allow Spurs to go bust and disappear as a football team. Even so, this neat arrangement could be seen as breaking the spirit, if not the letter, of the League's rules. Scholar worried that the League would try to act against him, but decided to brazen it out should it come to any sort of conflict.

Scholar had no reason to like the Football League Management Committee. It consisted of the chairmen of all 92 clubs and was weighed down by old-fashioned traditionalists very like Richardson. Most of them, he believed, understood nothing about business. After all, at least 80 out of the 92 had not made a profit in years. They had run their clubs into the ground and were largely responsible for the financial shambles in which soccer had found itself. He was not about to let them do the same to Spurs.

The League had done nothing to prevent the insane transfer-fee inflation of the late seventies that had done so much damage to a lot of clubs, including Tottenham. In fact, the League had profited from the madness by taking a percentage of each fee. Scholar was soon on record as saying that 'Soccer's great problem is that those in authority do not employ good business principles. Perhaps they have forgotten them. Some in senior positions never knew any.'

Scholar and Bobroff had been forced to play a sort of chess game against Richardson, carefully assembling their blocks of shares and quietly moving them around the board before the knock-out blow could be delivered. When it came to dealing with the League they were in a game that was much more to their liking: poker.

By now everyone knew the dire financial straits through which Tottenham was sailing. If the League tried to cut the financial lifeline held out by flotation, the club might actually go down. In these circumstances Scholar felt sure that the fans, the press and the other big clubs would put enormous pressure on the League to allow the plan to go ahead. The final sanction, the ace in the hole, would be the bald accusation that the League management had pointlessly and stupidly killed off one of the oldest, best loved and most famous teams. No football worthy would want to live with that accusation for the rest of his life.

In the event, to Scholar's surprise, the League did nothing to enforce a strict reading of their rules. 'We kept waiting for somebody to tell us we couldn't do it, the League, the FA or somebody,' he said later: 'but nobody did. It just seemed that nobody had ever wanted to, so nobody had ever tested the rules.'

The flotation was a huge success. On 13 October 1983, 3,800,000 shares in Tottenham Hotspur PLC, costing £1 each, sold out within minutes and the issue was four times oversubscribed. Scholar ended up with a 29 per cent holding, Bobroff with 16 per cent. The other three directors, Douglas Alexiou, Frank Sinclair and Peter Leaver, had just under 1 per cent. There were no other large and potentially troublesome stakes in the new company.

A glance at the new share register revealed that many subscribers were Spurs fans buying small blocks of shares to feel involved in the club rather than in the hope of making a profit. The issue had provided an extra £3.8 million which, together with the previous £1.3 million flotation and general tightening up of financial management, wiped out all the debts inherited from the old board.

Scholar was still a tax exile, technically resident in Monte Carlo and barred from the chairmanship of a British company, and so Bobroff became chairman of the new PLC. But Scholar joined the board as the largest single shareholder and, with the support of Bobroff, had total control of the company and spent most of his time running it. Alexiou stayed on as chairman of the football club subsidiary. Bobroff, meanwhile, continued to divide his time between Spurs and his property company, Markheath Securities. There was much sanctimonious and sentimental talk about giving ownership to the fans, the people who really deserved it. But the more hard-nosed realised that the fragmented shareholder list gave the board a big advantage over any other company. There were more than 14,000 shareholders, the vast majority likely to be fans with an average shareholding of less than 300. Because they were so widely dispersed, and because they probably did not take much interest in financial matters, they were unlikely to be very active or demanding.

The main worry facing any company issuing shares – the danger of a takeover or meddling by hostile financiers buying big blocks of shares – did not arise. Unlike Richardson's shareholders, the fans who had rushed to support the share issue were unlikely to sell out easily to a predator as long as the team was performing well. At the same time, their individual stakes were so small that they had no chance of interfering with the management of the company. As Bobroff was later to say when the share price dipped badly in 1985: 'I've never heard a fan complain about the share price. All they complain about is the football results; even if we win 5–0'.

5: FOOTBALL ISN'T WORKING

As one of the new breed of eighties businessmen, Irving Scholar was mesmerised by the world of advertising and the black arts of image-manipulation that could apparently conjure huge sums of money out of nowhere. Exploiting Tottenham's unrivalled network of supporters in the media, one of his first moves at Tottenham was to appoint Saatchi and Saatchi, the leading advertising agency of the time, as special advisers to the club.

The Saatchis were soon convinced that there was a vast pot of money to be had by involving advertisers and sponsors at every level of the club. Football was an 'under-exploited property'. In marketing terms, as Scholar himself began to say once he picked up the jargon, the club was 'an Aladdin's cave of untapped riches'. The old board had even failed to get a sponsor for the team's shirts, years after Manchester United, Liverpool and Everton had profitably turned their players' shirts into mobile billboards for multinational corporations. This was remedied at once with a £450,000 package with Holsten, manufacturers of a type of lager known to the fans as Gnat's Piss. The deal had been unveiled at a home game just before Christmas 1983 with Page 3 girls, in stripped-down versions of the team colours, and Glenn Hoddle, dressed as Father Christmas, dishing out promotional freebies to a generally unimpressed crowd. The main difference, as far as the fans were concerned, was the change of the away strip from a light blue colour, described as 'tasty', to a horrible bilious yellow which made the players look like mobile cans of lager, as intended.

This was a start, but from any advertising person's point of view the most exciting thing about soccer was the phenomenal extent of brand loyalty. Over the years the Saatchis and other leading agencies had spent millions of pounds of their clients' money trying to get people to look at themselves as a Pepsi Cola drinker and not a Coca-Cola type, to plant the conviction that they were 'with the Woolwich' or that they were one of nature's Volvo drivers as opposed to a Volkswagen fan. Yet soccer had some sort of magic ingredient that meant kids went to see one game and were hooked for life. The psychology behind this was obviously all very deep, and doubtless homoerotic at some murky level. But the results were plain to see. People had been known to change their brand of toothpaste, switch their political allegiance, change their nationality, convert to another religion and divorce their wives; but nobody ever changed their football club.

The potential was at least as great as the rock music business where a combination of blind fan culture and sophisticated marketing had transformed a cottage industry dominated by penniless hippies into one of the most important capitalist concerns in the world. Scholar and his advisers were convinced they were on the threshold of doing something similar with football. They were entering virgin territory where vast profits were to be had.

Scholar had already put his toe into the water by spending £100,000 on a series of TV ads for Spurs' home match against Coventry City, the first game of the 1983–84 season. The rationale was that Spurs had a lot of nominal supporters who had come to White Hart Lane in their youth, but who now stayed away. They probably now had children or grandchildren, and if they could be encouraged to turn up for the Coventry game the kids might get the bug, just as Scholar had done.

The ads were the first ever put on TV by a football club,

and showed the team emerging from the tunnel, smiling and ready for the game. Normally the players were led out by Steve Perryman, the captain, but for advertising purposes he was replaced by Ossie Ardiles who was better known to casual supporters and general punters. The obligatory touch of televisual surprise was provided by Mrs Ridlington, a bespectacled, white-haired granny who was pictured following the team on to the pitch, bedecked in her supporter's scarf, leading a team of 'celebrity supporters' including Peter Cook, the ageing satirist. The idea was to show that the supporters were somehow part of the team, to stress Spurs' sentimental connection with the old East End – now more of a heritage-style concept than a reality – and to show that going to a soccer match was a perfectly normal, comfortable and respectable thing to do, and not merely the preserve of hooligans and deviants.

The ads were a great success, in a way. But they didn't do much for the new regime's image in the eyes of the team's most loyal fans in whose interests, according to the propaganda, the club was now being run. Thousands of curious and casual punters turned up, which meant that a lot of regular, faithful supporters could not get through the crush in time for the kick-off. Some of them missed the first half and, when they did finally get into the ground, found that their traditional standing place, which many regarded as their own slice of terracing by way of squatters' rights, had been occupied by Scholar's Mrs Ridlington wallies, decked out with their recently acquired heritage-style rosettes. The exercise was good PR in terms of the Great British Public (the GBP as it is known in advertising circles) and added a few thousand pounds to the gate receipts for the Coventry game. As it happened, the game was a dull 1 – 1 draw, with Hoddle scoring with a penalty. The new fans melted away and the exercise did little to prevent the inexorable decline in the crowd sizes over the next few years.

But Scholar, with the encouragement of the Saatchis, was already looking beyond soccer to other sports like golf, boxing, tennis and athletics where every drop of profit was wrung out of events through sponsorship and the sale of TV rights: a process known as 'sports-ploitation' in the United States, where it was most advanced.

The Americans had an enormous and efficient sports sponsorship machine, but they had no soccer. Britain, in contrast, had soccer but no sports sponsorship machine – at least nothing to compare with the Americans. Soccer was British, 'the game we taught the world to play', and advertising was American. And until the 1980s the two worlds simply did not collide.

The Americans had led the way by turning sports like golf, tennis, athletics and other Olympic events into virtual branches of the advertising industry. The economic equation was simple enough. Putting the brand name like Coca-Cola on the shirt of a sportsman in the final of some event likely to draw a worldwide TV audience of hundreds of millions was much more effective than paying for TV advertising time.

The main organiser of this activity was Mark 'The Shark' McCormack, head of the vast International Management Group, the leading US celebrity sponsorship empire. McCormack started off in the 1960s as golf champion Arnold Palmer's lawyer, persuading him to set up a company to collect royalties from his endorsement of golf clubs and a personalised range of golf clothing – the great grandfather of all those designers' logos and straightforward free advertisements splashed all over tracksuits and leisurewear today. After huge financial success with Palmer, McCormack added Jack Nicklaus to his stable, creating Jack Nicklaus-brand leisurewear. One result was a worldwide plague of the hideous, stretchy black nylon polonecks favoured by 'golf's human miracle machine'. But it was McCormack's move into tennis which had really shown the financial potential of sport.

John Newcombe was an early tennis signing. McCormack organised a range of clothes decorated with a manly logo based on the player's famous moustache.

In return Newcombe was obliged, on pain of breach of contract, never to shave his upper lip. McCormack's greatest-ever tennis success was Bjorn Borg, described as 'a bionic money-making machine who can sell anything'. Boring Bjorn brought in so much cash that McCormack was obliged to open his own bank in Monte Carlo, Scholar's tax haven.

The jewel in McCormack's crown was the Wimbledon tennis Championships which he had effectively bought outright and turned into a global brand name. He bought and sold TV rights, and organised sponsorship and corporate entertaining on a lavish scale. He did not even need to build the luxury boxes needed to separate executives and ordinary punters at soccer grounds. The riff-raff were simply kept entirely out of the commercial bit of the stadium, allowing the quality to be housed in marquees which were much cheaper and which, as a bonus, added to the theoretically outdoor and sporty nature of the event. Every aspect of the Championships was exploited for profit, from the Championship logo which was licensed to sportswear manufacturers, to the 'placement' of fizzy drinks, enjoyed by players between games. Even 'grass-cutting rights' were sold to a razor-blade manufacturer who, after paying a suitably enormous sum, was allowed to say that their blades had cut the grass on the Centre Court.

All this activity was backed up by an army of 'enforcers': ferocious American lawyers ready to leap down the throat of any person or company who claimed even the most tangential connection with Wimbledon without paying for it. By 1983 McCormack's IMG was valued at about $500 million, and was shortly to bid $20 million for the television rights for the 1984 Olympic Games in Los Angeles. The organisation represented over 250 clients, mostly sportspeople with a smattering of general celebrities. IMG had even handled the merchandising aspects of the Pope's 1982 visit to Britain. But the group did not represent a single major British soccer star.

Various attempts had been made to introduce soccer

to the USA and Japan, but it had not caught on. The Japanese found it unspeakably barbaric and suitable only for simpletons and morons. The Americans found it just the opposite: effete and overcomplicated. It was all too fiddly and boring, with little physical aggression, no recognisable superheroes or supervillains; only one or two goals were scored in the average match and therefore there were few opportunities for TV-led razzmatazz. The game had no foothold in the colleges and universities that dominated the grass roots of US team sports. And since soccer was a game at which the derided Mexicans excelled, and world domination was not assured, it was always unlikely to catch on in USA, even if the Americans could force themselves to understand it. Soccer was the only sport in the world, said one American football commentator, where 'nothing happens'. Evidently he had not heard of cricket.

When Scholar arrived at Spurs, Saatchi and Saatchi and other major marketing outfits were beginning to fight the Americans for a slice of the booming international sports sponsorship action, and various agents and other moneymen were beginning to sniff around soccer, especially the World Cup, as their chance to beat the Americans at their own game.

Before Scholar arrived at Spurs all manner of companies used the Tottenham Hotspur logo for merchandising purposes without paying a penny. The Richardson board had simply not bothered to copyright the symbol or even realised that there was money to be made by forcing the purveyors of tacky souvenirs, unofficial programmes and team posters who hung around the ground to pay for the privilege of using the club's name. In short, they had made the elementary error of treating the Spurs as just a football team and not a brand name. The ubiquitous symbol of eighties 'post-industrial' commercial activity, the little 'c' with a circle round it, was promptly added to the club's cockerel and football logo.

Meanwhile, Seb Coe was on TV advertising Horlicks (of all things). But soccer endorsement had not moved

47

on much from the days of the 1966 World Cup final when George Cohen, the full back in England's winning team, could find nothing more profitable to advertise than embrocation oil. 'Prior to each game,' the excruciating blurb ran above Cohen's grinning mug shot and spidery signature, 'I use Elliman's Athletic Rub. It is a "must" in my pre-match preparations. Available from chemists. Three bob.' Other players endorsed and advertised football boots, but the market for these was restricted to people who actually played the sport. Unlike running shoes, which were just starting to take off as a fashion accessory, football boots had studs which made them impossible to wear at a disco.

The Football League Management Committee, to Scholar's disgust, was still arguing with clubs over the right to wear sponsors' logos during televised matches, a rule which dramatically reduced the value of potential sponsorship deals. When they finally agreed to televised logos in 1983, the argument over the exact size of permitted logos went on for years. In 1982, the League had allowed its knockout competition, the League Cup, to be sponsored by the Milk Marketing Board, partly on the worthy grounds that milk was a healthy drink at a time when alcohol was being blamed for a lot of soccer hooliganism. But it was still a long way from trying to sell grass-cutting rights at important matches, or allowing players to run to the touchline and ostentatiously gulp Coca-Cola every few minutes in the manner of Mark McCormack's tennis players at Wimbledon.

But looked at positively, the lack of sportsploitation and American interest in British soccer presented enormous opportunities. Soccer was ripe for development by braver and more knowledgeable souls such as Scholar himself, who were prepared to take on the Football League authorities and their tradition-bound, anticommercial attitudes. Scholar began working more closely with Saatchi and Saatchi's sponsorship department, which was just as determined to get in on the ground floor of this potentially vast new industry. He was duly invited to the Saatchis' London HQ for a special presentation of the agency's thinking.

The basic idea was that football was being ruined by overexposure. Advertising the Coventry game had been a good start, a step in the right direction, but it had been a one-off and only partly based on a proper strategy. Football was a product like any other, and had to be treated like one. The price people were prepared to pay for it was a matter of supply and demand, like anything else. Too much supply, and down went the price.

Spurs were lucky to fill half their ground for most matches, and they were one of the best supported teams in the country. When you looked at the likes of Wrexham, then in Division Two, the position was insane. Wrexham had a ground capacity of nearly 30,000 but rarely got crowds of more than a few thousand; 30,000 was a pretty good average for League club capacities. Multiply the empty spaces on the terraces by the number of clubs and you had a supply of three million tickets chasing a maximum demand of 500,000 consumers every Saturday. Supply outstripped demand by a factor of six to one. No industry could live with fundamental figures like that. Not even the British car industry had overproduced on this scale. There were too many matches, too many obscure competitions, too many players nobody had heard of and not enough identifiable stars, such as Ossie in the Mrs Ridlington advert, for them to latch on to and feel involved with.

The Saatchis had helped Margaret Thatcher to win the 1979 general election with the slogan 'Labour Isn't Working'. Now it was a case of 'Football Isn't Working'. The only way forward would be rationalisation on an even grander scale than that recently meted out by the Tories to the overproducing nationalised industries. Each industry had been crawled over by accountants to find something – anything – that could be profitably produced; all the rest had then been abruptly abolished.

The profitable bits of soccer were plain for all to see. England's 1982 World Cup matches drew domestic TV audiences of over 10 million. The 1970 FA Cup final between Leeds and Chelsea had drawn a new record domestic audience of almost 20 million and, although soccer's rating had declined since the 1970s, the advertising and sponsorship potential was still correspondingly huge.

Big games were watched by all kinds of people who knew next to nothing about soccer and would never dream of standing on the terraces: most women, for instance. Events like this were very definitely in Mark McCormack territory, though fortunately he had not yet tried to annex them to his empire. They were 'events' of national importance, such as a war or a royal wedding, which everyone watched, either because they were interested or simply because everyone else was watching. The way to unlock the profits was to develop the 'event-like' nature of football, as the Saatchis called it, and get the same bandwagon rolling. Ideally Spurs should stop playing football matches for the gratification of a few thousand football fans who, for some bizarre reason, enjoyed standing in a freezing concrete enclosure every other Saturday, and start staging 'football events' for the TV millions.

The logical conclusion was to drastically reduce the number of games Tottenham played, concentrating on 'event' games against Arsenal, Manchester United and Liverpool. There would be far fewer matches, but each one could be hyped to death like a big rock concert, heavyweight boxing bout or Papal visit. Once the punters had been hooked in, an enormous merchandising business could then be locked into place, exploiting the 'I was there' factor. People were happy to pay through the nose for the honour of wearing 'Pink Floyd – The European Tour' T-shirts. They bought the commemorative Pope-on-a-Rope Soap, or whatever McCormack's franchisers had come up with during his British visit. But not even the most demented Spurs fan was going to be suckered with a souvenir '1983–84 Spurs Versus Lincoln City (League Cup Round Two, Second Leg) – I Was

There' pyjama case, because the 1983–84 League Cup (second round, second leg) against Lincoln City was not 'an event'; it was a 'non-event' which Spurs lost 2–1.

In May 1984 Spurs had a handy 'event' match coming up in the shape of the UEFA Cup final against the Belgian club Anderlecht at White Hart Lane, the first Cup final of any kind since Scholar and Bobroff's takeover. It was not exactly on the scale of Bob Geldof's Live Aid which took place at Wembley the following summer. That was an 'event-like' occasion which was to electrify the advertising world with its awesome money-raising power. (Years after Live Aid it was remembered in ad land how one viewer had become so involved that he had mortgaged his house and given the money to the organisers.)

But the UEFA Cup final was an event nevertheless and, in line with the new Saatchi thinking, Scholar set out to auction the TV rights to the highest bidder. The attempt ended in total failure. The BBC and ITV, who for years had profited from presenting a united front to the soccer authorities, refused to bid against each other, and Scholar was obliged to accept the measly sum of £30,000. It was a bitter experience for Scholar, who became more determined than ever to find some way of breaking the TV duopoly and forcing the soccer authorities to hold out for more money for televised soccer.

The final itself ended in a 2–2 draw before Tottenham won on penalty kicks which, as a device for settling drawn matches, is merely a more televisual version of tossing a coin. This was a dramatic but ultimately unsatisfactory end to a not especially entertaining European campaign. After battering the hapless Irish team Drogheda 14–0 on aggregate in the first round, Spurs had several narrow scrapes, including another win on the penalties lottery in the semi-final.

Just before the final itself Burkinshaw rested most of his best players and fielded five reserve team players in a League match against Southampton who smashed the weakened side 5–0. Spurs were fined £7,500 for effectively throwing the game. This form of cheating had shown just how desperate Tottenham were to win a European trophy and, far from glorying in his team's Cup win, Keith Burkinshaw saw the League's rebuke and fines as part of a general malaise surrounding the club. Tottenham had always had a reputation for playing skilful, fair and attacking football. Now, as Burkinshaw saw it, the need to win at any cost made it hard to resist a more cynical and unattractive approach to the game. It meant defensive, cautious and boring play.

Burkinshaw had a more immediate concern: the new regime's attitude towards spending on new players. The prospectus issued at the time of the flotation had made it quite clear that extra spending on players could take place only if the PLC was in profit overall. And the directors had promised to 'finance the net cost of players' registrations having regard to an appropriate return to investors'. This would rule out buying of players in years when the PLC had done badly and, even when there were profits to be had, had set up a conflict between business and football success. Buying of extra players was to be regarded as 'an appropriation of profit'.

Burkinshaw had also been upset by the decision to spend £100,000 on advertising one game – money which, in the depressed transfer market, could have been used to buy a player of the sort he now desperately needed. Alan Brazil and Steve Archibald, the two strikers who had played a vital role in Burkinshaw's scrappy European campaign, were to be sold to Manchester United and Barcelona, two of the few clubs still able to pay 1970s-style fees, for a total of £1.7 million. Brazil, who had been with the club for just over a year, realised a profit of £250,000. And Scholar's winnings on Archibald were £170,000 after four years' service. No players of comparable ability were bought to replace them.

Burkinshaw resigned from his position as manager. 'There used to be a football club over there,' he said as he left White Hart Lane for the last time. The prospectus issued at the time of the Stock Market flotation had officially described the PLC's future as being based on 'the promotion of goods and services associated with the Spurs name', which would make it a 'broadly-based leisure group', that would grow by 'taking advantage of the Spurs name and reputation'. Burkinshaw disappeared to spread his gospel of attacking and skilful football in the desert, becoming manager of the Bahrain national football team.

The resignation created only limited interest, and was mainly seen as sour grapes. Burkinshaw was replaced by his former assistant, Peter 'Shreevsie' Shreeves who had joined the club as manager of the youth team in 1974. Shreevsie, not to be confused with Greavsie, was an unimposing figure with sharp, ratlike features, who spoke with a thin nasal whine, giving away his upbringing in nearby Islington, the heart of Arsenal territory. He would run through soccerspeak phrases such as 'I fink we did quite well there, but we was very disappointed about the second harve' quietly and quickly, his thin lips hardly moving.

Shreeves inherited a squad weakened by the profitable sale of Archibald and Brazil. But he was always seen as a stand-in manager, very much in the shadow of Scholar and the board, who were interfering in the organisation of the club on a scale not seen since the 1950s, before the Nicholson era. Scholar's total grip on Tottenham was partly due to his return from Monte Carlo. He still kept his bolthole there, but he was now officially resident in London, allowing him to take the chairmanship of the Tottenham FC, the footballing subsidiary of Tottenham Hotspur FC, which was still chaired by Bobroff. Douglas Alexiou stayed on as vice-chairman, providing the last link to the old regime.

Between them Scholar and Bobroff had turned the company round in remarkably short order. The debts had been wiped out by the share issue and the company was moving strongly into profit, helped by the start of a general upsurge in the economy, and the leasing of the empty executive boxes. After an uncertain start the boxes had sold well, leased to blue chip companies such as ICI and Rio Tinto Zinc. The whole operation was back on target and generating £750,000 a year. Banqueting in the equally plush International, Centenary and Northumberland suites was profitably subcontracted to Letheby and Christopher, the posh catering firm. With extra revenue from higher admission charges to the rest of the stand, and new income from renting out the Bill Nicholson conference-cum-banqueting suite, hired out at £1,500 a day to groups of 100 (inclusive of morning coffee, biscuits, lunch and car parking), the West Stand was now generating at least an extra £1 million a year.

The PLC's first annual report showed the scale of the financial recovery. Overall the new regime had created about £2 million extra income a year from commercial activities to set against the continuing losses of about a million a year from football. But so far all efforts had been concentrated on bringing financial stability to the club. The next stage of Scholar's campaign for profit would mean taking on the Football League, and that would involve a much more public profile for both himself and the financial side of the business.

Scholar began campaigning for a new 'SuperLeague' which, in line with the Saatchis' thinking on the event-like future of the game, would be based around matches played between English soccer's Big Five clubs: Manchester United, Liverpool, Everton, Arsenal and Tottenham.

The SuperLeague concept dated back to the mid-seventies when the big clubs began to establish a huge gap between themselves and the rest of the League, partly because of the increasing involvement of TV. The Big Five realised that TV was interested only in screening their games, and yet the money they paid for the right to screen the games was paid to the Football League whose Management Committee distributed it evenly between the 92 clubs in the League's four divisions.

The Big Five accounted for almost a quarter of Saturday afternoon attendances and were amongst the few clubs that were solvent. But within the administrative structure of the League they had little power. Each club affiliated had one vote in elections for the Mangement Committee and on important policy matters. As a result, the League rules and business practices were heavily slanted in favour of the smaller clubs, at the expense of Spurs and the other four glamour clubs.

To counter the League Management Committee, the Big Five chairmen, including Scholar, had begun to hold meetings in the discreet location of the Park Lane Hotel in Mayfair. Scholar worked closely with Martin Edwards of Manchester United, the biggest English club in financial terms, swopping money-making ideas and plotting a joint strategy for their dealings with TV and the Management Committee.

Scholar's impulse to keep hold of as much TV money as possible was not, as the smaller clubs sometimes said, evidence of simple greed. It was a matter of basic economics and sound business practice. The cameras came to White Hart Lane, Anfield and Old Trafford because the big teams had spent millions on star players, or at least resisted the temptation to sell good players as the smaller clubs always did. Looked at in purely financial terms Spurs would be better off selling all their first team, cashing up millions, and sinking down into Division Four where they would still get the same amount of money from TV. As Scholar saw things, it wasn't the big clubs who were being greedy or unfair: it was the small clubs who were riding on the back of the big clubs' expensive efforts to stay at the top.

The way the TV money was divided up was only part of the problem. Just as bad was the amount of money that the League had obtained in the first place. They had handled negotiations with the TV companies badly and the amount of money paid for the right to televise live matches for the first time in 1983 was only £5.2 million, a pitiful sum as far as he and the Saatchis were concerned. And the League had allowed the TV companies to ban the wearing of shirts with sponsors' logos on them during televised games, which drastically reduced the potential of his sponsorship package with Holsten.

So long as the structure of the League remained the same, TV would have two aces up its sleeve. The smaller clubs knew that the TV audience for their games was very small and that, on their own, the money they could expect from TV rights would be basically zero. If the large clubs pressured the League to hold out for more money the TV people could just threaten to walk away. TV could then rely on the small clubs to revolt, using their superior voting power to force the League to settle for less, rather than nothing.

The arrival of sponsorship as a vital part of the finances of larger clubs had, by the early 1980s, given TV its second ace. They knew that sponsors were interested only in seeing their logo on telly, and the League's supine acceptance of the sponsored-shirt ban during televised matches had given them another important bargaining chip. Without TV exposure Spurs would be scarcely in a better position than the small clubs. Rochdale, denizens of Division Four, were sponsored by the local All In One Garden Centre and were reduced to posing with a giant watering can, the Centre's logo, in the middle of their team photograph where the trophies should have been.

The TV people now wavered about the lifting of the ban in return for lower fees, arguing that the difference would be made up by higher sponsorship income. If the League, already under pressure from the small clubs to accept whatever offer was on the table, refused, they would threaten to walk away. The big clubs would not appear on TV and their vital sponsorship income would collapse.

The League's TV contract had been negotiated in 1983 when Scholar had been busy sorting out the flotation of the PLC. But the contract was due to come up for renegotiation in 1985 and he was determined to have a personal role in negotiating the deal. The SuperLeague plan which he had asked the Saatchis to draw up was crucial to this. If the League settled for too little money or insisted on sharing the cash equally between all clubs, the Big Five would walk out of the League, set up their own competition, and do their own deal with TV.

Manchester United and Everton had threatened to do something along these lines in 1982, but the plan had been too vague. The smaller clubs, confident of their ability to vote out any major changes, had been dismissive. 'This SuperLeague idea,' boasted Ernie Clay of Fulham, 'has about as much chance of getting through as Arthur Scargill admitting he needs a wig.'

In 1982 the drama had ended in the normal League fudge and hand-wringing in the form of a special Commission under the chairmanship of Sir Norman Chester, an ancient worthy and the League's trouble-shooter since the 1960s. His report had recommended a slight reduction in the number of clubs in Division One. Typically, nothing had been done to implement the report which, according to legend, was gathering dust on the 'Chester shelf' at the League's headquarters set in genteel Lytham St Annes, a posh seaside rival to Blackpool on the muck-strewn Lancashire coast. 'File it on the Chester shelf' had become a football in-joke for matters that were to be locked up forever in chains of inactivity.

Scholar said he hoped that it would not come to a breakaway, but he was determined that if the big clubs had to threaten a breakaway, the threat had to be real. If there had to be some sort of shoot-out, he wanted to make sure he had a loaded gun. The Saatchis had already presented Scholar with several SuperLeague proposals based on differing numbers of breakaway clubs. The option Scholar and the Saatchis settled on was similar to the Scottish Premier Division, consisting of ten clubs which would play each other four times a year. This would produce an annual programme of 36 matches per team, compared with 42 matches in a Division One season where 22 teams played each other twice. A ten-club solution would increase the proportion of SuperMatches and would appeal to TV, but it would also suck in enough medium-sized clubs to keep things interesting, and would leave the League with only the real duds.

And so Scholar set off to join the League's negotiations with the TV, buoyed up by Spurs' good performance in the League under the team's new manager, Peter Shreeves. Despite the weakened squad, Tottenham had started the season well and even looked like outside contenders for the League championship. Liverpool were faltering slightly and the championship looked more open than it had for years. At the end of the season Tottenham had finished third in the League, behind the runaway winners Everton. Liverpool finished in second position, one place ahead of Spurs on goal difference. It was the team's best League finishing position since 1978.

The main feature of the season had been the defence of the UEFA Cup for which, as holders, Tottenham had automatically qualified. After despatching various unlikely central Europeans, and some more Belgians, the team reached the quarter-finals where they lost narrowly to Real Madrid. This was disappointing, but not the end of the world. Spurs were heading for either the runner-up or third place in the League, and it looked like Glenn, Ossie and the lads would be back in the same UEFA competition next season, plonking some more obscure European also-rans. So long as nothing went wrong, this would give Scholar the extra attraction of European soccer to offer the TV people during the negotiations.

But something did go wrong, terribly wrong. The end of the 1984–85 season turned into a nightmare of disasters and hooliganism which so badly affected the reputation and image of soccer that some feared it would never recover.

6: THE EGO HAS LANDED

In the early 1980s Millwall were the nightmare club of English soccer; permanently short of cash and weighed down by an awful hooligan problem. The image was summed up by the skinhead supporters' favourite chant:

> We are Millwall
> No one likes us
> We don't care.

The club's problems were a direct result of the closure of the surrounding London docks. Its natural supporters had been dispersed and many of those who remained were unemployed and as skint as the club. The Den, Millwall's ramshackle north Lewisham ground, had become a sociologist's paradise of alienated youths and unemployed dockers shuffling around a grim concrete enclosure, with the dereliction of pre-boom Docklands as a backdrop.

Millwall hooligans had been causing trouble for years, but in 1985 they excelled themselves during an away FA Cup tie against Luton, occupying the pitch and taking part in a full-scale battle with the police, who were heavily outnumbered. The abiding image of the incident was of a Millwall skinhead putting the boot into a policeman who was trying to give the kiss of life to a collapsed colleague.

The toll of 47 seriously injured people established a new record in the unofficial Hooligan League. Next into the fray were the Chelsea mob, still in the grips of the Syndrome, who smashed up the stands at the Chelsea stadium during a League Cup semi-final against Sunderland, after which the club's chairman planned to put a twelve-foot electrified fence around the pitch until he was banned from doing so by the Greater London Council.

Events at Luton and Chelsea were followed by a riot by a Manchester City gang at Notts County; a fight between Leeds United and Birmingham City supporters that left a fifteen-year-old boy dead; and the arrest of 70 England supporters following mass looting in Helsinki.

The violence that marred the second half of the season was capped off on the last day of the League season when a stand at Valley Parade, the ground of Division Three Bradford, caught fire. Hundreds of people were trapped in the blaze and 57 people were killed. The whole event was broadcast on TV and the next day the papers were full of horrendous pictures of traumatised victims crawling out from the billowing clouds of black smoke.

But the horror was not over. A fight during the European Cup final between Liverpool and Juventus at the Heysel stadium in Brussels led to the collapse of a wall that crushed hundreds and killed 39. Liverpool supporters were squarely blamed for the deaths, and all English clubs were banned from playing in Europe.

English soccer could therefore not have been in a worse position to reopen the negotiations with television, the commercial relationship which Scholar now believed was so important to Tottenham's future. The botched 1983 contract had now run its two-year course and Scholar was ready to play a much more central role in the talks. He had tried to get himself elected to the Management Committee in 1984 but had been voted down by the smaller clubs who were suspicious of his motives. And from their point of view, they were right to be suspicious. Douglas Alexiou, Tottenham's vice-chairman, had queered the pitch for Scholar's election campaign by revealing the Big Five's real objectives in their dealings with TV: 'I'm sure the top clubs would be magnanimous and give some of the money to small clubs,' he disingenuously told the press, 'but it's essential that we keep the lion's share.'

But despite its worries, the League had invited Scholar to join a special sub-committee established to advise on relations with TV. In readiness for any type of show-down, which would involve pulling the Saatchis' detailed SuperLeague plan out of the hat, Scholar had also played a part in getting the agency appointed as special TV advisers to the League on a six-month contract. The TV committee was chaired by Sir Arthur South, the chairman of Norwich City, but the star member was Robert Maxwell, owner of the *Daily Mirror* and one of the richest men in the country.

Maxwell's involvement in soccer began in 1981 when he bought Oxford United, whose Manor Ground stadium was 400 yards from Headington Hill Hall, the family residence. Maxwell had added various personal touches to the Victorian pile, including a gigantic stained-glass window representing himself as Samson.

Oxford were one of the least glamorous teams in the League. The club had only joined the League in 1962, when they replaced Accrington Stanley in Division Four. They were officially nicknamed 'The Us' but in the football fashion stakes they were definitely the 'non-Us': owned by Bill Reeves, a local dentist, saddled with accumulated debts of £162,000, and losing £2,000 a week.

At the time Robert Maxwell was far from being a household name, and was not well known even in his adopted home town of Oxford. In the business world he was notorious for a 1971 Board of Trade report on his business dealings involving Pergamon, which denounced him as being unfit to run a public company. That particular débâcle had followed failed attempts to buy the *News of the World* and the *Sun*, in the late 60s, which gave Maxwell some notoriety in both the City and and the media. But in the world of dentistry he was an unknown quantity altogether. Reeves had never heard of him and the club's approach to him came purely by chance.

In December 1981, with Oxford just days away from

closure, a minion in the club's office, who also worked for Pergamon, suggested cold-calling Maxwell as a last desperate chance. He was tracked down on the telephone to Montego Bay, Jamaica, where he was taking a family holiday. Maxwell listened quietly as Reeves explained the club's dire financial circumstances before booming back across the Atlantic in his deep foghorn voice: 'Don't worry. Tell the bank that I will personally underwrite the wages bill.'

Arrangements were made for Maxwell's private company, Headington Investments, to keep Oxford going into the New Year, when he could have a closer look at the books. He duly turned up at the Manor wearing a furry Russian *chapkah* hat and baggy overcoat against the January cold, striking a bizarre figure among the tracksuits of the assembled squad as he embarked on a pompous stately tour of the dilapidated 11,000-capacity ground. To get into the spirit of things, the new chairman even wore an old-fashioned supporter's ribbon rosette with a bull's head, Oxford's logo, in the middle. The main effect of this was to make Maxwell look like he had escaped from the county agricultural show.

He patronised the players, explaining that the odds stacked against the club were nothing compared to his own triumph over adversity. Out came the story, which became a big part of the Maxwell soccer legend, of how he had 'fallen in love' with soccer as a child when he had watched Arsenal play a friendly match against a local team in his native Czechoslovakia.

Robert Maxwell had been born in 1923 as Jan Ludwig Hoch, into a large, poverty-stricken Jewish family in rural Carpatho-Ruthenia, a miserable slice of territory now located in the eastern tip of Czechoslovakia. Most of his family had been murdered in the Nazi holocaust and he had narrowly escaped the same fate by breaking out of a Hungarian prison and making his way to Yugoslavia where he combined trading in cheap jewellery with work for the anti-Nazi resistance.

Towards the end of the war Maxwell joined British

military intelligence and, as a linguist fluent in half a dozen languages, began working for the Allied occupation authorities in German. The post gave him his first major break in business. He used his specialist contacts to buy German scientific manuscripts for next to nothing, publishing them in Britain at a good profit. It was this activity, later repeated in his dealings with the Communist authorities in eastern Europe, which led to the foundation and success of Pergamon Press.

Maxwell had done something similar with Oxford United: buying from desperate people on his own terms. His first move had been an attempted merger with nearby Reading FC, creating a new club called the Thames Valley Royals. The Manor and Reading's Elm Park grounds were to be closed and the Royals would build a new stadium at Didcot, halfway between the two.

The merger had been kept secret until April 1983 when Maxwell called a press conference at the Football Association's Lancaster Gate headquarters. Jim Smith, the Oxford team manager, first heard about the plan when Maxwell called him an hour before the kick-off at a routine away match against Doncaster, announcing that he was now manager of 'The Royals'. Smith, nonplussed, broke the news to the players after the match. Unless Maxwell was planning to field 22 players in future, half of them were out of a job.

The fans rose in revolt, organising petitions and demonstrations which Maxwell ignored as simply sour grapes from people who did not understand how to run a business. But the opposition had been more serious at Reading where the directors booted the pro-Maxwell chairman off the board and rejected the merger, wrecking the plan for good.

After this Maxwell turned his guns on Oxford City Council, threatening to close down United unless they came up with money for ground improvements. Taking fan pressure more seriously than Maxwell, the council came across with £250,000, which was almost twice what Maxwell had paid to buy the club in the first place. As a result Oxford soon had one of the better grounds in the lower divisions. It also provided a handy city-centre parking space for Maxwell's personal helicopter, with the floodlights used as night-time landing lights.

But Maxwell was still not satisfied. 'I am a first division chairman and I need a first division club,' he declared and began sniffing around a variety of football's financial corpses, including Birmingham City, before making a bid for Manchester United. Like Scholar, Maxwell was convinced that ownership of a major club such as Manchester United or Tottenham, combined with a new TV deal, would be highly profitable.

In February 1984 Maxwell offered £10 million for the privately owned club, but United's chairman Martin Edwards upped the price at the last minute to £15 million. Maxwell, whose accountants had put United's true worth at about £8 million, withdrew with much bluster about sharp practice. (At the time Tottenham were worth about £10 million, mainly because the club had more valuable property.) Maxwell did, however, keep his options open, buying a block of shares in the club and negotiating a contract to land his helicopter in the Old Trafford car park.

A month later he bought Derby County for £850,000. Derby were one of the more famous names in the League, twice League champions in the 1970s under the management of Brian Clough. But the team had done badly after Cloughie left to manage Nottingham Forest in the 1980s. They had been in Division Two for four seasons and were facing relegation to Division Three with debts of £1.5 million.

By now it looked like Maxwell was playing a football version of Monopoly, buying up as many properties on the board as possible. The League's rule prevented anyone from owning more than one club, but Maxwell and his lawyers skirted this by transferring formal ownership of Derby to his son Ian. Ownership of Oxford and Derby gave the Maxwell family two votes inside the Football League, where Maxwell senior was working closely with Scholar to boot out the old guard and squeeze more money for televised soccer out of the TV companies.

During the closed season Maxwell finally registered as a figure with the general public by acquiring the *Daily Mirror*. Once again Maxwell had swooped on a company eager to sell, this time Reed International, the Mirror Group's corporate owner, which was struggling with stagnant sales and endemic over-manning problems. Maxwell bought the whole group, including the *Sunday Mirror*, the *People* and the *Daily Record* for £113.4 million.

Scholar admired and respected Maxwell, who he always called Uncle Bob, for the way in which he had turned Oxford United around and out-manoeuvred the League over the Derby purchase. Both men shared the same smouldering contempt for the League Management Committee, who they saw as a bunch of blithering amateurs standing in the way of soccer's profitable future as a branch of the media and advertising businesses.

Most club chairmen were entirely ignorant of the internal workings of the media. Even Scholar was not a media professional and relied heavily on the advice of the Saatchis. But Uncle Bob actually owned a large slice of the printed media and was expanding rapidly into cable TV. More importantly, he had the money and a team of expert lawyers at hand to make things happen. He had already proved his effectiveness by getting the 1983 TV shirt advertising ban reversed with an impressive show of legal bluster. The BBC's case against the ban was based on the convenient assertion that shirt advertising breached the Corporation's founding charter. But Maxwell got his lawyers to crawl over the charter and the BBC executives crumbled at once.

Now Maxwell was demanding a similarly tough attitude in the new round of talks. Preparing the way, he proclaimed that televised soccer was worth at least £10 million which, translated from his usual megaphone diplomacy, meant that his bottom line was probably around £5 or £6 million, the figure the Saatchis had calculated the BBC – ITV duopoly would be prepared to pay based on soccer's actual ratings and the cost of making other programmes that would attract the same number of viewers.

The TV executives were just as aggressive in their counter-attack. They had been angered by Maxwell's legal action in 1983 which broke the gentlemen's agreement that TV contracts should be a matter of amicable discussion. They couched their offer, in effect, as an ultimatum. The duopoly, headed by Jonathan Martin, head of sport at the BBC, and his ITV counterpart John Bromley, offered only £4.5 million for a package of nineteen live League games of their own choosing and an unlimited number of *Match of the Day*-style highlights programmes: take it or leave it.

The TV executives' hands had been strengthened by a media campaign centred on the decline of soccer's place in national life which the Saatchis later described as 'systematic denigration' of the sport. But after the terrible events at Luton, Bradford and, above all, Heysel, Martin and Bromley did not have to look far for ammunition.

The deaths at Heysel had been shown live on television. They had revolted the ordinary TV audience and had a sobering effect on ordinary soccer fans. Emergency safety inspections carried out by local authorities in the summer of 1985 had shown that many grounds were in a terrible condition, a series of 'disasters waiting to happen', especially when added to the hooligan factor. Charlton Athletic's dilapidated Valley stadium had been closed down on the spot after being officially described as 'a death trap'.

The TV companies were not going to pay extra millions when the only new 'attraction' soccer had come up with since the last deal had been screens full of sickening violence, death and destruction. The picture painted by the TV people got blacker and blacker. Attendance at soccer matches had declined almost every year since the war and in statistical terms there was now doubt about the game's claim to be the national sport. During the

66

heyday of televised soccer in the 1960s and early 1970s, the championship had been an open, exciting competition with lots of teams across the country in with a chance, and had attracted a genuinely national audience. In the decade following 1964, when *Match of the Day* started, seven different teams had won the League. But in the next decade a single club, Liverpool, had won the championship seven times. Most seasons effectively ended after a few weeks, when Liverpool had established their traditionally huge lead, and the rest of the matches were pointless and boring.

The way things stood, Liverpool's grip on the game looked set to tighten. The only other clubs with a realistic chance appeared to be Manchester United and Everton. The League had become a local competition. Nobody outside the North West, or even the city of Liverpool, got a look in. The TV audiences generated by soccer in richer and more appealing TV regions such as East Anglia, the Midlands and the South, were pitiful.

As soccer was changing in these negative ways, TV had also been transformed. The arrival of video recorders had been a big hit with soccer's traditional market of skilled working-class males ('social group C2' in marketing speak) and social trends surveys revealed that the biggest Saturday-night entertainment was now watching a video film while eating a takeaway meal. Audiences were down across the board. TV viewers were more fickle than ever before and demanded novelty. Darts and snooker, the new TV sports that had arrived in the early 1980s, had left soccer far behind in the ratings. Even American football had found its niche on Channel Four and, in terms of the number of viewers it attracted divided by the amount of cash the Americans wanted for British screening rights, it was a much better bet.

But snooker was the real winner. It filled hours and hours of airtime and was phenomenally cheap to produce. Eighteen million had watched the 1985 World Snooker Championship final. The winner, Steve Davis, immediately joined the celeb circuit. He was profiled in the *Observer* where, in paragraph after paragraph, he revealed how he lived with his mum and that the high spot of his daily routine was eating Marmite on toast for breakfast. He at once gained the nickname Steve 'interesting' Davis, which was designed as a slight, but in which he gloried.

Even taking into account the possibility that half the viewers were in a coma, snooker still represented much better value for money than soccer, and was much more attractive to advertisers too. Nobody got killed live on TV during snooker tournaments; there were no hooligans (unless you counted 'Hurricane' Higgins, one of the more popular players); and you could stop and start play easily, slotting in ad breaks as required.

Live soccer, in contrast, had to run for a marathon 45 minutes before a single advert could be shown. When adverts could at last be screened during the half-time break, a far smaller proportion of the audience could be relied upon to watch them. The minute the half-time whistle blew, most of the punters would disappear to the toilet or the kitchen. The more traditional viewers would doubtless go and microwave a cup of Bovril or stick their feet in their new chest freezer to simulate the dimly remembered reality of actually being at a soccer match. It was all very different from the ad breaks in snooker which fitted seamlessly into the flow of an evening's semi-comatose viewing.

Then there was the problem of the zap button which, to the horror of everyone in TV, all the punters now possessed. It was an established fact that viewers had taken to channel-hopping in a big way, reducing their attention span to seconds. Thirty seconds of the sort of midfeld slog that stretched out for 90 minutes in many English League games would lose half the audience. Ten minutes of boredom and everyone apart from the featured teams' committed supporters would hit the button. Televised snooker, in contrast, was constructed as a series of short 'cliffhangers', like the twists in a soap-opera plot, which, although not very exciting in themselves, glued the potatoes to their couches as they idly wondered what was going to happen next.

Jonathan Martin of the BBC summed up the duopoly's case: 'Football rates itself far too highly and has no God-given right to be on television. It is not our job to under-write and subsidise the game. We don't depend on football and if it loses its slot there is no knowing if it will ever get it back.' The ultimatum could not be clearer: either the League and the South committee accepted what was on the table, or the TV companies would walk away.

The Management Committee collapsed at once and recommended acceptance of the offer to a meeting of all 92 club chairmen. But Maxwell and Scholar bitterly attacked the deal and demanded a harder line. 'The game has sold itself too cheaply to television in the past,' Maxwell fumed. 'Football fills a lot of time on the screens. We must be run as a business and not kill our own audiences.' Swayed by this talk, and the opinion of influential people in the game, such as Nottingham Forest manager Brian Clough, who believed televised soccer was mainly responsible for soccer's decline in the first place, the League allowed its TV subcommittee, now effectively led by Maxwell and Scholar, to try for a better deal.

The approach they chose was the basic business tactic of trying to get the two TV companies to bid against each other; but the duopolists were having none of it. They called Maxwell's and Scholar's bluff and announced failure to reach agreement. Their offer was still on the table but until the League accepted it, the 1985–86 season, due to start in a few weeks, would be the first since 1964 not be televised.

Sir Arthur South resigned from the TV committee, the Saatchis were told they were no longer required as advisers to the League, and Maxwell dropped out as well, castigating the League Management Committee for its ineptitude over the years. Scholar was left at the centre of events, catching flak from all sides. The smaller clubs, as the TV camp had correctly calculated, saw Scholar and Maxwell as the villains of the piece and were campaigning for immediate capitulation.

Even the Big Five were shaky, worrying as ever about their sponsors. But Scholar had already established the bottom line: the Saatchis' professional study, showing that soccer as it stood was worth £6 million to TV. Martin's talk about not needing or wanting soccer on the box was arrogant hogwash. The game delivered its particular audience like anything else across the spectrum, from opera to game shows, and if the price was right they would buy. The main thing was to whip the smaller clubs and their sheeplike chairmen into line. In the past the Big Five had threatened to break away from the League if the small clubs did not do what they were told. But there was no point in waving about a fearful deterrent unless you were prepared to use it. TV had dropped its atom bomb on small-time soccer and there were white flags all over the place.

The only answer was to launch an even more devastating counterstrike. Scholar rolled his ultimate doomsday machine on to the launch pad: the SuperLeague.

7: THE *SONGS OF PRAISE* EFFECT

HMS *Spurs* had gone down the slipway of the 1985–86 season from the high point of the opening game and had kept on going. Gates for the early part of the season were down by a quarter and as the season went on more and more supporters drifted away.

Some fans already complained that the new West Stand had sterilised the atmosphere at White Hart Lane. They were more thinly spread round the ground, with more seated, and were much more subdued. This had not bothered the executive box customers who, behind their double glazing, were equipped with speakers and a variable sound control to hype up the sound like canned studio applause when they felt like it. But for the ordinary fans on what remained of the terraces, the West Stand destroyed the feeling of camaraderie that was one of the main attractions of the Saturday ritual.

As supporters fell away the ground got more and more morgue-like. Sometimes the loudest thing in the stadium was the whack of the ball being kicked, and the abuse shouted at each other by the players echoed around the half-empty concrete bowl like in an indoor practice match. All the time the West Stand loomed over the passionless spectacle like a huge white elephant. Excluding games against teams such as Manchester United, who brought their own fans in large numbers, the average gate in the first season was around 20,000, and by the second half was down to under 15,000.

Attendance at a Division One match against Birmingham City reached a new record low of 9,359. The collapse in gates was being reflected right across the League, but it was not just a matter of numbers; the very nature of football supporters had changed. The unemployed underclass was still turning up, and so were the ostentatiously rich executives, insulated behind the glass of their executive boxes. But the remaining 80 per cent of the population, the 'ordinary' and family based supporters whom Scholar and the Saatchis had tried to attract with their Mrs Ridlington adverts, deserted the game, perhaps for good.

Soccer grounds had become a metaphor of sorts for the new divided Britain pundits said Mrs Thatcher's free-market policies had brought about. The University of Leicester even set up a special sociology unit to investigate the phenomenon. The broad conclusion was that male members of the underclass had been stripped of all dignity and had reverted to a fierce masculine pride. The terraces inside football grounds were the only place where they could gain any respect in the form of great symbolic displays of unrestricted rage and hostility.

The main target was no longer opposing fans, but the police. Many of the more hardened underclass males, especially in the wake of the vicious battles of the 1984 miners' strike, sincerely wanted to inflict severe physical harm on policemen, and the fact that the miners had adopted the mindless 'Here we go, Here we go' soccer chant during episodes such as the Battle of Orgreave was causing great sociological excitement.

The blockheaded response of many clubs had not helped. After hooligans began to dominate the headlines in the early eighties, Allan Clarke, the manager of hooli-ganised Leeds United, had advocated the public flogging of offenders as a sort of pre-match deterrent and new form of entertainment. Clarke offered to do the whipping himself. Now, in the wake of Heysel, most Division One clubs had thrown up menacing ten-foot mesh fences round their pitches, which mainly had the effect of spurring the hooligans on to greater efforts.

Denied the fairly harmless mayhem of running on the

pitch they remained penned up like the ANIMALS and SCUM they were castigated for being. At Chelsea they took to smashing up the stands and throwing the debris on to the pitch, in the hope of provoking a police charge leading to a pitched battle inside and outside the ground.

At Tottenham, Scholar, who had the advantage of having actually attended soccer matches as an ordinary fan, was much more low key and effective in his anti-hooligan measures. Instead of cheap and nasty barbed wire, he spent a lot of money on less provocative measures such as extra entry- and exit-points to the ground, discreet security patrols, club stewards and closed circuit TV. As a result, and because most of the East London underclass seemed to gravitate to clubs such as Millwall and West Ham, Spurs escaped the worse effects of the sociology boom.

But there was nothing Scholar's enlightened policies could do to prevent underclass violence in general. White Hart Lane was located in the north London inner-city 'riot belt' that had periodically exploded since 1981. Two months into the 1985–86 season, the most horrific of a series of battles between the police and local youths took place less than a mile from the Spurs ground at Broadwater Farm. During the riot PC Keith Blakelock was battered and hacked to death with baseball bats and machetes. Spurs were forced to cancel a mid-week match to avoid overstretching the police. The incident had nothing to do with Spurs or football, but the match cancellation linked the club's name to the violence and added to the general feeling that soccer grounds were dangerous places located in horrible inner-city areas. All this was stirred into the general equation – soccer + underclass = crime + mayhem – that had lodged in the imagination of the nation's Mrs Ridlingtons.

The PR consequences of Broadwater Farm were only one of a series of problems facing Spurs for which the club would not be held responsible and over which Irving Scholar had no control. After the triumphs of the takeover, the flotation and the UEFA Cup win over the past three years, things were now going wrong.

The ban on English teams in Europe hit Tottenham straight away, losing the club up to £1 million in the extra gate receipts it would have got from the UEFA Cup games it was due to play during the season. The fans could find no compensation in the team's performance in domestic competitions that, anyway, had been devalued by the European ban.

Spurs were knocked out of both Cup competitions before the season was halfway through. With no prospect of a place in the UEFA Cup there was absolutely nothing left to play for. Even the executive boxes were in trouble. The government had banned alcohol at all football grounds and this was bound to hit crucial catering revenue. Nobody wanted to buy an alcohol-free executive champagne suite.

Half-year financial results covering the first part of the 1985–86 season confirmed the dramatic decline in the PLC's fortunes. A profit of £821,000 in the previous six months had been turned into a loss of £528,000 and Bobroff announced there would be no dividend. The PLC's share price collapsed to about 50p, which was only half the issue price, and would probably have gone down further if not for the arrival on the scene of Isadore Brown, an eccentric soccer-supporting Anglo-American millionaire.

Brown had been born in Manchester but made his fortune developing shopping malls in New Jersey, and now announced his intention of buying Spurs, sweeping up the club's shares at the bargain price of 54p each. Brown built a big stake in the PLC forcing Scholar, to his immense irritation, to invite him to London so that the board could size up this curious predator.

Brown flew in, waving his money about in stereotypical cigar-chomping-rich-Yank fashion, and telling the press that he had no particular interest in Tottenham Hotspur: he just wanted to buy 'any First Division club which is up for sale. Find me one and I'll buy it. I have money, that's not a problem'.

The problem was that, to his surprise, Tottenham was the only club he could buy into on the Stock Exchange and so he zeroed in, building up a 14 per cent stake and demanding a seat on the board. 'I have considerable stock in this company, I think they realise they have to treat me right,' he said before meeting Scholar and the board, and began outlining a sinister-sounding plan to turn White Hart Lane into a leisureplex and shopping mall. Scholar humoured him with the full patronising gringo treatment, palming him off with the dubious honour of watching a gruesome 0–0 draw with Luton from the Directors' Box. Brown returned to Heathrow clutching the standard autographed football and various rubbishy trinkets from the souvenir shop.

A predator as wealthy and determined as Brown would have been treated much more seriously by any other company, but Scholar and Bobroff knew that 14 per cent was about as big a stake as he was ever likely to get. The board and its close allies had more than 40 per cent of the shares and most of the rest were in the hands of the fans who, according to legend, kept them in frames on their toilet walls and would never sell them to anyone. The idea that something can't be bought or sold is baffling to Americans but Brown eventually realised he had hit the rock of fan loyalty. When the share price revived slightly he became bored, sold his stake at a big profit and troubled the board no more.

The Brown affair seemed to prove that the board was invulnerable to takeover no matter how financially weak the club was, or how low its share price dropped. All they needed to do was present a united front to the world. Fan loyalty, or at least inertia, would do the rest. This was comforting. On the balance sheet the club's financial difficulties were nothing like as bad as they had been in 1982 when Scholar had taken over. But beneath this superficial calm, the crisis he now faced was potentially much worse. In 1982 Spurs and soccer in general had been victims of recession and bad management practices that could be put right quickly. Scholar had bought

Tottenham at the bottom of the market when the general economic scene could only get better. Now the upturn was beginning to arrive for the economy, but soccer was being left behind.

Other businessmen might have taken a leaf out of the TV companies' book and walked away from football. Robert Maxwell, after his run-in with the League over TV rights, had put his soccer interests on the back burner and passed day-to-day control to members of his family. But Scholar was a genuine fan. On a personal level, the empty echoing scenes at White Hart Lane hurt him as much as any other fan.

Scholar had done everything he could to run the club more efficiently, but the problems he now faced were beyond his control. The collapse in gate receipts was sure to mean continuing thumping losses for the PLC's basic football activities. The City and normal investors were avoiding Spurs' shares like the plague, and so, for the time being at least, there would be no funds available for profitable diversification.

Only the possibility of a new deal with TV, backed by the threat of the SuperLeague, held out the prospect of any new money at all. Scholar had begun sounding out the possibility of a new deal between TV and the big clubs at the start of the season. On paper the prospects looked good. If the £4.5 million was still on offer, the ten clubs involved in Scholar's scheme would get £450,000 each, instead of the £49,000 due if the TV money was divided between all 92 clubs in the normal way. In other words, a deal with just the ten SuperLeague clubs would be equivalent to a TV – League deal of £41 million, a much bigger figure than even Robert Maxwell had dreamt of.

There was mild interest from the TV companies, but their basic line, that soccer needed TV more than TV needed soccer, was proving to be correct. The soccer TV blackout had not hurt audience ratings, at least not on the scale of the catastrophic decline in attendance at soccer matches. The new TV sports of snooker and darts were still doing well and the hunt for new televisual sporting sensations had taken an aquatic turn with live kayak racing, water polo and even an underwater ludo championship. The TV companies were content to let soccer stew in its own juices, confident that the clubs would drop their hard line and settle on their terms. They had heard the SuperLeague talk before and as far as they were concerned it was an internal League dispute in which they were not interested. They would not even begin to negotiate until any new SuperLeague organisation was an established fact.

Scholar and his Big Five allies reacted by upping the stakes. At a meeting at Old Trafford in September, the Big Five leaked the Saatchi-inspired SuperLeague plan to the *Daily Mail*, which splashed the story as 'SUPERLEAGUE REBELLION'. The talk was now of a new competition involving twelve or eighteen clubs, and not ten as the Saatchis had originally proposed. The expansion of numbers reduced Spurs' potential income, but in the pandemonium which was about to break out, the expansion proved to be a clever political move. As many as fifty clubs might think they had a chance of getting one of the non-Big Five places in the new set-up, after a couple of seasons at least.

The response from the League was typically muddled and the reaction from individual clubs quickly degenerated into dog-eat-dog. No-hopers such as Doncaster Rovers were apoplectic, and the medium-sized clubs condemned the move, while simultaneously putting out discreet feelers about their chances of joining.

The consternation at the League's Lytham headquarters soon subsided into the normal demands for meetings, and meetings about meetings. League secretary Graham Kelly, a plump, bespectacled and quietly spoken bureaucrat, began repeating the word 'compromise' like a mantra. After meetings with League President Jack Dunnett, the amiable old worthy from Notts County, Kelly offered to reform the League structure, hinting at more powers within the administration and a greater share of future TV money for the big clubs if they dropped the SuperLeague plan.

But the real pressure came from Gordon Taylor, secretary of the Professional Footballers' Association, who threatened to lead the players out on strike if the SuperLeague went ahead. This was not as daft as it sounded. A successful exercise in 'player power' back in 1961 had liberated footballers from the almost feudal restrictions of the minimum wage and one-sided contracts. Although tiny, the union had a lot of respect and affection from players, partly because membership was a badge of professional status which, to many footballers, with their poorly educated and working-class backgrounds, meant a lot.

There were still feelings of rough-and-ready solidarity which stretched like a web through the small and closed world of professional football. Many big-money players had personal friends amongst the lowly-paid players stuck in the smaller clubs who would now almost certainly face redundancy if the SuperLeague went ahead. The more standard Division One club players, including many in the Spurs squad, were looking forward to easing their way out of soccer, extending their short professional careers by playing with dignity for another ten years with the lower division clubs. Then there was the possibility of managing a small club. The late Cyril 'Nice One Cyril' Knowles, a much-loved Spurs player in the 1970s, had ended up as manager of Hartlepool United and would face an uncertain future if the SuperLeague went ahead.

Taylor came over in the media as a thoughtful and moderate man with right on his side. And by taking the role of David against a group of obviously scheming and probably greedy Goliaths, he immediately got the public on his side. He at once accepted that there would have to be some changes in favour of the big clubs. That was only fair. He admitted that there were clubs in the lower division that were a bit of a shambles, but there were others who had struggled to find an appropriate niche in their small-town surroundings.

He pleaded emotionally and effectively on behalf of

78

once great clubs such as Preston North End which would be destroyed by the SuperLeague. Clubs like these were victims of economic changes beyond their control: the closure of traditional industries, the arrival of motorways that enabled new generations of soccer fans brought up on *Match of the Day* to become travelling supporters of the Big Five. Preston had moved with dignity to cut its cloth to its new reduced means and become a friendly small-town club.

It was true that the big clubs had been subsidising the small clubs. But they had left out the contribution made by the smaller clubs who scouted out and trained raw young players. Gary Lineker, shortly to emerge as the star of the England team's creditable performance in the 1986 World Cup, might well have spent his vital teenage years working on his father's fruit and veg stall in Leicester market if he had not been taken on as a professional by Leicester City, one of the clubs threatened by the scheme. The SuperLeague was in danger of killing off the geese that laid the golden eggs. This was a powerful argument with the players who packed a meeting in Manchester to pledge total support for a strike.

The threats and counter-threats continued into December. League soccer had now been off the screens for half a season and the Big Five were coming under intense pressure from their sponsors. The counter-argument that lack of TV coverage encouraged people to turn up at football grounds collapsed for good as attendances continued to plummet. The Saatchis' 'event-like' view of soccer matches, which held that the presence of cameras added to a sense of occasion, was vindicated. TV had come to play such a huge role in people's lives that most thought that if things were not on telly they were not important, or perhaps did not exist at all.

At soccer games some fans would even try to position themselves near the corner flags or behind the goalposts, like human sponsors' messages, so they could wave to their families when the cameras came in for a close-up. People enjoyed the sense of occasion that the cameras gave to any event. It was the '*Songs of Praise* effect': empty churches would suddenly be bursting at the seams once the faithful realised that they might be on telly. The Archbishop of Canterbury had never complained that televised Church services were killing off the Christian religion.

By now the Big Five were desperate. With no TV exposure for three months and no progress towards an alternative SuperLeague deal, Philip Carter, the chairman of Everton and the unofficial representative of the Division One clubs, reopened talks with TV. He was in a weak position. After all the talk of SuperLeagues and demands for extra money Carter was forced to accept £1.5 million for TV rights to what remained of the season: £3 million less than what had been on offer earlier in the year. The TV executives, rubbing salt into the wounds, had also demanded a three-year contract at the reduced rate of £3.1 million per season for three seasons and access not just to nineteen games, but as many as they wanted.

Without changes to the League structure Spurs' income from TV would be only £34,000 a year, the income generated by just three executive boxes. If they liked, the TV companies could show every game of the season. That worked out at less than £1,000 per game for exclusive world television rights. This was total humiliation. And there was no escape from it until 1988 when the contract would again come up for renewal.

The SuperLeague was shelved in Scholar's thinking, at least for the time being, blocked by the threat of a players' strike. The only way forward was to transform the League into something like the SuperLeague and, above all, to make sure that he and the other big club chairmen were in control of it. In December 1985 Gordon Taylor of the PFA, the only person who had emerged from the saga with any credit, organised a crisis meeting at a hotel near Heathrow to discuss the future of the League. Scholar, Carter and Martin Edwards of Manchester United represented the Big Five and lined up against a small-club delegation led by Lawrie McMenemy of Sunderland, Bill Fox of Blackburn Rovers, and Ron Noades, the combative chairman of Crystal Palace. There were no League Management Committee members present.

The two sides agreed, in effect, to turn the existing Division One into a SuperLeague of sorts by 1988 by reducing the number of teams from 24 to 22. Although the original Saatchi target of ten clubs was nowhere near being on the agenda, there was an understanding that, if things went smoothly, a further reduction from 22 to twenty or eighteen might be possible in the future. As part of the deal there would be automatic relegation into the netherworld of the GM Vauxhall League for clubs who came bottom of the fourth division. That would slowly get rid of the basketcases. They would be steadily replaced by more efficient semiprofessional clubs who would be less of a strain on League resources.

This fate had already overtaken several clubs including Accrington Stanley, Burton Swifts and Bradford Park Avenue: all the big names in Hovis and Bovril land*. They had sunk without trace, making way for more cost-conscious southern outfits including Wimbledon and Maxwell's Oxford United.

Progress in these SuperLeague-ish directions would be underwritten by giving each Division One club two votes instead of one at League meetings and by increasing their representation on the Management Committee. The cause of the drama, the division of TV money, would be

---

* Bradford Park Avenue was booted out of Division Four in 1970 after winning just five out of 140 League games and finishing bottom of the League three years running. The club subsequently went bust, but there have been various heroic relaunch attempts. 'It won't be a six-month thing; we want to make nice, steady progress,' said the club's chairman in 1988, adding forlornly, 'At the moment we have no ground, no manager and no team.'

changed to allow the big clubs to keep a bigger share of what was available. And the big clubs would be released from the levy on their gate receipts that was paid to the smaller clubs.

Taylor emerged from the horse-trading clutching, Chamberlain-like, a piece of paper which promised a footballing equivalent of peace in our time. After some more wrangling, further threats of immediate breakaway by the SuperLeague, endless jokes about turkeys voting in favour of Christmas, more strike threats, media hysteria, League ineptitude and sundry futile small-club revolts, an amended version of the Heathrow Agreement was accepted by a majority vote at a meeting of all 92 clubs in April 1986. The main amendment was that the existing League Management Committee should resign and seek re-election, which they promptly did.

The Division One clubs swept the board in elections for the new committee. Philip Carter, chairman of Everton, stood against the outgoing President Jack Dunnett of Notts County and beat him. It was the first time in a hundred years that an incumbent President had not been re-elected.

Scholar preferred to remain on the sidelines. He did not have the deal he wanted with the TV companies, but he could at least again see the way forward. He had won the respect and support of Robert Maxwell in the process; and that might come in handy some day. And he was ready to fight TV again in 1988 without being hogtied by the League. His hand would be much stronger then and he could expect the duopoly to crumble, as Maxwell was predicting, under competitive pressure from the new satellite TV stations which were likely to be starting up by then. Scholar would have to bide his time.

Spurs returned to the screens along with everyone else in the second half of the 1985–86 season, but their performance was still dismal. Liverpool, in contrast, had bounced back from the Heysel tragedy to 'do the Double' of winning the championship and FA Cup. Only West Ham and Everton had stayed within chasing distance of

Liverpool in the League. Maxwell's Oxford United won the Milk Cup, but with no European or UEFA Cup places to play for, the season had been basically a waste of time for everyone else.

The collapse in attendances after the start of the season continued and spiralled further as a result of poor play and lack of Cup and European interest. The average gate for the season worked out at 21,000, the lowest ever recorded, and a third down on the previous season. It was the worst League performance, both in terms of gates and results, since the club had been repromoted to Division One and the squad was deeply demoralised.

The sour departure of Keith Burkinshaw, who had put the Cup-winning team together, had not helped. Peter Shreeves, though popular with the players, had the dis-advantage of having been Burkinshaw's deputy and seemed to lack the authority needed to whip them into line. Asked what he thought about his team's performance after a late-season thumping by Coventry City at home, Shreeves asked rhetorically: 'What's the bottom line in adjectives?' The board at once came up with the answer: 'sackable'.

Shreeves went to manage Queen's Park Rangers and was replaced by David Pleat, a strange-looking man sporting the part-teddy-boy, part-Dracula hairstyle of the sort made popular by ageing TV snooker players. He was lured from Luton Town, which he had steered into Division One with limited resources, making him the ideal man to shape a new team without spending too much money.

Pleat announced the arrival of his brisk new regime on the first day by ending free lunches for players and abolishing the club's policy of paying green fees at their golf clubs. In terms of footballing tactics most of his attention was applied to the unglamorous subject of defence. Under Shreeves the team had been scoring lots of goals, more, in fact, than anyone except Liverpool and Everton, but had been let down by conceding too many.

Pleat reorganised the squad introducing the continental

'sweeper' system, which involved one team member playing behind the defenders. When the 1986 – 87 season opened the team had a new, fresher look thanks to the tactical changes. The new attacking style suited striker Clive Allen who scored a hat trick against Aston Villa in the first game of the season. Allen scored eleven goals in the first eleven League games; Spurs even topped the table for a week.

Chris Waddle, the Geordie signed from Newcastle United at the start of the previous season, found form and was working well with Hoddle. Waddle and Hoddle were both in the England national team causing endless tongue-twisting problems for foreign commentators and confusion for the GBP who had taken their normal passing interest in England's performance in the 1986 Mexico World Cup. Waddle was conveniently identified as 'the one with the funny hairstyle', which was basically a reverse short back and sides – all bristles on top with long blond locks stretching over his habitually hunched-up shoulders. Waddle was known to Spurs fans as 'Widdly Waddly' because of his awesome dribbling abilities, or more simply as 'Wad' because of his allegedly huge salary. Together with Hoddle, who was worshipfully known as 'God', they were 'Wad and God', another great Spurs double act to rival Greaves and Gilzean (the G-Men), Ossie and Ricky, Scholar and Bobroff, and Chas 'n' Dave.

Scholar allowed Pleat to strengthen the squad with the purchase of Nico Claesen from Standard Liège, bringing net spending on players to about £2 million in the year since Waddle arrived from Newcastle. New managers always spend money on players when they arrive and Pleat, a legend for building teams on the cheap at Luton, was parting with the bare minimum to keep the team up to Big Five standard (by way of comparison Alex 'Fergie' Ferguson, who arrived at Manchester United in 1986, spent over £4 million in his first full season).

Despite Pleat's parsimony Spurs came third in the League, reached the semi-final of the League Cup, now sponsored by Littlewoods, and the final of the FA Cup where they lost 3-2 to Coventry City. Clive Allen scored at Wembley, taking his goal total for the season to 49, including 33 in the League – the best performance by any striker since Manchester City's Francis Lee in 1972. The team was doing well but Scholar knew it would cost millions more to replace the rest of the existing team, and then more again to provide a squad with strength and skill in depth to match Liverpool and win the League, which was all he really cared about.

The European ban had reduced soccer income but, paradoxically, pushed up the cost of players. The very best players, such as Liverpool's Ian Rush, wanted to play in Europe and there was a queue of Italian and Spanish clubs waiting to buy them. The new going rate was £2.5 million per player, treble what Spurs were able to pay at the time, and the inflationary effects were felt right across the domestic transfer market.

If events had followed the plan Scholar had in mind when he took over the club, Spurs might by now be able to contemplate team-building on this grand scale. But the catastrophes of 1985 and 1986 had changed all that and delivered him back to square one. The dramatic fall in gate income combined with spending on new players had produced an annual loss of £730,000 on a turnover of £5 million: a situation that would probably lead to a normal company being closed on the spot. Yet all around the economy was starting to take off, led by a property boom.

Scholar had at least been able to use his expertise to sell the club's training ground in leafy Cheshunt on the rising market, clearing the current losses and providing a small capital sum of £1 million. The lesson that until a new deal with TV was sorted out, football was dead as a paying proposition, was not lost on the Tottenham Hotspur PLC's board. The only way to profit was to pitch into the new 'enterprise culture' economy which was starting to roar outside the walls of White Hart Lane. The Big Bang in the City, heralding a new era of easy credit for hectic business expansion, had taken place just a few weeks into Pleat's first season as manager. Just as Scholar was attempting to run his sport like a business, business was beginning to be run like a sport.

The newly deregulated financial institutions were falling over themselves to gamble on all manner of fanciful and speculative leisure and consumer schemes, ranging from chains of post-modernist pizza parlours to 'niche shopping' wheezes specialising in the sale of socks. In contrast Scholar's long-term plan to tap the 'Aladdin's cave' of merchandising and marketing seemed very modest.

In this new environment all that was needed to raise huge sums of money was the 'bottle' to 'go for it', to use the terminology ushered in by the Big Bang, plus the involvement of a credible figure with a strong business track record. Scholar and Bobroff were respected in the City for their solid property-dealing experience, but what was really needed was an expert in the new game of conjuring vast profits out of virtually nothing: a mergers and acquisitions man.

PART
TWO

8: THE TORY, TORY GAME

The Network South East commuter train from Liverpool Street station in the City of London to the northern suburb of Edmonton passes through one of the worst urban disaster areas in Western Europe. For much of the way the line is elevated, appropriately emphasising the gulf between rush-hour commuters, as they rattle on their way to the suburbs from gleaming hi-tech City offices, and the inhabitants of the dismal panorama on display beneath.

Two minutes out of the station the train jolts violently as it collides with the worn-out points at Bethnal Green Junction. The dust and noise of skyscraping City redevelopment gives way to a sociologist's paradise of cheap post-war council blocks, overcrowded Victorian villas split into dozens of tiny bedsits, grubby high streets, cratered roads, beat-up cars and rubbish-strewn streets.

First stop is London Fields — a name which so cruelly contradicts the grim inner-city reality of its location that Martin Amis was inspired to use it as the title for a novel about the nature of duplicity. The train then clatters on through the nuclear-free, but cockroach and rat-infested, borough of Hackney: the Naples of the north, only uglier, and one of the poorest municipalities in Britain. To the right is Hackney Downs Comprehensive School, periodically closed following reports of playground drug dealing. From here the train crunches on through Stoke Newington into the joint rail-underground complex at Seven Sisters where the tunnels hold the record for the most muggings anywhere on the London tube system.

Then it's onwards to Bruce Grove, the station serving Broadwater Farm, another pastoral misnomer. Three stops later commuters arrive in the relative tranquillity of Edmonton, with connections and rush-hour direct lines to prosperous retreats in leafy Hertfordshire. But first they must pass through the most famous, rather than infamous, name of the line: White Hart Lane.

The Jewish community that had arrived fleeing East European pogroms at the turn of the century, and had originally formed the backbone of Spurs' support, still has a big presence in the area. Stoke Newington, two miles to the south of White Hart Lane, boasts the densest concentration of Orthodox believers outside Israel and New York. Until it upgraded the ancient local telephone exchange, British Telecom complained that it was over-loaded and was knocked out of action every Friday. Half the phones in the area were simultaneously taken off the hook to mark the start of the Sabbath.

But for many of the less religious families Hackney and Tottenham had been only a stop on the way to establishing themselves in more solidly middle-class territory, either in Essex (the traditional aspiring East-Ender territory centred on Chingford and Chigwell) or to the professional northwest London suburbs of Hendon, Muswell Hill and Finchley, where Irving Scholar's family had established itself.

Their place had been taken by West Indians, Cypriots and Asians, a new generation of poor immigrants likewise hoping for better things. By the mid-1980s another group had been stirred into the Spursland's traditional mix: young white professionals sucked in to work in the booming financial institutions at the other end of the train line. They settled like pioneers in pockets around the stations and were soon joined by professional 'gentrifiers' who specialised in snapping up the area's dilapidated Victorian villas, restoring them to a synthetic version of their original bourgeois splendour and selling them on at a huge profit. By 1984 the first wine bar opened in Stoke Newington, causing such amazement that the *Observer* wrote an article about it.

After that it was house-to-house combat as the yuppies, as they were known, bought out the locals and extended their enclaves. Soon the area's main shopping street was a bizarre mixture of dowdy kosher butchers and trendy estate agents; post-modernist designer boutiques nestled incongruously next to cheap and nasty nylon and plastic discount emporia; minimalist combined art gallery and vegetarian quiche establishments were backed up against reeking kebab shops and greasy cafés. As property prices in the area surged ahead on a tidal wave of easy credit, some of the more enterprising locals got in on the act, buying and 'doing up' houses and flats to sell to the arriving young City people, trendy designers and media persons.

Soon the new prosperity had trickled down to the terraces of White Hart Lane. Below the level of the executive boxes, the more traditional soccer supporters crammed the streets around the stadium with their XR3is and 'Rascal' Bedford vans and carried on business at half time with portable telephones.

Spurs supporters had always regarded themselves as a cut above the rabble who followed northern teams such as Liverpool and Manchester United. The northerners had in turn seen Spurs fans as a bunch of typically arrogant, 'flash' Cockneys. In the mental world of the northern soccer fan, Spurs' great 1961 Double was a typically crafty cheat by the moneybags Cockneys who had bought expensive players such as Jimmy Greaves as part of the country's first 'million pound soccer team'.

When portable phones started appearing on the terraces, the traditional stereotyping had been given a new twist by the growing north-south economic divide. Liverpool kept winning everything on the pitch but at least Spurs' fans could find comfort in the presumed financial success of their club.

Some Spurs fans called Liverpool supporters 'the thieves' or, adopting Mersey slang for the same thing, 'the scallies'. In dull moments during the normal crushing

Liverpool victory on the pitch, some fans would take wads of notes from their wallets and wave them at 'the thieves' as a wind-up. This was partly a dimension of the standard competitive macho scene, with depth of bank balance substituted for length of penis. It was also a reminder that, whatever happened on the field, the enterprising Tory-voting, *Sun*-reading, share-owning Cockneys and not the unemployed, Labour-voting, *Mirror*-reading, poverty-stricken scallywag Scousers were the real winners.

It was this spectacle that inspired comedian and Spurs supporter Harry Enfield to create Loadsamoney, the wad-waving plasterer who briefly mesmerised the nation at the height of the property boom and had a top ten hit with 'Doing Up The House', a novelty rap record. Enfield tried out his act at the seedy Tunnel Club in south London, where it was a great hit. The Loadsa character was then fleshed out to wear the standard uniform of logo-splattered leisurewear and trainers. Unlike the subtle and witty FA HIT sported by Irving Scholar's Range Rover, the personalised number plate on Loadsa's XR3i was more blunt: BA2 TARD.

Loadsamoney quickly became a mainstream TV sensation. The joke was less popular on Merseyside, where thousands of unemployed local building workers had been reduced to travelling to London on the 5 a.m. 'Giro express' every Monday, sleeping in grotty Portacabins all week and working off the cards as cheap labour for real-life Loadsamoneys on the capital's building sites. They would return home like refugees under police supervision every Friday night to see their families and watch Everton or Liverpool win, which was all they had left by the way of dignity. When Loadsa became a national hero instead of the hate figure Enfield had intended, the character was dumped. His next creation was Buggerallmoney, a skint Geordie Newcastle United supporter with more than a passing resemblance to Chris Waddle, who 'smerked tabs', drank 'nuerkee brern' and loathed all southerners as 'poofs'. Buggerall was not a success.

Scholar had meanwhile pitched into the rising property market, plugging the gap in Spurs' trading profit by selling off the club's training ground in suburban Cheshunt. The sale raised £4.5 million, £3 million more than the asset value placed upon it at the time of the flotation three years before. The working capital provided was immediately earmarked for expansion and diversification into areas such as leisurewear, tapping the new Loadsamoney market.

To do this meant buying up promising companies and welding them into a single money-making machine under the banner of Tottenham Hotspur. Scholar was not an expert in the tricky area of corporate acquisitions and not especially well placed to attract the sizeable loans that would be needed for rapid expansion. He knew that there were plenty of successful businessmen who, like himself, supported Spurs and might be happy to help the cause.

A trawl through the executive box list, combined with discreet feelers put out through the Spurs business circuit, came up with the name of Tony Berry, one of the greatest acquisitions and mergers specialists in the country. The cult of the A and M man began in Wall Street where people such as Michael Milken, Martin Siegel and Ivan 'Greed is Good' Boesky had thrown financial caution to the wind, borrowing billions to buy companies, breaking them up and selling them on after a few minutes of ownership, paying back the loans and reaping massive profits. The same game had spread to London on the back of the government's Big Bang deregulation of the City.

Like Scholar and Bobroff, Berry was another self-made man, and one of the new generation of aggressive, risk-taking entrepreneurs. His reputation was based on the way he had built his Blue Arrow staff recruitment business from virtually nothing to become one of the most dynamic companies in the country. In 1981 he had been sacked from his job as finance director of Brengreen, a contract-cleaning company run by David Evans, a childhood friend who had gone on to become the Tory MP for Welwyn and chairman of Luton Town football club.

Like many people in the enterprising eighties, Berry had plenty of opportunities to use the well-worn cliché that getting the sack, and thus release from the bondage of salaried employment, had been the best thing that ever happened to him. He invested £350,000 in a holding company that controlled Blue Arrow, then a chain of nineteen secretarial agencies based in London. Within a year Berry's company had been making profits of £200,000 a year and in July 1984 went on to the Unlisted Securities Market valued at £3 million. A year later Blue Arrow bought out the Brook Street and Reliance Service agencies, catching the upturn in the economy and latching on to the trend for a more casualised workforce. Berry had obtained the money for this rapid expansion from his merchant bank, County Nat West.

Berry's link to the bank was the cornerstone of his success and, at times, it was hard for City analysts to work out who was leading whom in the relationship. Aggressive merchant banks like County were playing a larger role in takeovers and each had its 'Golden Boy': a young outsider untainted by any contact with traditional manufacturing and 'old money' and addicted to the new game of multi-million-pound financial poker. Their role was to seek out takeover opportunities and do the deals. The banks would then supply almost limitless credit, creaming off their share of the profits and pushing their client, with reputation appropriately enhanced, on to his next triumph.

Berry was County Nat West's Golden Boy, a man with the Midas touch who was unafraid of any challenge, exuding the required Total Confidence, and always charming and determined to live the good life. Soccer fitted perfectly with the required democratic, man-of-the-people profile of the new City whiz kid.

Berry had been born in Tottenham into a family of Spurs supporters, and in his youth had been both a boxing champion and a promising schoolboy soccer player. At one point he had considered a career as a professional footballer and underwent trials for Spurs youth team. He had been rejected but now, like Scholar, he had the money to make some of his boyhood fantasies come true. He told the *Financial Times*: 'If my father was alive today he would say that to be chairman of Blue Arrow is really good, but if you are on the Spurs board you've really made it.'

When Berry joined the Tottenham board he was about to prove he had really 'made it' by pulling off his most audacious takeover so far: the purchase of Manpower, the giant US recruitment and labour agency which, in contrast to Blue Arrow's original nineteen branches, employed 700,000 people in 32 countries. County Nat West had arranged for the issue of £837 million worth of Blue Arrow shares to provide the cash needed to snatch Manpower from the Americans. This was the biggest single call on shareholders ever made in Britain and amounted to a gigantic IOU to be paid off from future profits.

The deal went through in August to Berry's complete satisfaction, raising the takeover mania gripping world financial markets by another notch. But City regulators soon began to smell a rat. There was deep suspicion, as well as amazement, that County Nat West had managed to sell all the shares needed to finance the Manpower takeover. The reality, uncovered by an enormously complex Department of Trade investigation followed by a £35 million fraud trial, was that the bank had bought many of the shares itself. This had the desired effect of hyping up the price of the shares. Ernest Saunders of Guinness had already been found guilty of the same scam.

Although he later lost control of Blue Arrow, Berry was not accused of being involved in the corrupt dealing. The £440,000 he invested in Tottenham Hotspur PLC to buy 400,000 shares was much more straightforward, and very small beer in comparison.

The moment Berry's involvement was announced Tottenham Hotspur PLC's share price shot up. City people rushed to get a slice of the latest Berry bonanza and share in the Midas touch. Because of the increase in the PLC's share price Berry's investment had been paid back with an instant theoretical profit the moment he set foot in the Spurs boardroom. But it was realised that if Berry ever tried to sell his shares to realise his profit, the process would go into reverse, the share price would collapse and he would probably lose every penny of his investment. Such was the ephemeral nature of many of the paper fortunes being built up at the time: everything depended on keeping up the momentum.

Sometimes these thoughts would bubble up from the City's collective subconscious to produce nightmarish images of brick walls, missing rungs at the top of mile-high ladders, and saturated markets where there was simply nothing left to buy. But these worries were quickly lost among the howls of 'no limits' in the City.

With Berry on board Spurs had at its disposal a man who could disappear into the bowels of the City and re-emerge with a cheque for the best part of a billion pounds. Getting the much smaller sums of money needed to buy or start up the companies needed for diversification would be easy enough. Berry's arrival, in its way, had provided as much money as the flotation that had wiped out the Richardson debt. The new money he was certain to bring in could be used more positively.

During the traumas of the 1985–86 season Irving Scholar's friends swore that he had suddenly aged as a result of the pressures and problems crowding in from all directions. He had never stopped displaying his own brand of the required Total Confidence, but the signs of strain could be seen in new bouts of chain-smoking and his suddenly greying hair. Now he was fired up again, back on course, more impatient for success than ever and bursting with expansionary ideas.

Paul Bobroff, with his naturally more conservative frame of mind, had been much more cautious about Berry's arrival. Unlike the flamboyant Scholar, he was a quiet man who rarely joked and did not join in Scholar's jovial banter about soccer trivia. Generally he was seen by people as a bit of a cold fish. Unlike Scholar, who was now devoting almost all his time to Spurs, Bobroff was still deeply immersed in the affairs of his property company, Markheath Securities, and tended to see the club more as a simple business proposition rather than an all out quest for footballing glory. He was also more acutely aware that Berry's success was mostly a case of being in the right place at the right time to be spotted by County Nat West. If his bankers failed to back him, or got into cash difficulties of their own, his success could disappear as quickly as it arrived. But that did not seem very likely in early 1987, the high point of what became known as the financial 'go go' years. For now they were all Golden Boys together: a trio of young financial strikers whose fancy footwork was a match for anyone in the country. Scholar was to play the role of midfield general, controlling the pace and setting up scoring opportunities for others. He would continue to tighten up the club's management, minimise the inevitable losses resulting from the activity of football itself, and supervise the steady growth of merchandising. Beyond this he was itching to resume his battles with the Football League and the TV companies, working with Robert Maxwell to unlock the Aladdin's cave of TV money.

Bobroff's job was to take charge of the next phase in the development of White Hart Lane. The debts caused by the West Stand had now been wiped out and, after some discreet but effective lobbying by Scholar, the soccer alcohol ban had been lifted from the executive boxes, making them highly saleable again. The fans had got used to the higher prices charged for entry to the stand, even though tickets at White Hart Lane were the most expensive in the country.

Plans were now in hand for a new East Stand which would be built to the same standard and financed in the same way, extending the number of executive boxes from 72 to 108. The development proposal was not popular with many of the fans, who complained that the West Stand had created a sterile atmosphere at the ground, and hated the way that the stadium had become a continuous

97

building site. But the worst complaint was that the hallowed Shelf, where the hardcore supporters stood, was destined for redevelopment.

A small minority of the fans organised themselves as a pressure group and started pestering the board over the plans. They were generally ignored as a nuisance, though Scholar was more sympathetic and even took the trouble to point out that part of the Shelf would be allowed to stay intact. This seemed to satisfy most of them, even though it was part of the plan all along.

Bobroff had more on his plate than a few moaning fans. As part of the Golden Boys approach, Bobroff's Mark-heath, booming away on the back of the bullish property market, was to play a large part in managing the development. This would prevent cost over-runs of the type that had floored the Richardson board. Since he had the model of the West Stand to work with, the development was seen as one of the simpler and duller aspects of Spurs' expansion and Bobroff was left to get on with it with only limited interference from the rest of the board.

Berry's job was to head off into the more uncharted waters of expansion into leisure markets. Scholar had already pointed the way by buying Hummel UK, taking Spurs into the profitable business of selling replica football strips, mainly to children and teenagers. The replica industry had been started by clubs working with Adidas, the German sportswear company which had cleaned up by transforming its functional running shoes, tracksuits and sports gear into fashionable, and highly marketable, leisurewear.

The roots of this perplexing trend stretched back through the rock industry to the avant-garde New York art scene of the 1960s. Comic books, soup cans, old advertising images, brand logos and random collections of junk from Manhattan scrap heaps were declared to be 'pop art' and started changing hands for rapidly escalating sums. A watered-down version of the fad eventually reached the high street with a new trend for plastering logos and symbols on clothes and carrier bags. Fuddy-duddies in the 'straight' marketing world were amazed by the punters' sudden willingness to pay for the privilege of turning themselves into walking billboards, but cashed in gleefully.

Demand for sports clothing bearing a logo of some type had been assiduously hyped by the rock industry. By the mid-1980s, some of the biggest-selling rock and rap acts were based almost entirely around worship of particular items and brands of sports clothes. At some concerts fans would take off their smelly Adidas or Puma sportshoes and start waving them above their heads like old fashioned soccer scarves as a symbol of loyalty.

Football was slow off the mark in attacking profitable sucker markets like these, encumbered by hopeless reactionaries who still tended to look upon it as a sport instead of a shopping experience. There was no such sentimentality in the rock industry. The core activity of composing and performing live music, the equivalent of fielding a soccer team, had first shrivelled beneath the marketing exterior to occasional 'stadium clanging' by SuperGroups (often at Wembley) with most of the creative work being done by computers, robots and accountants.

Manchester United had been the first to exploit teenage sportswear-and-logo fetishism. In 1975 the club hit upon the idea of producing an 'official' version of its strip to give it, in marketingspeak, a Unique Selling Proposition, making it different from the otherwise identical red and white strip worn by, for example, Crewe Alexandra. The strip was made more expensive and flashy by reverting to old-fashioned winged collars and the addition of various superfluous stripes on the shorts and socks.

The idea made use of one of the marketing industry's favourite and most successful ploys, known in the trade as the 'apron tug'. This involved recruiting the nation's children as salesmen. United-mad kids turning up at the local park in a shirt that was merely red would be mercilessly ridiculed by peers decked out in the new official United kit, and could be relied upon to pester, moan and sulk until they got the same. The fact that the new kit was almost twice as expensive as the simple red soccer shirts, which now mouldered on the shelves of old-fashioned outfitters, added to its exclusivity and attraction to the kids.

Using these methods United and Adidas had apparently been released from the basic laws of supply and demand where sales go down when the price goes up. For the kids there was only one thing worse than not having the official strip and that was having last year's official strip. And so each year the design was changed slightly; the most minute changes to the shape of the collar, or the addition or subtraction of a stripe on the shorts, would do the trick. The kids would do the rest, with their limitless whingeing and nagging abilities, forcing parents to buy household peace by making a repeat purchase. More money was made by marketing marginally altered 'souvenir' kits worn in big matches like Cup finals. To pick the last few pounds out of parents' wallets, the same formula was applied to the team's away strip.

When Scholar arrived at White Hart Lane, Spurs' shirt deal was with the French company Le Coq Sportif which kept most of the profits for itself. Scholar decided that there was no reason why Spurs should not cut out the middle man by controlling shirt manufacture and distribution directly: like the stock market flotation, nobody had bothered to think about it.

In 1985 Scholar signed a four-year deal with a little-known Danish shirt manufacturer called Hummel, obtaining the right to franchise the brand in the UK. Hummel UK was set up as one of the first subsidiaries of the PLC and was provided with headquarters in a warehouse in Enfield, a couple of miles to the north of White Hart Lane. A marketing manager was poached from Adidas to run the business and the company at once began marketing replica Spurs shirts.

The move was not a great success. Like many of

Scholar's business negotiations, it was thought to have great potential, as part of the untapped Aladdin's cave. Larger companies like Adidas and Umbro marketed the shirts of dozens of clubs, giving them all the advantages of economies of scale and a virtual stranglehold on outlets. It was hard for Hummel to elbow its way into such a small, well-oiled and carefully targeted market. The shops were reluctant to do anything that might upset the big companies which supplied best-selling Manchester United and Liverpool shirts and therefore had no interest in helping Hummel and Spurs to establish a strong presence.

With Hummel struggling, the board decided to expand its way out of trouble. Hummel UK began pitching for the licence to produce and distribute the other big clubs' shirts. When Manchester United's contract with Adidas came up for renegotiation in 1987, Hummel UK bid for the contract, offering £100,000 more than Adidas's proposed £1.5 million advance against royalties. Martin Edwards, the Manchester United chairman, decided to play safe, sticking with Adidas, and nakedly using the Hummel offer to lever up their bid.

Hummel UK also copied Adidas by expanding into leisurewear for adult football fans, rather than football strips for teenage players. Glenn 'God' Hoddle had even been persuaded to model the gear under the snappy slogan 'Hoddle in Hummel' leading to the inevitable accusation of being 'a poof' from rival fans. Hummel had no particular manufacturing or marketing experience in the field of general leisurewear, at least not on the scale of Adidas. Another problem was that the whole sport-as-fashion scene was led by young black people, some of whom still regarded soccer as an activity for lumpen whites: fair enough in an age when a few soccer fans would still throw bananas and make monkey noises if a black player appeared on the pitch.

The sports gear that young blacks had turned into popular fashionwear involved the trappings of black-dominated sports such as basketball and athletics. It was also unisex. In contrast to the lithe black disco dancers performing astonishing feats on the dancefloor in skin-tight athletics gear, the spectacle of thousands of pasty-faced white men lumbering towards White Hart Lane wearing 'Hoddle in Hummel' shirts that barely covered their beer bellies was hardly going to set the fashion crowd alight.

The leisurewear development had therefore been no great source of profit but it plodded usefully along, expanding the number of outlets available to Hummel UK. One of Berry's first moves was to build on this base, buying two fashionwear companies to add expertise in the general fashion field and expand the operation away from the Adidas/Umbro dominated sector of the market. According to plan, once a new and profitable clothing company had been established within the PLC, Hummel UK and Spurs would have both the resources and clout for a renewed attack on the replica kit goldmine.

Berry organised the purchase of two other clothing companies: Martex, a ladies' fashionwear distributor whose outlets and experience was to be used to counter the overwhelming male bias of Hummel UK's market; and Stumps, which made cricket clothes and Nicholucci brand tennis gear (made not in Milan, but Leicester). These would be used to get a foothold in posher outlets. The acquisitions were partly debt-financed, which was Berry's normal operating method. They were to be paid for with a combination of cash raised from the sale of shares and loan notes, a form of IOU that, in theory, was the equivalent of printing £50 notes. Just like the real thing the issuer had to promise to pay the bearer the denominated sum but, unlike the real thing, as Scholar knew, the promise had to be honoured.

The IOUs worried Scholar because if Spurs ever got into serious debt the holders of these notes would be able to demand a liquidation of the club to get their money back. It was far less safe than borrowing money from the banks who would face a PR disaster if they ever threatened to close down a much-loved institution like Spurs.

But in the heady atmosphere of expansion these fears were put to one side as Berry and the board planned their next coups. These included the acquisition or establishment of a computer-software company, a book-publishing house and interests in souvenir manufacturing, including the production of teddy-bear mascots for the England national team. The acquisition of a computer subsidiary, Synchro Systems, looked like an especially shrewd move. In the wake of the hooligan problems of 1985 the Government was planning to force all 92 football clubs to bring in club membership schemes. These would amount to official registers of their supporters. Scholar was lobbying hard against a compulsory scheme but, at the same time, Spurs had introduced a voluntary membership scheme costing £80 a year which involved preferential treatment in the allocation of tickets. The software Spurs had chosen to keep its membership list up to date was highly sophisticated and offered many possibilities for updating individual attendance records, targeting of junk mail and other marketing ploys.

As with the Hummel UK operation and the united front Scholar had attempted to organise against the TV companies, the aim was to involve the other big clubs, offering the same software system to them. A good start was made by selling an adapted version of Synchro software to Manchester United; if the government's national football supporter registration scheme ever became a reality, the market for specialised computer software would be considerable.

Scholar was meanwhile expanding his own main area of responsibility within the PLC, which was the club itself and the profitable operation of White Hart Lane. The team was performing well under Pleat and gates had returned to their pre-Heysel levels, helped by a good run in the FA Cup. More importantly, a deal between Scholar and boxing promoter Barry Hearn added £400,000 in profit when White Hart Lane was used as the venue for a boxing match between Frank Bruno and Joe Bugner in October 1987. The fight grossed up almost £3 million.

'Five pop concerts and one fight like that in a year and we'd make more money from the ground than we do from all our soccer,' Scholar enthused, adding a jibe at the expense of the local council: 'It is laughable that a major sporting venue, which is the biggest ratepayer in the Borough of Haringey, is used no more than thirty times a year.' What the locals would make of the likes of Phil Collins or Megadeth emerging every week from a cloud of dry ice to thunder away at 10,000 decibels was another matter. The number of heavyweight boxers willing to fight in the middle of nondescript Tottenham, when much bigger and more 'event-like' venues such as Wembley, Las Vegas and even Zaire beckoned, was strictly limited.

As part of the general commercial development, retail outlets had now been added to the original club shop to tap the existing market and all three were packed with 'Hoddle in Hummel' gear and other vital supporter equipment. The old-fashioned, heritage-style fan outfit of bobble hat and scarf was still available, but it had been joined by a baffling range of baseball caps, key rings, miniature replica FA Cups, posters, books, wallpaper and even Tottenham Hotspur brand aftershave, which at least had Scholar's reputation with the ladies to recommend it.

The club had come a long way from the days when the most visible retail operation was ex-player Dave Mackay's dowdy novelty souvenir tie shop located next to a kebab stall in the desolation of the Seven Sisters Road on the route from the tube station to the ground. (Mackay, a former Tottenham centre half, captain and 'hard man', had meanwhile decamped to Saudi Arabia, following the same desert trail to riches and obscurity taken by Keith Burkinshaw.)

The upgrading of the souvenir shop was followed by the introduction of an 0898 number, the money-spinning new service from British Telecom based on identifying callers' numbers and charging them a fortune for listening to a recorded message. The service had been monopolised by the porno industry who advertised a series of uniformly filthy and merely suggestive messages to its target audience of wankers.

Tottenham Hotspur lined up next to sundry HOT NYMPHOS to provide SPURSLINE under the banner of ALL THE NEWS AND MORE FROM THE CLUB YOU ADORE, a rhyme worthy of Chas 'n' Dave, who provided a suitably time-consuming introductory jingle: 'Congratulations you are through to Spurs, Spurs, Super Spurs, Oh! Super Spurs, Super Spurs, Super, Super, Super, Super Spurrrrs'. There were eleven programmes a week, each four minutes in length. It would have cost the punters £25 to listen to them all, with profits shared 50–50 between the club and the telephone company.

At first the line contained a lot of genuine information about the fitness of various players and so on, which was immediately 'lifted' and quoted by tabloid sports hacks before the press office had the chance to get the normal anodyne line straight. After this, dull and evasive material was substituted. The fans derided the service as rent-a-cliché after investigating it at their employers' expense. But it would still be jammed with thousands of calls if there was a major development of some sort at the club.

In the summer of 1987 the line was humming as fans attempted to find out what was happening to manager David Pleat, the hero of the revived team performance. After just eighteen months with the club, Pleat had fallen victim to another phenomenon of the 1980s: rampant tabloid muck-raking. On 26 June the *Sun* splashed the huge front page headline:

SPURS BOSS IS CAUGHT KERB CRAWLING

The story revealed that Pleat had been stopped and cautioned by the police in the West End. The paper had then mounted a heroic search for a prostitute prepared to say that she had been propositioned by him. They came up with 'Vice Girl Wendy', who provided the material for a double-page spread on the inside pages headed: 'WE DID IT IN A CAR PARK – Vice Girl Wendy reveals secrets of her sleazy sex sessions with the kerb-crawling soccer manager'.

The board gamely refused to comment on the story which, at this stage, rested solely on the unsupported statements of an anonymous policeman and a decidedly sleazy-looking hooker who may or may not have met Pleat. This level of evidence was good enough for visiting Arsenal fans who turned up at the next home game triumphantly wearing T-shirts decorated with the *Sun* front page. The controversy rumbled on through the final weeks of the season that saw Spurs finish third in the League and included a disappointing 3−2 defeat by underdogs Coventry in the FA Cup final at Wembley.

Pleat's subjection to tabloid monstering, as the process of dragging celebrities through the mud was known in the *Sun* newsroom, had naturally shaken him. After the success of 1986−87, when the team came close to pulling off the hallowed League and Cup Double, the team lost its way the following season, despite a promising start. Now Spurs fans, as well as their rivals, were less inclined to let Pleat forget the 'We did it in a car park' episode, and began to blame his unwillingness to spend on players for the loss of form. Rumours began to spread that the board was already looking for a new manager, but the main effect of this was to destabilise the team even more.

In October the *Sun* monstered the Spurs manager again, this time by marching up to the front door of the Pleat family residence in suburban Luton, demanding answers to fresh allegations from a prostitute. The *Sun* reporters and photographer had a bit of luck by catching him in the bath. He was duly pictured half naked, dripping wet and looking startled next to the front page headline: 'PLEAT HAGGLED OVER THE PRICE OF HIS VICE'.

The *Sun* story played up to Pleat's stingy reputation, reporting prostitute Heather Barrett, 24, as saying: 'I told him it was £15. But he wanted it for a fiver. I told him to **** off.' For good measure the paper reported that Pleat had once complained to the local council about noise made by courting couples in the park next to his house.

This was too much for the board and Pleat left the club. Suitably chastened and ashen-faced, he disappeared to take on a team in Greece before resurfacing after a decent interval to manage lowly Leicester City.

As Scholar saw it, what was bad luck for Pleat could be good luck for Spurs, at least in one respect. The crucial position of team manager had fallen vacant at just the right time to attract the man hyped as possessing 'the greatest football brain in Europe'. His name had been whispered all over White Hart Lane during the Pleat crisis: 'El Tel' the recently deposed Cockney king of Barcelona.

9: HOMAGE TO CATALONIA

The style of Barcelona's Camp Nou stadium is part Roman Amphitheatre, part *Blade Runner* film set: a gigantic symmetrical hysteria machine plastered with sponsors' messages and advertising, rising in a series of concrete spirals to enclose 110,000 seats arranged on three circular tiers.

Irving Scholar's plans for Tottenham were to a large extent based on copying the commercial approach of Barcelona, one of the most successful European Super Clubs. He was a regular visitor at Camp Nou, both as a businessman and a fan. One of his most exciting visits had taken place in April 1982, just as he and Bobroff were putting together their bid for Tottenham. The occasion was the second leg of the European Cup Winners' Cup semi-final. The first leg, played at White Hart Lane, was drawn 1–1 showing that in footballing terms the clubs were evenly matched. But in the financial stakes it was no contest. The gulf between the top European clubs and the English Big Five was as great as that between Tottenham and the basketcase English Division Four clubs.

When the ragbag of Tottenham supporters, including Scholar, reached Camp Nou, they were reduced to wandering about like pitiful East European refugees let loose in a Californian shopping mall, eyes glazed by the scale of abundance and financial power all around them. The American concept of the sports 'event' was fully on board at Barcelona, and each match was accompanied by elaborate and carefully constructed frenzy: pop singers, marching bands, celebrity appearances, fireworks, flags, parachutists and balloons all played their part. The home fans were armed with drums and trumpets and would parade up and down the spacious aisles adding to the cheerful bedlam.

Spurs were beaten 1–0 and lost the semi-final 2–1 on aggregate in two nasty games riddled with professional fouls and bookings. Scholar was naturally disappointed by the result, but was lost in admiration for Barcelona, not least because the profits generated by all this diversified commercial activity were used to buy the world's best players. At Barcelona, soccer was merely the flagship for a range of activities based on the club which included the operation of a 1,500-capacity skating rink, a basketball team and a 60,000-capacity secondary football ground-cum-athletics stadium. It was all underpinned by a membership scheme with 100,000 subscribers, offering spin-offs such as travel deals, insurance and discounts in local shops. This had enabled the club to buy the best players on the international market. In the season after the Cup Winners' match against Tottenham, Barcelona paid £4.8 million for just one player, the Argentinian star Diego Maradona. This was ten times what Scholar had paid to get control of Tottenham complete with 22 players, White Hart Lane and acres of prime residential development land in Cheshunt.

Despite this gulf in available resources, Scholar's control of Tottenham had made him a figure on the European soccer circuit, where Tottenham could rank themselves in the top twenty in terms of reputation, if not trophies won. Shortly after officially becoming chairman in 1984, his access to Barcelona had been increased by the appointment of Terry Venables, a former Tottenham player, as Barcelona's team manager.

Venables, who had arrived from Queen's Park Rangers where he had been both team manager and a director, was a controversial appointment. His first move was to sell Maradona, then believed to be the greatest player in the world, to Naples for a new world transfer record of

£5 million. He then used the money to import less glamorous, but more reliable, British players capable of putting his new tactical invention of 'pressure football' into operation.

Tottenham had been the first English club to benefit from the Venables largesse when he bought striker Steve Archibald for £1 million a few weeks after his arrival. Scholar personally supervised the deal and, along with other Big Five chairmen such as Martin Edwards of Manchester United, became a regular visitor to Camp Nou. He would return from his Euro jaunts to the humdrum of White Hart Lane full of enthusiasm as he poured out the details of what the Europeans were doing on the business side. The child in him would again come to the surface, just as it had done when he took Mo Keston on to the roof at White Hart Lane, as he dreamily set out what Spurs could do with the same resources.

Venables was enjoying life at Camp Nou. At last he had the resources and the personal salary, rumoured to be in the region of £500,000 a year, which he thought he needed and deserved.

After the purchase of Archibald, the rest of the Maradona millions were eventually spent on Gary Lineker, whom Venables bought from Everton, and Mark Hughes, the rough-and-tumble Manchester United striker. It seemed that Venables was determined to create a British team playing in Barcelona's colours in exile: the sort of dream team composed of the best players in the English League which fans sometimes fantasised about.

During a period of record balance of payments deficits, it was said that he should be given the Queen's Award for Exports instead. At Barcelona managers and players lived in the full glare of media interest and were treated like film stars. Individual hairdryers, shower units and jacuzzis were provided to help with the increasing grooming requirements needed to meet the new high standards for international players originally established by George 'El Beatle' Best and boosted in the 1970s by Kevin Keegan's perms.

110

It was all very different from facing the showers at Rochdale and Grimsby Town, the prospect that Venables had faced as a member of the Crystal Palace team in his last season as a professional player. There was even an ornate Christian chapel attached to the changing rooms, which would have been useful for Spurs' Glenn Hoddle, who had recently become a born-again Christian. 'Hoddle's found Jesus,' they joked on the White Hart Lane terraces. 'It must have been one helluva pass.' The more hard-hearted observed that there was 'one born again every minute'.

Like others from his home town of Dagenham, Venables took to the Mediterranean lifestyle in a big way, quipping that the only thing he missed about London was the sausages. Even this was no problem: the nearby Costas boasted every type of English culinary horror demanded by the hated hordes of 'filthee Ingleesh', many of them also from Dagenham, who populated the coast for most of the summer. Unimpressed by Venables' record at QPR, which few of them had ever heard of, the Barcelona fans sneered that Nunez had apparently picked up his new manager on the beach.

It was true that Venables, the archetypal sharp-suited, quick-witted Dagenham boy with the chunky frame, flash persona, Essex guffaw and impressive vocabulary of swear words, cut a strange figure in the cultivated and exotic world of Barcelona. But he soon won the locals over. In his last season as manager of QPR he had surreptitiously learned lingaphone-style Spanish from a *Teach Yourself* book which he studied on the coach to away matches, only to realise that in Barcelona people spoke Catalan – an entirely different language. He soon got on top of the local language making him a fully polished polyglot, able to converse with ease in four tongues: Cockney, Spanish, Catalan, and Soccerspeak – of which he was the acknowledged world master.

Venables' ignorance about Spanish geography said a lot about his background and experience of life. He was highly intelligent, had the confidence to learn quickly and put what he learned into practice. Yet he was almost completely uneducated. Venables boasted he never read a book at school and had no intellectual pretensions outside football management. He could therefore be forgiven for not knowing that Spain and Catalonia, of which Barcelona is the capital city, are very different and effectively hostile nations.

Terry 'Tel' Venables was born in January 1943 in his grandmother Millie's house in Vallance Avenue, Dagenham. At the time his father Fred, a semi-skilled docker by profession, was in the North Atlantic serving in the Merchant Navy. Venables' mother Myrtle soon returned to her job working in a local café and so the infant soccer genius was raised by his grandparents, who were Welsh and had moved to Dagenham from the Rhondda.

He was brought up in a small council house in Bonham Road in the middle of a huge 1930s estate built to house workers in the new power stations, car and cement factories lining the Essex bank of the Thames to the east of the old London docks. Even though people were poor by today's standards, Dagenham was always more prosperous than the traditional East End. The council houses, though modest, were solidly built, and many were semi-detached with small gardens. The families who lived there had shown the initiative to move, like Venables' grandfather, from the more depressed areas of the country to work in the new industries. They represented a very special sort of working-class community, a lively mixture of confident and relatively well-to-do Scots, Welsh, Geordie and East End self-improvers.

Much later, in the 1980s, the policy of selling council houses was a huge hit in the area. Former tenants enthusiastically did up the exterior of their council semis, copying the villas they had seen on their holidays, in a distinctive mixture of mock Tudor, Moorish and Greek Taverna styles which became known as Costa Del Dagenham. At about this time the council commemorated the Terry Venables connection by naming a Dagenham

112

street after him (he also received the ultimate 1980s accolade of being an answer to a Trivial Pursuits question).

When Venables was growing up in the prosperous 1950s, Dagenham's wealth was boosted by the booming Ford plant, on the A13 trunk road between the East End and tacky delights of Southend, which dominated the area, churning out the first mass-market Cortinas. The stereotype of the free-spending Essex Flash Harry was being born.

For younger people this new financial confidence often took the form of forays into the insecure, but glamorous and increasingly linked, worlds of showbiz and professional soccer, safe in the knowledge that a well-paid job in the car factory was always available if things did not work out. When Venables began his professional career Dagenham had already provided soccer with Jimmy Greaves and Alf Ramsey, the former Tottenham full back who won the World Cup as England manager.

This was the world of the teenage Tel. From the start he was a show-off, even by local standards, always demanding to be at the centre of attention. As a schoolboy he divided his time between football, at which he had to be the best, and putting on singing-and-dancing shows at the local youth club in which he always took the leading role. He was thus the star of both the Dagenham Schools football team, the best in the country, and the Happy Tappers, a local song-and-dance ensemble.

He was friendly with Brian Poole, later of Brian Poole and the Tremeloes fame, and was established on the fringes of an emerging Dagenham pop scene which was to become a southern rival to Liverpool and the Beatles. Venables might have tried the pop music route to glamour and stardom if his natural talent on the field had not decided matters. When he was fourteen Venables was training regularly with West Ham, the nearest professional club, under the supervision of Malcolm Allison. Tottenham, Fulham, Chelsea, Arsenal and Wolves were also interested in signing him up. Manchester United was so keen to get him that they even arranged to fly Fred and Myrtle to Belfast so they could watch him play in the England national youth team, which made a big impression in an age when air travel was a rare luxury.

Venables was naturally excited by the prospect of playing for a big club like United or Tottenham, the team he supported as a boy. But Jimmy Greaves, another Essex lad, talked him out of signing with either. Greaves had started with Chelsea, a middling Division One club, gaining some solid experience before moving on to the big time with Tottenham. He advised Venables to do the same and follow his path to Chelsea. Venables agreed, partly because his schoolfriend Allan Harris had signed for the club. He was fifteen and went fully professional in 1960, two years later.

Venables continued to live with his parents, enabling him to invest most of his gigantic £20 weekly pay packet, which was more money than the family had ever seen at one time, in the first of a series of small businesses. Aged seventeen he registered himself as a limited company to market the Thingymawig, an invention which he believed would make his fortune. The Thingymawig was a hat that women could wear over their curlers but which had either blond or dark brown alleged hair on the outside. The idea was that women would pay handsomely to be able to move about in public without having to wear a scarf over their curlers in the style of Hilda Ogden, star of the new ITV show *Coronation Street*.

The idea collapsed under the weight of its essential daftness. But Venables was not deterred and continued his ducking and diving, forever coming up with get-rich-quick schemes ranging from general buying and selling to a tailoring business targeted on fellow soccer players, none of which made much money. He kept up his contacts on the pop network, was friendly with Tommy Steele, and would often be seen hanging around the Soho expresso bars after training, writing songs with Tony Hiller, who had the advantage of being able to read music, and then trying to sell them to Denmark Street music publishers.

Basically Tel was a Frank Sinatra man, a smoothie and a crooner. The nearest he ever got to the more avant-garde side of pop was a vague friendship with Kenny Ball and his Jazzmen, who also came from Dagenham. His songwriting efforts were thus mainly wasted in the emerging era of the Beatles and Stones, though Hiller did later find modest fame and fortune by writing 'Save All Your Kisses For Me' which won the Eurovision Song Contest.

Fortunately Venables was having much more success with soccer, settling into the young Chelsea team managed by Ted Drake. At this point Chelsea liked to be known as Drake's Ducklings, optimistically comparing themselves to Manchester United's Busby's Babes. In reality the Chelsea team was mediocre, and in Venables' first few seasons finished in the middle of the Division One table. As Jimmy Greaves had predicted, this suited Venables who quickly became a 'midfield general' type, able to shine without too much difficulty.

After Chelsea dipped into Division Two Ted Drake was sacked as manager and replaced by Tommy 'The Doc' Docherty, at the time a fashionable Scottish hard man. Docherty ruthlessly cut out a lot of the dead wood, which was to be his forte in more than one football management job, and made Venables the team's captain at the young age of nineteen. This was fine at first with the two strong and showy personalities working together. But Venables then made the mistake of changing Docherty's tactics on the field. The changes improved Chelsea's performance and they won as a result, but Docherty was furious at Venables' insubordination and began to needle his captain.

Docherty ridiculed Venables for his pop music activities, which was not difficult, especially his hobby of entering talent contests at Butlins (he once came second to the Bachelors) which the manager said was interfering with soccer. Venables ignored the warning and took up

115

a singing engagement at Hammersmith Palais, crooning a couple of Sinatra numbers with the Joe Loss orchestra at the old-fashioned *Come Dancing*-style dance hall, complete with reflective spinning globe. Venables had risen to the occasion by wearing a pair of winklepickers of heroic pointiness and applying half a jar of Brylcreem to his dark, slicked-back hair. Docherty was unimpressed and temporarily dropped him from the team as punishment.

There was another clash a few months later when Venables and other Chelsea players were accused of drinking heavily and misbehaving at a party. There had always been a certain amount of laddish looning about amongst the Chelsea players: the sort of thing that later, in a much more publicity-conscious age, became the forte of Paul 'Gazza' Gascoigne.

Venables himself was reputed to have once stuck his bare backside out of a hotel window. This time he and others were accused, falsely as it turned out, of taking part in a late-night drinking session likely to affect match fitness. There was great shock when Docherty, after hearing the rumours, phoned Dagenham and found Fred on the end of the line. 'This is Tommy Docherty,' he snapped. 'Tell Terry he's not playing tomorrow. And he's not captain any more.'

The Venables–Docherty needle match continued for another two years. Both were natural leaders and competed for the loyalty of Chelsea players such as goalkeeper Peter 'The Cat' Bonetti, striker Peter 'Ozzie' Osgood and George 'Doomed' Graham, later Venables' rival as manager of Arsenal in the 1990s. Graham, a fellow smoothie and Sinatra fan, got his nickname during the constant Docherty bollockings. Graham had arrived at Chelsea from lowly Aston Villa, giving him the chance to aim for the big time. 'You were doomed, George,' The Doc would rave at him, 'doomed until I saved you from Aston Villa.'

In the summer of 1966 Venables finally fell out with Docherty and was transferred from Chelsea to Tottenham for the large fee of £80,000. By now Venables had settled down a bit, and after marrying Christine at age 23, finally left home and moved to Loughton, a posh Essex suburb near Chigwell, to which go-ahead Dagenhamites aspired. His singing, showbusiness activities and general larking about were sidelined as he concentrated on making the grade at Tottenham and getting on the right side of Bill Nicholson, the Tottenham manager.

Whereas Docherty ranted and raved, Nicholson was a quiet, though sometimes gruff, man who commanded the automatic respect of his players. There was never any chance of Venables cheeking austere 'Old Nick' or disobeying tactical orders during games. The cocky Venables style was cramped further by the other Spurs players. At Chelsea he had been the acknowledged star and was looked up to by his team mates: a big fish in a small pond, as intended. At Tottenham he was just another member of a squad dominated by great players and strong personalities such as Dave Mackay, and was much further from the centre of attention. He did at least have the satisfaction of being in a Cup-winning team at Wembley. Tottenham beat Chelsea 2−1 in the final. He did not score, but the victory was reward enough, made all the more sweet by the sight of Docherty fuming on the Chelsea bench.

Venables had finally reached the top flight as a player but the experience quickly turned sour. He was not a hit with the White Hart Lane crowd who saw him as a poor replacement for John White, a popular player who had been killed by lightning while playing golf. Tottenham supporters decided he was a typical Chelsea dilettante who was not prepared to get stuck in with the required gusto. They called him 'Terry Vegetables' and gave him the bird for the slightest mistake on the pitch. Like Alan Gilzean and Jimmy Greaves before him Venables became increasingly unhappy. Unlike Greaves he managed to stay off the booze. Greaves eventually pulled himself together and was reprofiled as 'Greavsie', the populist TV commentator. Gilzean went off to play in South Africa but later returned as player-manager of Stevenage Town, ending up as the manager of a local haulage company.

Venables' consolation was not drink, but his huge wages, which he ploughed back into his increasingly diverse business interests. The Thingymawig marketing invention was now long forgotten, replaced by a general trading company which he ran himself, saving on secretarial costs by learning to touch-type. He was also dabbling in the more traditional footballer sidelines of pubs and restaurants, helping his father Fred buy the Royal Oak in posh Chingford, Essex – the suburb soon to become famous as Norman Tebbit's parliamentary constituency.

In terms of soccer, things were going from bad to worse. Venables lasted just three full seasons with Tottenham before being transferred to QPR at the end of the 1968-69 season. The £70,000 transfer fee paid by QPR meant, in market terms at least, he was still one of the most valuable players in the country. The move from White Hart Lane to Loftus Road, QPR's modest stadium in west London was a considerable drop in soccer's traditional pecking order. At the time QPR were a regular Division Three team who had been promoted through the second into Division One for the first time in 1968, inspired by Les Allen, a Dagenhamite who had been friendly with Venables in his youth and had played in Spurs' Double-winning team in the 1960s.

QPR had not been able to make the grade in Division One and had been immediately relegated. This meant Venables would be playing in Division Two for the first time since he started his professional career with Chelsea. Despite this, the move turned out well for him. He had little to live up to at QPR and stood out with his greater experience and touch of Division One class.

At QPR he was again the star of the show. Like Chelsea in the 1960s, the club's band of supporters was sufficiently small to be considered select. Loftus Road's catchment area included the BBC television centre and areas such as Notting Hill Gate and parts of Shepherd's

118

Bush and Hammersmith that had once been poor, but were now being settled by well-off media people and intellectuals. It was said that QPR fans did not shout or clap, but politely rustled their copies of the *New Statesman*.

The team itself featured intelligent and televisual players such as long-haired Rodney Marsh, the Rod Stewart of the soccer world, and flash Stan Bowles, who became a star as a result of his operatic televised arguments with referees. Manager Gordon Jago encouraged a laugh-a-minute attitude with endless silly stunts. Terry 'Henry' Mancini, a bald QPR player, famously played in disguise, wearing a long-haired wig, partly as an in-joke at the expense of Marsh, which Venables whipped off his head at the end of the match.

This sort of looning was meat and drink to Venables after his dull and unhappy period at Tottenham. With Jago's encouragement, he orchestrated and joined in the media activity whenever possible, making the most of the TV cameras whenever they turned up at Loftus Road. His biggest media success came in 1973 when the team was chasing promotion to Division One. During a crucial game against Derby County, Venables noticed the camera lining up to record a tight shot of his face. He obliged by smiling and wiggling his eyebrows up and down independently: the sort of trick he had perfected during his Hammersmith Palais and Butlins talent-show days.

The TV people included the shot in the opening sequence of *Match of the Day* and Venables at once became a hit with the mums and girlfriends who were supposedly obliged to sit through televised football against their will. Tel became a tabloid personality as a result, with photographers following him around for months shouting 'Wiggle yer eyebrows, Tel!' until their editors got bored and moved on to the next craze.

Venables, now 30, was slowing down a bit on the pitch but had reverted to his old Chelsea role of orchestrating the team as an unofficial player-manager and all-round tactical genius: 'I've got the brains and you've got the legs,' he would say to younger and fitter players. It worked. In 1973 QPR were promoted from Division Two. Venables, now too old to make the grade for Division One, was transferred to Crystal Palace.

This time Venables' move really did look like a trip to the knacker's yard. Palace was essentially a Division Three club operating in the footballing twilight zone of south London with a catchment area stretching into the unpromising rugger territory of suburban Surrey. In the early 1970s Palace had a freakish run up the League tables, grimly hanging on to a place near the foot of Division One for a few years before dropping back down to the third in consecutive seasons.

The move to Palace reunited Venables with Malcolm Allison, the loud-mouthed East Ender and former West Ham scout who had supervised his early career. 'Big Bad Mal' was typical of the new breed of media-wise soccer managers, complete with pithy wisecracks, exciting playboy lifestyle, quotable homespun soccer philosophy and his very own televisual gimmick: he ostentatiously smoked a fat cigar and wore a giant Humphrey Bogart fedora, which he duly chewed when Palace unexpectedly lost a crucial match.

Venables played only fourteen games for Palace before he limped out of the team, the victim of a form of arthritis. His playing career was over, but Big Mal signed him up as coach and, in effect, his deputy manager. The combined Mal – Tel brain power, and even more formidable combined mouth power, failed to get Palace out of Division Three but they did take the club to the semi-final of the FA Cup for the first time in its history. This was a major feat for a Division Three club, and attracted huge media interest. Big Mal fully exploited the limelight with Tel joining in, throwing his hyperactive eyebrows and cheeky chappie grin into the media mix and organising visual stunts. These included getting the team to turn up for big matches in 1930s gangster costumes in tribute to Big Mal's fedora.

The Allison-Venables double act lasted for two years after which Big Mal left to manage Manchester City, where he had established his managerial reputation ten years earlier.

Venables took over from Allison and, at 33, became one of the youngest managers in the League. He was again back on track as a man ahead of his time. He was again bursting with potential and at last had the opportunity to put his years of leadership experience as a team captain at Chelsea and QPR to good use. He pioneered a new varied coaching style which replaced the traditional drill techniques practised by Nicholson's generation.

Venables steered Palace from Division Three to Division One in three seasons, attracting big crowds, including a new 51,000 record club attendance for a crucial match against Burnley which secured promotion to Division One in May 1979. By now Palace had emerged as the new darling club of the newspapers, often called 'the team of the eighties' because of the team's young players and the club's knack of attracting more middle-class and 'family' supporters.

Venables' own media profile was higher than ever. He had graduated from wiggling his eyebrows to become a TV soccer pundit and post-match studio analyst. On top of this he had co-written a novel with Gordon Williams, who ghosted celebrity soccer columns in newspapers and magazines and wrote soccer programme notes. Williams also dabbled in the thriller novel market. He scored a minor hit with *The Siege of Trencher's Farm* which describes how a group of country yokels attempt to hack a visiting academic to death with blunt farm implements before he shoots them. (The novel formed the basis for the 1971 Sam Peckinpah film *Straw Dogs* which was slammed by *Halliwell's Film Guide* as a 'totally absurd, poorly contrived, hilariously overwritten *Cold Comfort Farm* melodrama with farcical violence'.)

The Venables-Williams novel was called *They Used to Play on Grass* and was based on the boardroom manoeuvrings at an imaginary club called the Commoners. It was set in a near future where all the old soccer grounds have

121

been replaced with modern EuroStadiums with synthetic Astroturf-type pitches. Venables claimed most of the characters in the novel existed in real life, though the names used were invented.

The novel was followed up by a TV detective series called *Hazell*, also co-written with Williams, and named after the main character, James Hazell. Venables said Hazell was based on Bobby Moore, the former West Ham player and England captain. Williams did most of the writing, and Venables' main contribution was the provision of pithy phrases which were put in the mouth of the character. 'He had a wad big enough to choke a spin dryer' was one of his favourites; he said that he had heard a Dagenham haulage contractor use it.

Venables did well in his first season as the Palace manager in Division One. The team even briefly occupied the top position after a good start, creating another wave of tabloid hyperbole about the abilities of the mighty Tel. But the team's performance slumped in the middle of the season and Palace ended in thirteenth place: respectable enough for a small club and one place higher than Tottenham that season.

The success was attributed solely to Venables' ability. This was fair enough given the limited resources available at Palace, and his abilities were finally recognised by the England national team's management who made him the part-time coach of the youth team. Since Venables was still young by soccer management standards he was surrounded by extraordinary hype about his 'potential' and had been marked down by some as a future England manager.

He was confronted with the more mundane business of persuading the Palace board to come up with some money to buy the new players needed to keep the team in Division One. The board appeared to be ready to give him the cash when they sold some land next to the club's Selhurst Park stadium to a supermarket chain. But the money failed to find its way into Venables' team building fund and Tel was soon on his way, taking up an offer to manage his old club QPR.

Rangers had not done well after Venables' departure and had recently been relegated into Division Two. QPR had a new owner, Jim Gregory, a ferocious millionaire secondhand-car dealer who had summarily sacked the ubiquitous Tommy Docherty, and so the appointment also gave Venables the satisfaction of putting another one over on his old foe, The Doc.

More importantly, Venables liked Gregory and his approach to business. Gregory's background was similar to Venables' and the two men got on well together. It was on the business side that Venables made the most immediate impact. Gregory and Venables decided to install the League's first artificial pitch, made from a substance called Omniturf which they had seen during a tour of sports grounds in Canada.

QPR's success under Venables was not as dramatic as Palace's had been, but the club did at least stabilise its position near the top of Division Two. He built a young squad, discovering and training one or two good players, including full back Terry Fenwick, and it soon looked like promotion to Division One was just a matter of time. The real triumph came in the FA Cup where the club reached the final in 1982 for the first time in its history and managed a creditable 1−1 draw with Burkinshaw's Tottenham before losing 1−0 in the replay.

Venables was again playing his favourite role of underdog soccer genius, fashioning success out of unpromising material and able to compete with the very best despite limited resources. The fact his team was beaten at the last hurdle in the FA Cup, and by such a narrow margin, only added to the David and Goliath mythology surrounding Tel, and a footballing defeat was transformed into a stunning personal PR victory.

Next season QPR were promoted to the top flight as Division Two champions, ten points clear at the top of the division. At the last home match of the season, Venables personally led the customary team lap of honour, taking the crowd's applause in the style of his old mentor Malcolm Allison. In the close season Gregory offered to sell the actual club to Venables, keeping hold of the Loftus Road ground himself. The plan was similar in some ways to Irving Scholar's emerging scheme at White Hart Lane; based on splitting off football from other profitable activities based on redevelopment of the stadium.

Venables was tempted by the scheme. Loftus Road had already gone through a lot of changes since Venables' time as a player, and was now virtually all-seater with a vastly reduced 25,000 capacity more in line with QPR's regular home attendances. There were few places for hooligans to run riot and the atmosphere was more like a large theatre or concert hall with seated fans in smallish stands tightly surrounding the plastic pitch. Gregory's plan involved the logical next step of putting on a stadium roof, which was to be mobile, like a giant car sun roof. This idea, copied from similar all-weather sports venues in North America, would make the stadium suitable for money-spinning indoor activities such as rock concerts and boxing matches.

The full plan did not go ahead, but Venables did become QPR's second-largest shareholder and managing director, working closely with Gregory on leisure development plans and finding the additional powers to his liking. The team did well in the first division but Venables was again thinking about the future. His attention was drawn to Europe where it was known that Barcelona was looking for a new manager. British clubs were now dominating European Cup competitions which, given their limited resources, was a mystery that could only be explained by the superior quality of English players, coaches and soccer managers. Barcelona and the big Italian clubs had already been raiding British clubs, exploiting the bargain basement prices of the frozen eighties domestic transfer market, buying up star players and attracting managers with sky-high salaries.

Venables had at last decided to cash in his potential for results or, as he put it in one of his favourite phrases, the chance to 'set out his stall'. The job in hand was to win the Spanish League, wresting the championship from Real Madrid, the traditional enemy in a ferocious needle match overlaid with heady Catalan nationalism. His tactical invention of 'pressure football' soon got results and in his first season in charge Barcelona won the League for the first time in nineteen years. Venables became a local hero and TV personality in his own right, forever cracking jokes like a stand-up comic, being cheeky, stealing cigars from his chairman José Nuñez, and boasting about what he was about to achieve in the European Cup.

Venables was showered with awards and gifts, most of which were repatriated to decorate the walls of the Royal Oak, the family pub in Chingford. After one appearance on TV in Madrid he was given an original painting by Salvador Dali, the famous surrealist. Even with all this interest the Barcelonese never quite managed the pronunciation of the Venables name, which his father Fred told everyone was introduced into England by the Normans. At first it came out as a respectful 'Señor Ben-a-bless' before the more friendly and pronounceable 'Meeester Terry' was substituted. Back home the tabloids called him 'El Tel', hyped his supposed salary towards the magic £1 million mark and speculated that his move to Barcelona was part of a carefully worked-out plan to gain international experience before becoming manager of England.

Back home Bobby Robson was not performing well as manager of the national team. He was therefore getting the standard tabloid crucifixion for failing to match Alf Ramsey's performance in winning, or even looking likely to win, the World Cup. Calls for Robson's instant resignation, if not public disembowelment, were an everyday staple and Venables was often touted as a possible successor. El Tel always denied any immediate interest in the post, saying it was a job for an older man and he was not the sort of person the aged and class-conscious worthies of the Football Association were likely to pick.

Anyway, he had his hands full with Barcelona where, for the first time in his career, he had created a record of success that he would have to live up to.

Barcelona did reach the final of the European Cup but lost on penalties to Steaua Bucharest of Romania, an underdog team doubtless steeled by the thought of what President Ceausescu would do to them if they returned from Romania's one and only European Cup final empty-handed. This was followed by a run of poor results in the Spanish League which saw Camp Nou attendances drop to 70,000, more than twice the average English Division One crowd, but a disaster in Spain. Unlike any of Venables' previous employers, Nuñez would accept nothing less than total success and Venables was sacked after the 1986-87 season. He was still popular with the Barcelona crowds, who theatrically waved goodbye with hankies at his last home match.

El Tel returned the compliment with the typically cheerful stunt of singing the old Sinatra standard 'My Way' in Catalan live on TV. His place was taken by Johan Cruyff, the chain-smoking former star of the Dutch national team, who was put on a £1 million bonus if he delivered the European Cup, but suffered a heart attack and underwent a by-pass operation soon afterwards.

With Venables on the float, the tabloid rumour machine went into overdrive, speculating wildly about his next destination. A holiday in Florida was enough to convince some that he was considering managing the US national soccer team: a thankless, but hugely remunerated, task. He was also said to be pondering a managerial offer from Juventus.

Irving Scholar had already made up his mind that he wanted Venables, and tracked him down in Florida with the help of Mo Keston, who had known Tel since he was a Tottenham player. After a quick discussion on the phone, Scholar flew across the Atlantic in Concorde, worried that Juventus or, even worse, Arsenal might snatch Venables from under his nose.

When the two men met, Venables had already decided

to go to White Hart Lane, so long as Scholar met a simple condition: money must be made available to buy new players and strengthen the squad that Pleat had left behind. He had seen a few video tapes of recent Tottenham performances and decided the team had potential. But he reckoned that about £4 million worth of new players would be needed to give the club a chance of making the grade in Europe.

In particular he wanted to bring Lineker with him from Barcelona. He reckoned he could persuade the England striker to go to White Hart Lane, but knew that his fee alone would be in the region of £1 million. This, Venables realised, was a lot by British standards, but should be possible given what Scholar had told him during his Camp Nou visits about the commercial developments at Tottenham.

Venables still had ambitions to run his own club some day, but he was less concerned about the role he would be given in the general running of Spurs. Venables could afford to bide his time. There was always the possibility of buying his own block of shares in the club if he decided to get more involved later.

It was agreed that Venables would not have a formal executive position at Spurs, unlike his time at QPR where he had been managing director. There was no question of him merely being the team coach as he had been at Barcelona. His role was to be somewhere in the middle, and Scholar was quite insistent that he would be kept fully informed about the financial position.

The meeting lasted only twenty minutes. Venables agreed to start work on 1 December, with a salary said by the tabloids to be in the region of £200,000, making him one of the best-paid managers in the League. On the main point, Scholar said he was quite happy to surrender complete control of the buying and selling of players within an agreed budget, just as Venables wanted. He sucked his teeth at the idea of spending £4 million on players, but agreed this would be possible if Venables raised about half this sum by selling off unwanted members of the squad. Tel's appointment was triumphantly announced in the press to the universal approval of the fans. Ever anxious to cash in, the PLC celebrated by running a 26-part Terry Venables Story on the 0898 Spurs Line which fans estimated would cost more than £50 to hear in its entirety.

Venables announced that the club was on the threshold of a new golden age. 'I have come to Spurs to win the First Division. I need it, I desperately want to do it, and I know it has to be next season,' he said. 'I'm supposed to have said it will take three years,' he added, 'that is nonsense. A consolidating sixth place is no good to me. I must be right at the top with Tottenham.'

10: FANCY FLICKS AND SWEET SHERRY

Irving Scholar's coup in bringing El Tel to White Hart Lane was hugely popular with the fans. The *Sun's* attack on David Pleat, forcing the manager out of the club, had left the team rudderless and floundering. The 1987–88 season had begun well enough, but a successful run in the opening matches quickly turned into a string of nine League games without a win.

By the time of Terry Venables' appointment as manager in November, the fans had already endured the particularly stinging humiliation of losing 2–1 at home to Arsenal and, as part of the new deal between the League which Scholar had helped to negotiate, the game had been televised live on Sunday. Even more disastrous for most of the club's executive-box punters was Black Monday, 12 October, when billions were wiped off the value of shares in the biggest Stock Market crash since the 1930s.

Board members such as Tony Berry were likely to be badly hit, but Tottenham Hotspur PLC itself had less to worry about than most companies. The PLC's share price had always followed its own course, determined partly by the large number of small supporter shareholders who were touchingly and conveniently uninterested in the value of their investment. The share price had already veered wildly above and below the 100p issue price, crashing to a low of 52p after the disastrous 1985 season and shooting up to 250p in the summer of 1987 on the back of news of Tony Berry's involvement. In early October the price had stabilised around the 200p mark, and so the Black Monday drop to 170p was not especially threatening.

In fact there were advantages, both for the club and for individual board members. After the crash, Chancellor Nigel Lawson quickly cut interest rates to prevent the Stock Market crash sparking off an economic depression, making borrowing far cheaper. The board was already contemplating the large loans needed to rebuild White Hart Lane's East Stand, bringing it up to the standard of the West Stand and providing more boxes, and to expand the Hummel leisurewear business. Lower interest rates made borrowing more attractive. Pleat's last season as manager had seen a useful improvement in the financial performance of the football club. Attendance was up by 24 per cent, recovering to pre-Heysel levels, providing an extra £1 million income in return for virtually zero extra spending. The team transfer account was £2 million in the black after the sale of Glenn Hoddle to Monaco and Richard Gough to Rangers.

The good news was reported in the half-yearly results published on 30 November, during the week in which Venables officially joined the club as manager. The financial press was suitably impressed: 'Mr Terry Venables has a lot to do to raise Spurs' flagging fortunes, but the latest accounts indicate that El Tel will have money to spend on players,' said *Investors' Chronicle* which, by now, was officially describing the PLC as a 'football club and sportswear distributor'. The *Chronicle* was further cheered by the renting of White Hart Lane to boxing promoters which, it was predicted, would bring in another £400,000 of additional revenue at once, with millions more to come in future. Even so, the magazine cautiously advised its readers against punting on the share price. 'For fans and admirers of El Tel only,' was the verdict.

When Venables gave his first press conference as manager at the end of November he was in confident mood. The team was in bad shape and had been demoralised by the loss of Hoddle as much as by the

130

departure of Pleat. But with £2 million in the transfer pot already and *carte blanche* to sell off sundry members of Pleat's squad, Venables was certain that the £4 million war chest he had been promised was in place.

'We have not got time to fanny around,' he told the assembled soccer hacks at White Hart Lane, repeating his ambition to take Tottenham 'right to the top'. This bold talk triggered off another bout of wild tabloid speculation about his player buying plans. The main rumour was that Tel was about to lure Lineker from Barcelona. But the speculation was premature. Venables' first signing was not one of the glamorous big names, but dull Terry 'Fenners' Fenwick, the square-framed Geordie full back whom he had nurtured during his time as manager at QPR and now signed for £550,000.

After all the hype Fenwick's arrival was a bit of an anti-climax, but Venables explained it all in suitably profound language: 'Players like Terry are vital to every side – I call them backbone players,' he later explained, apparently damning the player with faint praise. 'It can't always be showbiz-style and there are going to be days when you have to earn the right to play attractive football.' (A throwaway cliché that Fenwick was 'worth his weight in gold' was picked up and confirmed by the *Financial Times*. Gold ingots weighing Fenwick's 11 st 11 lbs would have cost only $586,000 at the time – much less than the transfer fee Venables paid.)

Fenwick's arrival firmed up the defence slightly, but the team continued to lose. The season was now a straightforward disaster with no chance of getting near the League title, and there was more concern about avoiding relegation. Tottenham had already been knocked out of the Littlewoods Cup by Aston Villa in the third round. That left only the FA Cup, the competition in which Venables specialised. Tottenham had been drawn away in the fourth round against Port Vale, who at the time were in thirteenth place in Division Three and had managed to get further than the third round of the FA Cup only once in twenty years. In the previous season the Valiants, as they are known, had been knocked out of the Cup 5−0 by Walsall.

Venables led the lads confidently on to the team coach, a monstrous 'first-class hotel on wheels' complete with on-board physio department, kitchen, gourmet chef, à la carte menu, stereos and video monitors on which Chris Waddle would play scratch videos made up of snippets from *Top of the Pops*. As a real-life pop star, who had a chart hit with 'Diamond Lights', co-recorded with Glenn Hoddle, Wadsy would sometimes join in, karaoke-style, on the coach microphone.

Some 20,000 people turned up at Vale Park, The Valiants' cavernous collection of old sheds, with travelling Spurs fans swamping the normal 3,000 home supporters. Venables installed himself in a small wooden hut by the side of the ploughed-up pitch and was soon leaping up and down, shouting abuse and encouragement at his players. Venables 'pressure game', with its heavy reliance on the offside trap, came unstuck at once. After twenty minutes Port Vale were 2−0 in the lead, mainly by employing the old kick-and-rush formula of booting the ball up the pitch for the forwards to chase. Tottenham pulled back a goal halfway through the second half and the result was 2−1 to the Valiants and total humiliation for Spurs and El Tel.

The consensus was that the Tottenham players had failed to get stuck in and the Valiants had won by dint of greater determination. 'They were like West Ham used to be,' said Phil Sproson, Port Vale's match-winning scorer, adding as a dig at Venables' preference for clever tactics: 'They were all fancy flicks and sweet sherry.'

Venables' honeymoon was now over with at least one section of the fans, who revived the old 'Terry Vegetables' jibe, updating it to 'El Veg'. Pro-Venables fans, prepared like Scholar to give him the benefit of the doubt, were known as the Vegetarians. He was ridiculed in *The Spur*, a new fanzine launched by supporters opposed to Bobroff's plan for the next stage in the commercial development of White Hart Lane. This had been unveiled in February and involved bringing the East Stand up to the same standard as the West Stand, increasing the number of executive boxes from 72 to 108, and abolishing the fans' favourite Shelf terrace. A pressure group called 'Left on the Shelf' was set up and immediately became bogged down in a tangled attempt to get involved with planning negotiations between the local authority and the club.

There might have been less unease amongst the fans about stadium developments if the team had been doing better on the pitch. The season continued with a series of poor performances dominated by the team's reliance on the offside trap. The team was now the butt of countless jokes about the failure of Venables' tactical flair. When Millwall lost to Arsenal at home as the result of a dodgy offside decision, the team's manager complained that the nearest offside player had been at White Hart Lane. As the run of losses continued through to the middle of the season there was even a fear that Tottenham would be relegated to Division Two.

But by the spring, after drawing a lot of games, Tottenham had amassed sufficient points to avoid relegation. With no Cup action there was nothing at stake, and nothing left to play for. The home crowds regularly dropped back below 20,000 and the last game of the season, an utterly futile match against boring Luton Town, attracted only 15,500. This was less than half the number who attended the same fixture in the previous season and, apart from the disastrous 1985–86 post-Heysel season, the worst turnout since the war for an end-of-season League game at White Hart Lane. Tottenham won the match 2–1 and ended up thirteenth in the League, the club's lowest finishing position since Scholar took over.

By now the players were almost as demoralised as the fans, especially as a lot of them knew they were for the chop during the summer close season, the traditional time when managers cut out dead wood and, if they can afford it, buy new players. Venables had decided on an almost complete demolition and rebuilding job. Clive Allen, holder of the Tottenham goalscoring record, and goalkeeper Ray Clemence left the team before the end of the season. Ossie Ardiles went on a free transfer to QPR and Steve Hodge was sold to Nottingham Forest, whose manager, Brian Clough, quipped: 'I haven't just signed a player. I've rescued a lad from hell.'

Other, more minor, players came and went before Venables reached for the cheque book in earnest. Striker Paul 'Stewy' Stewart came from Manchester City for £1.7 million and Paul 'Gazza' Gascoigne was bought, after much hard bargaining, from Newcastle United for £2 million; a new British transfer record. Including the fees paid for Fenwick and Bobby 'Mimmsy' Mimms, a goalkeeper brought from Everton to replace the ageing Clemence, Venables had spent over £5 million on new players in his eight months with the club.

Venables' performance was starting to open a fateful rift between Bobroff and Scholar, the partners who had organised the takeover of the club and had originally planned its profitable transformation. Bobroff and the rest of the board began to suggest Venables should go. The new manager was doing far less well than Shreeves, and was costing the club a fortune at the same time. At the very least, Bobroff demanded, there should be a freeze on transfer spending until Venables proved he knew what he was doing.

Scholar fought hard for Venables, insisting that the rest of the board backed him. Scholar had personally approved the purchase of Gascoigne after seeing him score for Newcastle against Tottenham in a League game. Bobroff was much more inclined to use any available cash for investment in commercial development, especially the building of the East Stand. In purely commercial terms there was not much premium in paying a fortune for players capable of winning the League championship while English clubs were banned from Europe, where the real returns were to be had. Investing money in the PLC seemed like a better bet in the short term. Profits would then be available to buy players in the early 1990s when the European ban would be lifted. Either way a choice had to be made. Money was in the bank for commercial development or for buying a new team. But the board, pulled in different directions by Bobroff and Scholar, decided to try to do both.

Bobroff was chairman of the PLC, but his real power on the board came from his relationship with the company's bankers. Under the Richardson regime, Tottenham had banked with Barclays, whose chairman, Sir John Quinton, was a Spurs fan and season-ticket holder. In terms of investor confidence, inviting Sir John to join the board, even in some basically ceremonial non-executive capacity, might have been a good move. But in August 1988 Bobroff suddenly switched the PLC's account from Barclays to the Midland, the bank used by his property company, Markheath Securities.

The bland official reason for the move was given to the press three months later in the annual report. 'The group has had many changes over the last few years,' Bobroff explained, 'and as the business has altered we have had a look at all other factors, including our bankers.' This was true, but the full story was more complicated.

The rumour was now circulating that Barclays had been unwilling to extend the further loans needed for the purchase of Gascoigne, and that Tony Berry had plugged the gap by arranging for his company Blue Arrow to lend more than £1 million to the PLC. The £2 million Venables believed was available to buy players had been spent instead on buying two clothing companies, Martex and Stumps, designed to give Hummel greater presence in the shops and expand the faltering leisurewear business out of trouble.

Whatever the reason for the switch from Barclays, the effect was to strengthen Bobroff's hand on the board. Money was still available from the sources that could be tapped by Tony Berry. Through the Midland's relationship with Markheath, Bobroff was now in a stronger position to control the supply of money in the form of

135

bank loans.

As manager, Venables felt entitled to sit in on board meetings. With things going so badly wrong on the pitch he missed the first four meetings after his appointment. When he finally turned up, he was asked to leave when financial matters other than those directly affecting the team were discussed. This was fine with Venables who had already told Scholar he was happy to play his Barcelona-type role of team coach, with only a small part in the running of the club, if that was what was required. Scholar had stuck by his word and found the money for new players. So everything appeared to be fine.

With Gascoigne on board Venables gathered his new squad together at Mill Hill, the new and inferior training ground that had replaced Cheshunt, and told them that they had to win the championship. Nothing less would do. The limbering up began with a series of pre-season friendly matches in Scandinavia. The team's performance was mediocre, but the tabloids played a blinder, obsessively following Gazza around and reporting a series of flamed-up encounters with Swedish blondes. The warm-up programme finished with an Anglo-Italian tournament at Wembley which involved playing Arsenal. The game was a disaster, a 4–0 defeat, and the Arsenal fans spent its entire duration winding up Gazza, booing and jeering every time he touched the ball: 'Whadda waste of money'.

As the League season approached every non-Spurs fan in the country was willing Tottenham to lose, just for the satisfaction of seeing Europe's biggest soccer brain and his multi-million pound team taken down a peg. A lot rested on the opening League match against Coventry City scheduled for 27 August.

The opening day of the season, or the Big Kick-Off, as it is known, is one of League soccer's finest moments. Players are fit, fans have been denied their weekly fix for months, all the disappointments of the previous season are forgotten and even the weather is normally good. There is everything still to play for and grandiose ideas of winning everything in sight romantically beat in the most unlikely hearts.

The Coventry game, and the start of the 1988–89 season, was particularly important for Spurs. It was the team's chance to put the débâcles of the previous season and the pre-season programme behind them. It was the first outing at White Hart Lane for Venables' new-look team, with Fenners at the back and Gazza, Wadsy and Stewy in attack, who in the heady start of season atmosphere, might reasonably be expected to get a bucketful of goals against Coventry, one of the weaker sides in Divison One.

On paper the game was so attractive that Scholar might have considered advertising it on TV, as he had done with a similar fixture against Coventry at the start of the 1983–84 season. It was a good job he did not: the match had to be called off because Bobroff's East Stand had not been completed in time and the ground, still full of rubble, was declared unsafe.

The first the players heard of this was in the middle of Saturday morning, by which time they were fully psyched up for the Big Kick-Off. They were told simply that the Coventry game had been postponed and to turn up at Mill Hill for a practice session instead. 'Everyone is in the dark and Terry looks mad,' noted Terry Fenwick in his diary, an Adrian Mole-type document full of wooden-headed observations and footie wisdom, later whipped into standard cliché-speak by a *Sun* soccer writer and published as *Earning My Spurs*. 'Just when you are looking forward to getting the season under way you get a sickening piece of news like this,' Fenwick whinged, 'dear diary' style, adding: 'I haven't felt so gutted for weeks.'

Scholar was even more gutted when, shortly afterwards, the League deducted two points from Tottenham's Division One total. In most seasons, two points either way made all the difference between winning the championship or coming second. Over the summer Venables had spent millions on players, with the sole aim of winning the championship. Commercial developments such as the East Stand were supposed to help the team achieve success on the pitch. Instead the opposite was happening. Spending on the stadium was drawing heavily on funds earmarked for Venables' team-building plans and now, for the first time, it had directly affected the all-important championship chances of the team.

Later in the season the League restored the two points and substituted a £15,000 fine. 'You can't put a price on the value of clearing our name,' Scholar told the papers, 'but at that price we'd buy two points every week.' The League's change of mind cheered Scholar up, but it did little to calm his rage over the mishandling of the East Stand. The cost of building work was now well over budget, which was a repeat of the management error that had led to the downfall of Richardson and the old board. It also reduced even further the money available for players.

The board acrimoniously decided to cover the extra costs with further borrowing, and another milestone in the deteriorating relationship between the cautious Bobroff and the excitable and impatient Scholar had been reached. After the fiasco of the postponed Coventry game, the team's next fixture was heaven-sent for the tabloids: an away match against Newcastle United, Gascoigne's old club.

The papers worked the underdog angle all week, contrasting Geordie grit and poverty with the millions spent by El Veg to no apparent effect. This was standard psychological warfare, which the hacks were only too happy to help perfect, dished out before any important match. Newcastle's manager, Willie McFaul, and remaining star players piled on the coals, claiming that Gazza was 'a fattie' and unfit. Newcastle were better off without him; and he would never make the grade amongst the fickle and flash southerners.

McFaul was whistling in the dark. They had good reason to fear Gazza, a player who, like Maradona, could win a game single-handedly. His main defect as a player was a slight weight problem, the result, according to legend, of guzzling chocolate bars. The better the player, the louder and more hurtful the abuse needed to be, and so Gascoigne was always going to be given a hard time. But McFaul stopped short of delivering the final psychological hammer blow: that Gascoigne was a traitor who had betrayed his mates for money. The Newcastle supporters, some of the most fanatical in the country, had no such inhibitions.

When the Tottenham coach arrived at the Newcastle ground it was mobbed by angry home fans screaming 'Judas', 'Fathead', 'Rich Bastard' and, worst of all, 'Yuppie'. Coming from other groups of fans, insults like these would have amounted to a superficial excuse to unsettle a rival team. But in Newcastle it was deeply and genuinely felt and, in Gazza's case, meant a lot.

In the northeast poverty was as bad as in Merseyside, at least for the sort of people who watched soccer. The Geordies did not even have the consolation of footballing success and the chip on their shoulders was correspondingly huge. Until the 1960s Newcastle United had been one of the greatest sides in the country, winning the FA Cup in three years out of five, but the club had suffered badly when a proper national transfer market began to operate in the 1960s.

It was just like the economy. The southeast, especially Londoners, got all the money, and if you wanted to work you had to move down to their filthy city, queue up at building sites and pay most of your wages to landlords who ripped you off with as much determination as everyone else down south, including the publicans, who served watery, overpriced beer, and the management at White Hart Lane who were now charging the highest admission prices in the League.

Richer clubs had plundered Geordieland over the years, luring away greats such as Bobby and Jack Charlton, plus many more workaday players like Tel's protégé, Terry Fenwick. Because of this, the fans believed, Newcastle had not won a major competition for more than thirty years and had spent long spells in Division Two. Spurs' rise almost exactly mirrored Newcastle's decline and, as every soccer fan in the north believed, the southern clubs, especially Tottenham, had bought their success. Now they had stolen Chris Waddle and Fattie Gascoigne, the cream of the latest crop.

Gascoigne knew and felt all this as much as any other Geordie. He had supported Newcastle as a boy and still saw himself as one of the lads. His first game for Newcastle, in front of his family and friends, had been the greatest day of his life. Now he regularly returned to play snooker and drink with his mates in the Excelsior Working Men's club in Dunston. He was capable of getting into a fight if anyone pushed the Yuppie Bastard line too hard, and was careful not to be seen using the car phone when driving around Gateshead in his new black Mercedes 190 2.6 worthy of an Arab potentate, complete with rear spoiler, low racing skirt and one-way reflective windscreen. (Other Tottenham players went in for more modest mid-range BMWs and even Sierras. Lineker, Tottenham's other England international, plumped patriotically for a boring grey Jaguar.)

Gascoigne had the same attitude as the Geordie bricklayers or electricians who went to London to part the southerners from as much of their money as possible and then came back, the Prodigal Returned, wearing the latest flash sunglasses, chatting up the girls, getting the rounds in and hitting the waterfront discos, nightclubs and postmodernist pizza parlours catering for the city's itinerant King for a Day trade.

But the Newcastle fans were having none of it. By now the story of how Gascoigne had fallen out with the Newcastle management was common knowledge. The club had offered him a package worth £1,500 a week to stay, a fortune by the standards of the fans he purported to be like, but he had turned it down, demanding more. Gascoigne's agent had then played the field, getting Manchester United, Liverpool and finally Tottenham to compete against Newcastle and each other.

In addition to his share of the transfer fee, it emerged that Manchester United had offered him a four-year contract with a £100,000 signing-on fee; a share of any profits made on his transfer to another club later; a £200,000 house and £15,000 car and a guaranteed average salary of £125,000 a year plus cash payments when the team won and £5,000 every time he played for the England national team. The total package was estimated to be worth at least £1 million; but Tottenham topped even this. He signed for the club, with the usual secrecy surrounding the exact nature of transfer deals for top players, amid claims that he had chosen a London club because Liverpool and Manchester United were traditional rivals of Newcastle, and that he did not want to let the fans down.

Members of the Newcastle team now queued up to reveal just how money-mad Gascoigne had been and how, when they had teased him about it, he reacted badly. The famous clowning would stop and his harder, self-interested side would come out: 'Yeah – that's right I'm going,' he was reputed to have snapped when news of the move to Tottenham broke, 'going to a better club, to make more money. I'm in demand and I'll do what's right for me.' Gascoigne had been unaware of the exact financial details which he had handed over to Alastair Garvie, one of the growing band of soccer agents, with the vague instruction to make him a millionaire.

Finally, it was revealed how Gascoigne had been obsessed with the idea that Newcastle had not paid him enough for the time he spent with the club. He had even whinged over the £2 million transfer fee – not his share of it (an undisclosed figure unlikely to be less than £200,000), but the fact that Newcastle got far more than they had paid for him as a player. Garvie, who was dumped at about the same time in favour of a new financial adviser, Mel Stein, later revealed: 'He didn't want Newcastle to have £2 million, because he felt they had him for virtually nothing.'

Now the Newcastle supporters had their chance to show what they thought of Gazza. From the minute the game started they pelted him with Mars Bars bought from a stall set up in the forecourt of a garage near the ground. This was partly the standard wind-up about Gascoigne's weight problem, with the added edge of pointing out his supposed commercialisation. The symbolism went deeper that this. It echoed the way racists threw bananas at black players at some grounds. It was nasty, and meant to be seen as such. Gascoigne was jeered with real hatred throughout the game, played badly in a 2−2 draw and came off before the end, booed all the way to the tunnel.

He avoided a second helping of abuse by leaving on his own, through a side door, in advance of the team coach. He did not play in the return match at White Hart Lane later in the year because of injury; but it was one of only a handful of matches he missed all season. Fenwick noted in his diary that Gascoigne had looked 'drained and emotionally tired' during the game and added, unhelpfully, that this was 'something he is going to have to learn to live with if he is to succeed.'

Gazza got back on the rails in the next match, scoring at White Hart Lane against Arsenal, but Spurs still lost the game 3−2, adding further to the gloom now simultaneously engulfing both the boardroom and training facilities. At the end of October Tottenham lost 2−1 away to Aston Villa and went to the bottom of the League with only five points from nine League games. 'What's the difference between Spurs and the Star of David?' ran the joke on the terraces. 'The Star of David's got six points,' came the reply.

At the next training session Venables walked straight past the squad heading towards his office. 'Everything OK?' he turned to say. The squad nodded. 'Now, you don't mind if I just go upstairs and hang myself, do you?' he said with a sardonic smile. Venables had spent £5 million on new players to get five League points; at this rate £80 million would be needed to win the Championship. He had been in charge for almost a year, and the team had won only seven games during that time. 'There is nobody more gutted about that than the manager,' Fenners observed.

Even though things were going badly wrong, and the tabloids were on his back, Venables remained popular with the players. He took them into his confidence – even Gascoigne, up to a point – and treated them like adults and equals. 'You do right by me,' his message seemed to be, 'and I'll look after you.' As a result there were no silly restrictions like requiring players to go to bed earlier on Friday nights or banning sex before important games, tactics to which other managers were said to resort. The relaxed and adult approach extended to the actual coaching where, instead of the endless knackering drill and physical exercise demanded by some of the more traditional managers, Venables kept things varied and interesting, tailoring coaching to each player's particular needs.

The whole approach had the younger, more easy-going feel which Tel had pioneered as a player at QPR and Crystal Palace. Tottenham players were often involved in the sort of larks and showbiz activity which had been Tel's forte as a youngster: Gazza was always up to some PR stunt or other. Years before, Tommy Docherty, Venables' manager at Chelsea, dropped him as captain for wasting time in this way, but Venables saw things differently. A touch of showbiz glamour was all part of the modern game, and it did no harm at all.

Naturally he did have to discipline players from time to time, but he never resorted to the ferocious bollockings in front of the whole squad like those dished out by Tommy Docherty. Venables' method was to take a player who was not pulling his weight off to one side and have it out in private. If the whole team had let him down he would position his assistant Allan Harris on guard at the changing room door to make sure there were no reporters, known as the 'rotters', about before delivering some well-chosen and psychologically cutting criticism. On these days the whole team would sit there silently like naughty schoolboys as the manager paced up and down, a pained and disappointed father figure, reeling off his complaints and asking for impossible explanations. By now the pressure was starting to get to all the players and especially Gascoigne, who had come from Newcastle not just for the up-front transfer money, but for the chance to improve his career prospects and market value by being in a trophy-winning team.

Part of the problem was thought to be Bobby 'Mimmsy' Mimms, the likeable goalie bought by Venables from Everton. Mimmsy kept making simple mistakes and letting in goals. After a particularly dire netkeeping performance against Derby County, Gascoigne began brawling with Mimms in the dressing room and the two of them had to be held apart. Things had calmed down a bit by the time Venables arrived to deliver the expected roasting. He used his ultimate sanction on Mimms: his long, silent, fuming stare. Gascoigne himself had received similar treatment after a mistake in a game against Southampton, which resulted in Tottenham being knocked out of the League Cup. 'Where were you?' he had pleaded, and Gazza had been reduced to hanging his head in humiliation under the steely glare, in front of the rest of the team, mumbling 'Sorry boss' like a naughty schoolboy.

After the early departure from the League Cup at Southampton, and with no chance of winning the League, the FA Cup held out the last hope of salvaging the season. A good Cup run and, even better, a Wembley appearance would wipe out the painful memory of the previous season's Cup defeat at Port Vale. It was not to be. The team was immediately eliminated, losing 1–0 to Bradford City of Division Two.

After this, rumours began to circulate that Venables would not be re-employed when his two-year contract came up at the end of the season. The *Daily Mirror* linked him to Portsmouth, where Venables' former partner at QPR had taken over and was looking for a new manager. The Portsmouth move came to nothing, but on the board the pressure on Scholar to get rid of the manager was becoming intense. Isolated on the board Scholar insisted that Venables should be given more time to prove himself. But the row was now bitter and the alliance between Bobroff and Scholar, the rock on which control of the club was based, was coming to an end.

Venables was staying, but Bradford sealed the fate of Mimmsy who was dropped from the team. He was replaced by Erik Thorstvedt, a beefy Norwegian netminder bought from the Swedish club Gothenburg. 'Big Erik' got of to a bad start by dropping the ball into his net on his White Lane debut against Nottingham Forest on live national television, thereby losing the match. He was given the derisive nickname 'Erik the Horse Vet' by some of the fans. The nickname was updated to the more respectful 'Erik the Viking' when the film of the same name was released, by which time both his and the team's performance had improved.

The revival began in February when Tottenham beat Norwich 2−1 at home, with goals from Waddle and Gascoigne, starting a long run of wins and draws. The El Tel magic seemed to be working at last and home attendances began to get better through the spring. By the time Tottenham finished beating Wimbledon 2−1 away from home on 15 April the team had played fourteen games with only one defeat, and were firmly positioned in the top quarter of the League. The general rejoicing in the changing rooms after the game was dulled by news from Sheffield Wednesday's Hillsborough stadium where an FA Cup semi-final between Liverpool and Nottingham Forest had been taking place.

Apparently there had been hooliganism of some sort and the game had been stopped after a pitch invasion. The first reaction was irritation: the Liverpool fans were at it again, perhaps threatening the chances of the European ban being lifted. As details of events up north began to get through, the mood changed from anger to stunned horror.

11: DICKHEADS WHO DON'T
GIVE A DAMN

The death of almost a hundred people during the 1989 FA Cup semi-final at Hillsborough was an entirely avoidable tragedy. The disaster was mainly the fault of the police who had relieved congestion at the turnstile entrances to the ground by opening an exit gate, allowing 5,000 fans to flood on to an already packed terrace. People at the bottom of the terrace were crushed against the security fence and many were killed by the sheer weight of people on top of them. Others managed to climb over the fence on to the pitch, but the police, assuming this to be hooliganism, tried to stop them.

The first unthinking reaction had been to blame the Liverpool fans, 'the thieves' as some of the Tottenham crowd called them. Memories flooded back to the Heysel disaster when a fight involving Liverpool supporters had caused the death of 41 people. The resulting ban from European competitions was deeply resented by clubs such as Tottenham which claimed to have overcome their own hooligan problems. Now, it seemed, Liverpool were at it again, destroying the chance of an early end to the ban.

TV and radio commentators broadcasting the Hillsborough game jumped to the same conclusion as parts of the security fence enclosing the Liverpool fans burst open, allowing hundreds on to the pitch, interrupting the game, and leaving the police to wander helplessly in the middle of the mêlée. Advertising hoardings surrounding the pitch were torn down in what appeared, at first, to be an act of sheer vandalism.

It took time for the commentators to realise the boards were being used as makeshift stretchers to carry dozens of limp bodies from the terraces, laying them out on the pitch. The death toll mounted through the evening and finally reached 96. It was the worst disaster ever to take place at a British sports event.

Most clubs, including Tottenham, at once removed security fences, the immediate cause of the Hillsborough deaths. Reaction to the disaster was dominated by muddled recriminations over who was responsible for the tragedy. (A report by Lord Justice Taylor, published many months later, squarely blamed the police, berated League clubs for the shabby and dangerous state of their grounds, and cleared the Liverpool fans of blame.)

The Football League Management Committee handled the crisis badly, joining in the unseemly search for scapegoats and failing to co-ordinate the response from the individual clubs who dithered over whether or not to call off games as a mark of respect. In the end they passed the buck by announcing that cancellation was a matter for the clubs (though none of them, except Liverpool, did so).

Proposals to cancel all remaining League fixtures and the FA Cup final merely succeeded in upsetting the families of the Bradford stadium fire victims, who had received no similar mark of respect, before quickly fizzling out, allowing the League and Cup programme to continue as normal. At the same time undignified moans about the financial implications, and the potential lost TV revenue and the cost of higher safety standards, merged with a tendency to blame the Liverpool fans for their own fate, presenting a deeply unattractive picture to the public.

At boardroom level the Hillsborough disaster was seen as more evidence of the need for stadiums that would have a far smaller capacity, with most supporters sitting down, which would be safer all round. The fact that this strategy fitted with the commercial equation outlined by Tottenham at the time of the PLC's flotation was a happy coincidence.

The following week Tottenham had to play Liverpool's neighbours, Everton, at White Hart Lane. The pain of the event was made all the worse by the fact that the game had been meant to be special. The team's performance had revived after the terrible start to the season. Tottenham had lost only one home game since November, and were set to finish sixth in the League, the best position they had achieved since Venables arrived at the club. The Everton match, the last home game of the season, was to have seen a lap of honour. Instead it turned out to be a completely miserable affair. The security fences were down already, but the crowd was almost completely silent as a mark of sympathy and respect for the small number of Everton fans who had made the journey.

After all the agony the season had continued as normal. Liverpool won the FA Cup, beating Everton in the last minutes of extra time in the final, but the championship had been settled in the last minutes of a game against Arsenal, which Liverpool lost, giving the title to Spurs' main rivals on goal difference.

Tottenham won nothing at all, but the fans could take some comfort from the improved form of Gascoigne who, it seemed, might finally lead them to the League championship in the next season. On a more personal level Gascoigne was coming closer to fulfilling his ambition of becoming a millionaire. Waddle had introduced him to Mel Stein, a lawyer who had branched out into the profitable area of sportsploitation. Gazza was already getting a lot of profitable media exposure, posing for the tabloids in a variety of stupid costumes and, under Stein's careful supervision, collaborating fully with his tabloid recasting as 'the Clown Prince of Soccer'. But the exposure was still mainly on the sports pages. Promotion to the front pages as a tabloid character in his own right would require far more TV exposure, and the way to get that was to secure a regular place in the England team in time for Italia 90: the football World Cup.

Gascoigne had aready played for England twice but

Bobby Robson, the mumbling manager of the national team, had refused to give him a regular team place, claiming that Gascoigne was immature and unreliable in important games. This had given the tabloids a new angle for their traditional sport of England manager bashing. The campaign had already featured countless demands for Robson's sacking, including the classic IN THE NAME OF ALLAH GO! run in the *Mirror* after England managed only a draw in a friendly game with Saudi Arabia, and was now reaching fresh peaks of hysteria as England continued to play badly in qualifying rounds for Italia 90.

Robson's refusal to pick Gascoigne, now touted as England's new hope, was fresh grist to the tabloid mill and they mounted a ceaseless campaign on Gazza's behalf. Robson held out against the pressure, but he did select Gascoigne as a substitute for a game against Albania at Wembley, a week after the Hillsborough disaster. Albanian football was almost as backward and isolated as the country itself which, at the time, was in the grip of the world's last avowedly Stalinist regime; as a result, the team was regarded as a bit of a joke. In the early 1980s comedian Alexei Sayle, who once professed sympathy with the Stalinist ideology of Albanian leader Enva Hoxer, satirised the tired genre of souvenir soccer records with a Marxist–Leninist version entitled 'Albania! Albania!; not half as repressive as Romania'. It seemed that Robson was joining in the lightweight atmosphere by including Gascoigne in the squad.

There was never much chance of Albania winning at Wembley and, with England 3–0 up in the second half, Robson felt secure enough to allow Gascoigne off the subs' bench and to see if Venables had succeeded in drumming some sense into him. But the England manager's suspicions were confirmed.

Gascoigne ran about the field playing up to the fans, and, in contrast to Robson's careful and cautious team tactics, played his own manoeuvres with Waddle, despite the yells from the bench.

Robson turned to his coach in exasperation and said:

'Look at that silly bugger. He's as daft as a fucking brush, isn't he? I told him to play over here and he's gone off to play with his mate. He's as daft as a brush.' England won 5–0, Gazza scored and the crowd loved it. But Robson was not impressed. After the game he told the papers that England had needed two balls: one for the team and one for Gazza. 'If the ball had been kicked out of the ground he would have chased it,' he said with an amused but dismissive shrug.

The tabloids' verdict was different. After months spent rubbishing Gascoigne as El Tel's overrated £2 million flop, he was elevated to genius status as the saviour of England's national team. Gascoigne turned up at the next England training session with a toilet brush stuck down the top of his socks, leaking the story of Robson's 'daft as a brush' remark to the tabloids who pounced gleefully. Under yet more pressure Robson began dropping heavy hints that Gascoigne would soon, once he gained a little more experience, become the star of the England team.

The Albania performance had given Gazza the desired publicity boost. Although he was still far from being a household name his performance had brought him to the attention of at least part of the Great British Public, rather than just soccer fans. Mel Stein moved into action to help him turn the publicity into money in the required way. Stein had already steered Gazza into a boot-endorsement contract that Gascoigne believed would at last make him a millionaire. He had turned up at the press conference at which the boot deal was announced, mildly ridiculed the actual boots and their manufacturer and returned to White Hart Lane, bouncing about and bragging: 'I'm Gazza, me; I'm loaded, I am, absolutely loaded!' Other moneyspinning ventures, including the copyrighting of the 'Gazza' trade name and the production of a joke book entitled *Daft as a Brush?*, were soon under way.

The new concentration on Gascoigne, combined with the strong finish to the season by the team as a whole, boosted the Spurs fans' expectations for the next season. Scholar was as excited as anyone and, in this mood, allowed Venables to buy Gary Lineker from Barcelona for £1.2 million. There had been rumours about a Lineker move for months, and now they were confirmed, expectations went into overdrive. Season tickets sold well as the fans told each other that their team, led by the international trio of Gascoigne, Lineker and Waddle, could not fail to win something next season: maybe the League; maybe even the Double. Arsenal, the reigning champions, would be put in the shade.

Venables' 'dream team', built around Gascoigne, Lineker and Waddle, lasted just seventeen days, when the news broke of Waddle's transfer to Marseille for £4.25 million. The first Venables had heard about it was when Scholar bowled into his office in a state of high excitement. 'You won't believe this,' Scholar gabbled, 'but we've had this offer of £2 million for Waddle.' Venables turned to Doug Livermore, one of his assistants, and shrugged: 'Yeah, so what?' Waddle was a vital part of his plans and, although £2 million was a lot for a player, it was only the going rate for an England international. Venables had no intention of letting him go. It would only mean spending the same amount or more to replace him with a better player.

Scholar persisted: 'But it's from Marseille,' he said. This excited a little more interest. The French club was owned by the free-spending Bernard Tapie, one of EuroSoccer's millionaire sugar daddies, as they were known. He was a man who might be prepared to pay a lot more if he had set his heart on getting Waddle. Venables set his own price: £6 million. If Tapie would pay that much it would be worth letting Waddle go, and replacing him with a couple of new players of comparable quality.

Scholar turned down the £2 million and, as predicted, Tapie immediately raised the stakes to £3 million. He was again rejected but was invited to London to discuss the deal in more detail. Scholar and Venables then secretly met Tapie at the Carlton Hotel to play an extraordinary game of multimillion transfer poker. So far Waddle had not been told about the proposed deal. Venables was still convinced Marseille would go to £6 million, if only to match the world record fee paid by AC Milan for Dutch goalscorer Ruud Gullit two years before.

When the bid reached £4.25 million Venables took Scholar to one side and said: 'Look I think we should tell the player.' He knew that Waddle would accept. His share of the fee would be at least £1 million and his salary would be enormous.

At 28 he had only a few years left at the very top, and a financial opportunity like this might never present itself again. Venables thought it was only fair to give Waddle the chance to set himself up for life. He was prepared to let him go on the clear understanding that all the money was to be spent on replacement players. Scholar agreed.

By now the £4 million player fund Venables had been promised when he joined Tottenham had been spent on Lineker, Gascoigne, Stewart and Fenwick. Letting Waddle go would be 'a wrench', as Venables put it, but it would top up his war chest with another £4 million and bring him back to where he started. With the team already strengthened in this way, another trip round the transfer market might mean finding another four Waddle-class players, buying them cheaply from poverty-stricken clubs such as Newcastle and completing the required trans-formation of his team.

What Venables did not know was that the Waddle Money, as it became known, would be sucked into the growing financial black hole of the PLC's debts. Within six months, instead of buying players, he would be asked to sell them.

Spurs fans felt cheated by the sale of Chris Waddle. 'Widdly' had been the outstanding star of the team, much more popular than Gascoigne. It was not as though, they innocently thought, the club needed money. The evidence was all around them every Saturday in the form of the continuous ground development which had reduced White Hart Lane to a permanent building site.

Tottenham's rivals were meanwhile spending money

like water on new players, getting ready for the most important season for years. The European ban on English clubs was under review and it looked like it would be lifted if English fans behaved well during the World Cup, due to take place at the end of the season. The team which won the League this year would be straight back into Europe.

Where was the sense, the fans asked each other, in putting Waddle's £4.25 million transfer fee in the bank when Arsenal, the reigning champions, were doing well? Manchester United had spent £4 million on new players and even humble West Ham had forked out £2 million. The golden scenario of Waddle, Gascoigne and Lineker bringing the League championship back to White Hart Lane, winning the World Cup for England and then leading Tottenham triumphantly back into Europe had been badly dented.

The better-organised fans, grouped around *The Spur* fanzine, began complaining and demanded an explanation, only to be fobbed off with the bland official line that Waddle had wanted to leave and there was nothing Venables or the board could do to stop him. The *Spur* people grumpily accepted this and wished their hero well. At the same time they launched a 'Buy Back Chris Waddle' campaign and solicited donations of £10,000 or more. (At Venables' old club Crystal Palace, now under the brisk and enterprising regime of property developer Ron Noades, a similar scheme had been set up for real. Palace fans were expected to contribute to a special fund set up to buy the players they had to pay to watch on Saturdays.)

'Buy back Chris Waddle' was a joke, but one which cut close to the bone. Tottenham fans already paid the highest admission fees in the League, and had coughed up a record amount for season tickets over the summer, partly because they wanted to watch Waddle. In other circumstances they would have been entitled to ask for their money back and the feeling spread that the board was cashing in on fan loyalty. The more informed were alarmed to read in the *Financial Times* (the new 'pink 'un' for shareholding soccer fans) that the Waddle sale had pushed the PLC share price up by 7p to 115p, showing just how much the interests of the fans and the money men, all vaguely presumed to be ignorant about soccer, were now moving apart.

Although few fans could identify him, a new chief executive had arrived: Bob Holt from Tony Berry's Blue Arrow empire. He had promptly included all the players in the balance sheet as assets, like so much livestock. Most fans had heard a garbled version of this complicated arrangement, and it did not sound very promising. Even the dimmest knew that assets had value only if they could be sold off.

Then the PLC's computer subsidiary, Synchro Systems, made a bid to help set up the proposed national identity scheme for football fans, which was part of the Government's muddled response to hooliganism. Football fans naturally despised the ID scheme and, paradoxically, Scholar had simultaneously slammed it in a speech to a Parliamentary committee. Speaking as 'a committed fan and supporter of our national game', he revealed that there had been only 73 arrests at White Hart Lane throughout the previous season, calculating that 99.99 per cent of Tottenham supporters were law abiding citizens. The only effect of the scheme, he concluded, would be to reduce attendance at soccer games.

Some fans saw Scholar's speech as pure hypocrisy, coming from the chairman of a club which hoped to profit via the PLC from the ID scheme. It was all part of a vague but growing feeling of unease about the club, a muffled 'sleaze factor' of partly understood and threatening financial developments. More and more faceless Men in Suits, faceless marketing and financial people like Holt, seemed to be hovering around the club.

This was followed by the sudden resignation of Bobroff, his reinstatement within a week and dark rumours in the papers of mounting debts, boardroom splits and unfathomable faction fights between groups of directors and financial advisors. There was talk of takeover bids and mysterious share purchases by sinister-sounding groups of foreign banks.

The Coventry fiasco, when a game had been cancelled without warning because of building work on extra executive boxes, still rankled. It sometimes seemed that football was an inconvenient sideline to the main activity of providing banqueting facilities and executive entertainment boxes.

Worst of all, the momentum of the previous season had been lost, and the team, after all the optimism of the close season, was not performing well. Tottenham had won only one of the first six games of the new season. Naturally the sale of Waddle was blamed and became the focus for the general unease and grumbles which now began to appear in the media. *The Spur*, which now sold to thousands of fans every Saturday, kept up an intermittent sniper campaign, but the main written broadside was delivered by Hunter Davies, a celebrity supporter and author of *The Glory Game*, a respected insider account of Tottenham's 1971–72 season. Under the headline 'SELLING SPURS SHORT FOR THE PROFITS OF DOOM', Davies commandeered a page in the *Independent* and set about a comprehensive demolition job.

'I have given the club total devotion for 30 years,' he wrote. 'I hate Arsenal. I'm sick as a frog when Spurs lose and gutted when Arsenal win.' Things had got so bad he was thinking of a switch between clubs, just like a fickle player on the transfer market. 'They don't give a damn, they have no faith, no loyalty,' he explained. Managers were at least as bad: 'Half of them don't know what town they are in.' He continued with a tirade against the Spurs programme and the whole merchandising business.

Merchandising was a soft and obvious target. The official Spurs Supporters' Shop, with its huge number of risible gimmicks, had now been extended to include a special Visa credit card with a Tottenham Hotspur logo on it, and Davies' overlooked Cockerel books, the PLC's moneyspinning publishing wing. Cockerel produced fan material and a series of bland biographies including *Waddle* by his financial adviser Mel Stein, and *Against All Odds*, a worthy tome about long-suffering defender Gary Mabbutt, who has diabetes. But alongside this profitable partisanship, the company had committed a remarkably brazen act of treachery by producing a book glorifying Manchester United, of all people.

No aspect of the club's activities escaped Davies' wrath. He hated the directors (they were interested only in meeting the sponsors); the new press box (moved to an inferior position so the grandstand view could be sold off); sponsorship by Holsten ('it's the kowtowing for money which sickens me'). And, horror of horrors, Davies brought himself to tap out the words 'I hate Gazza'.

Scholar replied with his own *Independent* article, just as bitter as Davies' in its way, which gamely answered the criticism point by point. The general line was that all the other big clubs had gone commercial first and Tottenham had been forced to catch up. Davies might not like the Spurs programme, he said, but that was a matter of personal taste and freedom of choice. Others liked it: children for instance.

Scholar then countered by acidly attacking the old non-commercial regimes at big football clubs across the country. He was echoing a telling remark made at a supporters' club dinner two years previously. 'Before the takeover,' he had said, 'I always loved the team, but hated the club.' Now Scholar wanted to know where the profits from the big crowds and gate receipts in the good old days had gone.

Until the 1960s the maximum wage for a player was £20 a week and transfer fees were just as small. Now Tottenham had to compete in a global market for players and had to make money to pay for it all. People might complain about development at the stadium, but it represented the future and at least it was safe. Less commercial clubs had horrible, insanitary grounds which were potentially lethal. To show how times had changed Scholar made a weak joke about a fan who had been pestering him about the quality of the White Hart Lane wine list. He then reached his emotional conclusion: 'I love Tottenham. If I watch two other teams I don't feel I want either to win — unless they are playing Arsenal.'

Scholar's dedication to the cause of soccer in general, and Spurs in particular, might have been calculated to win over disgruntled fans. But it failed to do so. Another wave of press reports revealed more about the boardroom splits and the increasingly fragile state of the PLC. The company had explained Bobroff's sudden departure as chairman of the PLC to 'increasing outside business commitments' and his equally sudden reinstatement a week later to 'representations from board members'.

This vague and unconvincing version of events was at once demolished by the *Sunday Times*' influential business editor, Jeff Randall: 'Pure guff' was how he put it, reporting instead a 'behind the scenes' power struggle. 'Bobroff left Spurs,' added the *Daily Telegraph*, 'after feuding with Scholar, reasoning: "You can't have two Popes in Rome".'

The papers blamed the row on the public disclosure of loans and guarantees worth over £4 million made to the PLC by Tony Berry's Blue Arrow in the autumn of 1988, which Berry had organised without telling the Blue Arrow board. The company had subsequently fallen on hard times and a Board of Trade investigation into its tangled finances reported that the Tottenham loan had been used 'in connection with the company's sponsorship programme' at a time when Venables was using most of the available cash to buy Gascoigne and Paul Stewart.

Bobroff had been horrified by the Blue Arrow revelations and worried that the 'stink', as he put it, might reflect badly on his own property company, Markheath, which was also going through a sticky patch. Bobroff had always been less than enthusiastic about Berry's activities at Tottenham and he found himself increasingly isolated on the board. Berry and Scholar then forced Bobroff's resignation, but this had alarmed the PLC's bankers, the Midland.

Bobroff had transferred the PLC's account to the Midland, the bank which worked with Markheath, a year before. The Midland was now nursing Tottenham's large overdraft, giving it a lot of power over the board, which was used to overrule Scholar and put Bobroff, very much their man, back in charge with a mission to make sure the debts were kept under control. Bobroff was already livid about the leaks to the papers, which had had the effect of undermining him. The mole hunt deepened the split even more and added a new feeling of bitterness. Scholar and Bobroff, who had worked so closely to get control of the club, could now scarcely bring themselves to speak to each other.

At the time few outside the closed circle of the board, the bank and the PLC's financial advisers knew these details. Despite all the rows the board had wisely decided to present a united front to the world: open warfare would destroy confidence in the PLC and make the financial position even worse. This façade of unity was soon subjected to its first major test. Although they knew few of the details, a well-informed and increasingly vocal minority of fans zeroed in on the December 1989 Annual General Meeting, determined to dig out the truth.

Until now the AGMs had been dull public-relations exercises. Serious investors rarely bothered to turn up, and were content to receive the annual report, setting out profit and loss, through the post. Some of the shareholding fans looked forward to the meetings as a chance to indulge in the fantasy for an afternoon that they had some control over the club. The board had been quite happy to patronise them, organising tours round the office complex inside the West Stand.

Apart from a smart area just inside the main doors, complete with a heroic bust of Bill Nicholson and an incongruous Tottenham Hotspur nameplate rescued from a redundant steam train, the complex struck them as

158

surprisingly spartan. There were blown-up pictures of previous stars and meaningless action shots mounted, Athena style, on blocks of wood, but apart from this the offices could have easily belonged to a small, down-at-heel engineering company.

There were few signs of the new corporate affluence and 'style' obsession: no vast World of Leather sofas or forests of potted ferns, and not so much as a brass uplighter. Instead it was all moulded plastic chairs and steel-frame tables. It was nothing like the echoing marble halls of Highbury, the Arsenal headquarters, declared a national treasure and said to be haunted by poltergeists. But the fans were still delighted to be on sacred territory.

The meetings which followed had presented few problems for the board. The fan shareholders were happy to nod sagely as the financial details flew straight over their heads, and wait patiently for what they were really interested in: the chance to play team manager for a few seconds by offering heartfelt tactical advice to club officials over the free tea and biscuits provided after the business section of the meeting was over.

This time things were a little more difficult for the board, but not much. Instead of a few dozen, 400 shareholders turned up. The crowd included a gaggle of investment bankers alarmed by the press rumours. They sat quietly amid the throng, exuding professional *gravitas* and taking careful notes as Bobroff announced annual profits down from £1.9 million to £950,000, despite a 42 per cent increase in turnover. Professional eyebrows were raised when it was explained that the balance sheet had been improved by writing down players as assets for the first time.

Even more worrying were the bank loans and overdrafts of £7 million revealed in the accounts. This borrowed money had been spent winding up the Hummel UK clothing company, which had made a heavy loss, and on investment in computer equipment needed to bid for the national soccer ID scheme. A banker asked if press reports that the debt had recently increased to

£10 million were true. Bobroff brazened it out, saying that it was 'not appropriate' to give more detail.

The fans were just as passive. All they wanted to do was help. They were reluctant to make a fuss and even the mildest of criticism was prefaced by lengthy expressions of loyalty to Tottenham Hotspur. They hardly recognised most of the board and officials sitting on the platform in front of them, and all eyes were on Venables. They were naturally subdued by meeting El Tel in the flesh, a meeting described by one fan as 'a pure and precious experience'. Most of their questions were about the state of the team and the players, rather than the PLC's bank balance.

'What happened about Chris Waddle? He was brilliant, the best. Why did you let him go?' one fan managed to ask. The standard line that Waddle had received a good offer and the board could do nothing to stop him going was trotted out, and that seemed to satisfy the meeting. 'Why are you getting rid of the Shelf?' another wanted to know. 'I love this club,' he added, quivering with nerves under the sympathetic gaze of El Tel. 'I want to bring my mates, but I can't because they are not members and they can't get in the members' end. Why are you keeping people away?'

Scholar, who sat through the proceedings with an expression of agonised sincerity clamped to his face, explained that the PLC was developing White Hart Lane into 'the finest stadium in the country, one of which we can all be proud' and, anyway, part of the Shelf would be preserved. Some fans aired personal obsessions and grumbles about the catering or the punctuality of the supporters' club coaches. Still others went on at great length about the Glory, Glory days, or simply declared themselves to be fans, asking when Spurs were again going to do the Double. That was an easy one for Scholar to answer: 'As soon as humanly possible'.

There had been only one really shaky moment when Bobroff was aked why he had resigned and then returned as chairman, and what was behind all the press reports

160

about splits on the board. The platform shifted uneasily in their seats and black looks flashed back and forth before Bobroff explained: 'We are a united board with a united strategy and policy. I am sure that over the next few months any concerns will be allayed.' This had caused a ripple of laughter to run round the room.

Otherwise, when things got difficult, Bobroff merely reminded everyone that time was pressing and Terry Venables, who was sitting on the platform next to him, was waiting to answer questions about the team. Venables duly took centre stage and the meeting came to life. 'Why do you insist on playing a left-footed player at right back and a right-footed player at left back?' asked one fan. Venables, although slightly bemused, answered, appearing to take all the loyal criticism and suggestions seriously, and displaying all the famous charm and wit until Bobroff suddenly closed the meeting bang on time. Unlike previous years, when directors had hung around to chat with the fans, they all scooped up their papers and disappeared immediately, mightily relieved that the façade of unity had survived the test.

One reason for the board's easy ride at the meeting was the improved form of the team, which was all the fan shareholders cared about. Signs that the El Tel magic might finally be working prompted even Hunter Davies to recant – up to a point. 'I do not hate Gazza. I take that back,' he wrote in *The Spur*. 'It is the Gazza image, his persona the papers have created, which I object to. Paul Gascoigne, Esq., is I'm sure, an engaging young man.' He had tried to turn his back on Spurs, but the strain had been too great and he had turned up at White Hart Lane as usual for a match against Millwall. Tottenham won the match, but he still did not enjoy it.

The board, having feigned unity at the AGM, had a few months of relative peace, underpinned by an apparently improving financial position. Half-year figures published in March showed a fourfold increase in profits to £1.1 million. The share price was strong, supported by a hostile takeover bid from Guy Libby, a financier with

161

interests in Crystal Palace.

The publication of the Taylor Report into ground safety in the wake of Hillsborough also meant good financial news for the club, in a way. Taylor had slammed soccer as a whole, asking rhetorically if 'some clubs are genuinely interested in the welfare of the grass roots supporters' as opposed to the executive-box clientele. Of the 67 recommendations he made, the most important and expensive was the idea that all Division One and Two clubs should provide all-seater stadiums.

Tottenham had already developed White Hart Lane along the lines required by Taylor, and had the overdraft to prove it. Now Tottenham's rivals were being placed in the same position, the PLC's debts seemed less onerous. Successful clubs such as Manchester United, where the cost was put at £10 million, and Liverpool (£7 million) would be able to afford this, but the building costs would be a severe handicap and they might have to borrow on the same scale as Tottenham. For smaller clubs, the cost was potentially ruinous.

As far as Tottenham's fans were concerned, the Taylor report was soon overshadowed by the team's activities on the pitch. There had been a rerun of the previous year; a rollercoaster season which started badly but improved in the second half. This time the revival had been strong enough to take Tottenham to a finishing position of third place in the League. Just as importantly, the England national team was limbering up for the World Cup, due to start in Italy the following month. The fans were naturally preoccupied by England's chances, especially as Lineker and Waddle, who was still regarded as a sort of honorary Spurs player despite his exile in Marseille, would be the stars of the team. Gascoigne was going to Italy too, but England manager Bobby Robson was still worried about his lack of maturity and had not yet decided whether he would be included in the team.

Scholar's feelings about the tournament were more mixed. Just before he set off for Italy in the middle of June the PLC's accountants had drawn up full-year figures showing losses of £2.6 million, caused by interest payments on debts of £12 million. There was no way Scholar could allow Venables to spend the £4.25 million from the Waddle deal on new players: the Midland Bank simply would not allow it.

His main hope now was that the World Cup would be a financial as well as a footballing success, showing sceptical financiers once and for all that soccer, if properly handled, was a truly international 'event-like' sport, capable of delivering enormous TV audiences ripe for sportsploitation. He was not to be disappointed.

PART THREE

12: THE TEARS OF TURIN

Football appears on the agenda of the general, non-fan public once every four years when the nation's living rooms are invaded by saturation coverage of the World Cup. People who do not watch a football match from one season to the next are suddenly hooked and, after heavy doses of Jimmy Hill every evening, may even be found sagely discussing the merits of the Egyptian sweeper system or finer points of Brazilian ball control during their coffee breaks.

The World Cup provides an irresistible mixture of mindless national chauvinism, extreme physical competitiveness and personal drama. As a televisual substitute for stuffing the foreigners with actual military aggression, it lies somewhere between the pomposity of the Olympic ideal and the buffoonery of the Eurovision Song Contest. And the competition is, by rights, British, because football is British. It is 'the game which Britain taught the world to play'. Great Britain is the mother of parliaments. Not every country has a parliament; but all of them have a national soccer squad. FIFA, the international football authority, has more national affiliates than the United Nations.

The fact that Britain gave this simple gift to the world is still a source of national pride. Even better, the World Cup is the one of the few major world-class sports events where a British team stands a decent, if uncertain, chance of winning. This happened within living memory, when in 1966 England beat West Germany 4–2 on the sacred turf of Wembley.

Coming soon after the start of televised soccer, England's 1966 victory had profitably increased the profile of the game in Britain, especially as the competition was held in England. But the financially inept worthies who ran soccer in those days had failed to cash in and the financial advantage had been lost.

Scholar, already working on a new and vastly more profitable post-Italia TV deal, was determined not to make the same mistake after Italia 90. England seemed to have a reasonable chance of doing well in the competition. The team had been playing well in the warm-up matches which manager Bobby Robson had used to try out new players, including Gascoigne. And the English TV audience had been starved of international competition for four years following the Heysel ban.

England had been placed in group F along with Ireland, Egypt and Holland, and all four teams would play each other in a mini-league system which formed the first part of the competition. The main danger was Holland, who had won the European Nations Cup, a mini-World Cup for European teams only, two years previously. But two teams would qualify from group F and go on to the later knockout stages. On paper it looked certain that Holland and England would go through, and only then would there be a chance of meeting more fancied teams like West Germany, Italy, Brazil and Argentina.

Even a modest performance by England, combined with a lifting of the ban on English teams in Europe, would transform British football's longer-term prospects. And there was a more direct reason why Tottenham could prosper. Scholar and Venables set off for Italia 90 confident that good performances by Gascoigne and Lineker would boost their tradeable value. Even if the players were not sold after the competition, any increase in value could at least be used to offset the PLC's debts because of the new accounting system which included players as assets in the balance sheet. It would then just be a matter of hanging on while the debts generated by

Berry's diversification and Bobroff's stadium building were brought under control.

Scholar had kept a low profile in Italy compared to other English football bigwigs. David Dein, the new owner of Arsenal, arrived in his yacht, the *Take It Easy*, and went to attend every England match, even though Bobby Robson had not included a single Arsenal player in his first-choice team. Tottenham, in contrast, had provided the two main stars, and Chris Waddle was still seen by many as a Spurs player in exile. Despite this, Scholar, preoccupied by the boardroom split, bank demands to reduce the PLC's debts and new League manoeuvrings over TV contracts, did not attend a single game until the semi-final.

The England squad had meanwhile set up camp in remote Cagliari, Sardinia, where Group F was partly based, surrounded by a small army of armed policemen ready to deal with any outbreak of the 'English disease' of hooliganism. As the fans were herded between squalid campsites and high-security stadiums, the squad became the centre of a commercial travelling circus of sponsors, players' agents, marketing men and tabloid hacks.

Leading the way was Jon Smith, one of only six people officially licensed by FIFA to organise international friendly matches. Smith was handling the exploitation of England's participation in the Italia 90 World Cup, worth, he later claimed, about £6 million. (Others put the figure closer to £1 million. Hype merchants, it was noted, are always keen to hype their moneymaking abilities.) Smith's activities included the production and marketing of the team's pop record, brand endorsement and 'product placement': an increasingly important subcategory of hype which, in this case, involved getting team members to mill about during filmed practice sessions nonchalantly drinking Coca-Cola.

Other sponsorship deals included carphones and clothing companies, though not 'Hoddle in Hummel' which, by this time, had gone bust. One of the most lucrative deals was with Mars, picking up on the

Gascoigne connection. The deal prompted the *Observer's* soccer writer Patrick Barclay to quip that Gazza had done more for Mars Bars than anyone since Marianne Faithfull.

Like any good PR man Smith had good connections in the tabloids and a lot of power over the tabloid soccer hacks, a craven bunch at the best of times, rationing their access to the players for interviews. The £100,000 sponsorship deal with Mars was thus reported in the *Daily Mirror* as a 'Mirrorsport Exclusive' under the headline 'THE MEN FROM MARS'. 'England medical experts recommend the players eat chocolate on the night before their big games,' the paper reported: 'Now they will turn to Mars to help them work, rest and play!' Smith later claimed that he had more or less written the story himself, and the *Mirror's* sportsdesk had been happy to insert it because it owed him a few favours. The story was described as 'headline driven'.

The money generated by Smith went into a pool shared by all the squad. In addition Lineker had his own fixer, sports PR expert Jonathan Holmes (who also handled Frank Bruno and Daley Thompson), and Gascoigne's interests were looked after by Mel Stein, Chris Waddle's adviser. To prove that business is business and knows no prejudice or sentiment, Smith's biggest individual client was Maradona, the *bête noire* of English soccer.

Gascoigne had only the slightest of grips on the details of the financial deals being done for him, now involving serious money after his graduation to a regular position in the England first team. He had made it to Italy after a good performance in a warm-up game against Czechoslovakia at Wembley where he had scored a goal and set up the other three in a 4–2 win. After that the tabloid clamour to include him in the squad had been irresistible, even though manager Bobby Robson still had his doubts.

True to form, Gascoigne was behaving like a spoiled brat in and around the squad's hotel in Cagliari. When the team was supposed to be relaxing on the beach Gazza was to be found in worst Club 18–30 mode, wearing silly sunglasses, Bermuda shorts, snorkel and flippers and

170

falling off a windsurfer, innocently chasing the other players' wives in a pedalo and splashing them with water, playing bumper cars with golf buggies, whacking other players on the back as he sped past them or pestering them to play table tennis with him.

More than once the team coaches had to rescue him from falling off his surfboard on to the rocks or roasting himself raw by overdoing the sunbathing: not that he lay still long enough to get seriously pink. Eventually Chris Waddle agreed to babysit, which was a daunting task. He got so used to Gascoigne's continuous whinnying that a sudden silence would fill him with dread and he would set off to check everything was all right. Invariably Gazza would be found in a room by himself, momentarily absorbed in some mindless football-related activity such as heading a tennis ball against the wall a hundred times. The worst thing was that Gazza was at it day and night, gibbering on to the other players until the early hours when, in desperation, he would be given a sedative injection so everyone could get some sleep. But then he would be up again bright and early, bounding into the breakfast room and throwing pieces of toast about.

When it came to doing the actual business during England's first game of the competition, against Ireland, it seemed that the sedative injections had finally had their effect. Apart from a few clever touches, Gascoigne was just as subdued as the rest of the players in a dire performance. Ireland played like a middling English Division One or Two team, which was not surprising since this was where most of their players came from. They played for a draw with a packed defence, whacking the ball up the pitch for their lone striker Tony Cascarino to chase. The fact that the game took place in a thunderstorm did not help.

The result was a 1–1 draw, which at least kept both teams in with a chance of getting through to the later stages. But the verdict was that England, the favourites, had blown it by descending to Ireland's level. Scotland had been simultaneously beaten by Costa Rica, reducing

171

the whole of British soccer to a laughing stock.

This did not matter too much, because the TV audience had still not woken up to the event-like significance of it all, and was still mainly restricted to football supporters and not the general public. England had to play Holland next in what was billed as the first crunch game of the tournament.

Dutch stars like Ronald Koeman, recently bought by Barcelona for £4 million, and Ruud Gullit (AC Milan, £6 million) were already on the record as rubbishing England as easy meat. They were particularly sneering about Gascoigne and Lineker, and said that England had only one world-class player – Bryan Robson, the veteran Manchester United midfield general. The Dutch promptly spiked themselves by managing only a 1–1 draw with Egypt, the fourth and weakest member of the group. Assuming England would beat Egypt, which they did, this set up the match against Holland as the decider in the group, kindling national interest to the point where large numbers of the ordinary public tuned in for the first time.

Fortunately for all concerned the England–Holland match was a cracker, full of drama and cliffhanging moments. It ended in a 0–0 draw, which, as it turned out, was enough to get England through to the next round. To their own surprise, the more casual viewers, the Great British Public, were now hooked.

The GBP did not really know much about tactics, or the names of the players. But one man stood out in the Holland game: Paul Gascoigne, who played according to type, charging about the pitch and trying all manner of reckless, and often futile, moves. Gascoigne's clownish televisual Gazza persona also shone through. At one point he clashed with Ruud Gullit and then cheerfully tugged at his dreadlocks. That was the great thing about Gascoigne, the analysts and commentators decided: he was an entertainer and nobody knew what he was going to do next. After one of his frequent rough and tumbles he might get up and thump somebody, or burst out laughing and hug the referee. The Holland match moved

Gascoigne off the back pages and made his every move front-page news. Gazzamania had arrived.

Already the advertising agencies were savouring the hype potential of the perplexing new TV and tabloid phenomena of Gazzamania, struggling to distil the exact nature of his appeal. 'He's like Eddie the Eagle with talent,' enthused John O'Donnell who, as creative director of the Collet Dickenson Pearce advertising agency, was paid to think about these things. 'He's such a popular figure that at the moment he could be used to endorse just about anything,' he told the *Sunday Times*. To prove it he was soon advertising Brut aftershave. Later, after Gerald Ratner described his jewellery as 'crap' in a misjudged PR scam, Gazza was brought in for an emergency PR campaign: 'It's world class, man' he was paid to say in a watered-down Tyneside accent. Real Geordiespeak was reserved for advertising his own autobiographical video under the snappy slogan: 'Howay lads! Get th'affishal video a this canny fella's leef story fa arnlee nine poond, ninety-nine pee.'

The consensus was that he had tapped the British love of an underdog. He was Mr Ordinary Bloke, not too bright, but suddenly successful on the grand scale as the underdog star who had only just made the grade in an underdog team. Gianni Agnelli, owner of Juventus, was thinking along the same lines, indicating the instant and huge increase in Gazza's transfer value. Gascoigne was 'a dog of war with the face of a child', he said.

Soon the intellectuals got in on the act. Back home Karl Miller, editor of the *London Review of Books*, decided that Gazza's appeal was based on a delicious sexual ambiguity: 'fierce and comic, formidable and vulnerable, urchin-like and waif-like, a strong head and torso with comparatively frail-looking, breakable legs, strange-eyed, pink-faced, fair-haired, tense and upright, a priapic monolith in the Mediterranean sun; a marvellous equivocal sight.'

The GBP was now looking forward to watching the antics of the priapic monolith in England's next match against Belgium, the first sudden-death eliminator. Almost 20 million tuned in to the match, along with 4.5 million Belgians, which was 45 per cent of the entire population. Tottenham's regular 25,000 supporters, who already knew all about Gascoigne, were now swamped by the TV millions, cutting a swathe right through the middle of England. Never again would Gascoigne's value as a player be based entirely, or even mainly, on his appeal to the White Hart Lane crowd. Now he was Gazza and had connected with a global TV audience. The football supporters on the terraces were a sideshow. The England supporters in Italy, between 5,000 and 10,000 strong, were even less important, playing the role of the invited studio audience in a TV spectacular, except nobody had invited them. Instead they had to pay at least £30 for their tickets (£100 on the black market), were not allowed to drink on match days and were indiscriminately herded around by the police who treated them as suspected hooligans, with the full support of the British sports minister Colin Moynihan, who had called them 'the effluent tendency'.

The Belgium game itself was another fast, end-to-end match with narrow escapes for both teams. England had two goals disallowed after questionable decisions by the referee and Belgium hit the post. Gazza was again at the centre of events, rushing about chaotically with the enthusiasm of a Sunday morning park player. With minutes to go he went on a fifty-yard run, dodging one Belgian after another until he was fouled just outside the penalty area. Gascoigne took the free kick himself: a lob of genuinely wondrous inch-perfect precision which David Platt of Aston Villa smashed into the net to score the winning goal.

Now England were playing well and were through to the quarter-finals and had a real chance of going all the way, with Gazza the undoubted star. The next hurdle was Cameroon who, according to the form book, should have presented few problems. Soccer sages said that

African soccer teams had a lot of potential, but they were not yet highly rated.

The general sniggering over stories about the employment of witch doctors and voodoo by teams in the African qualifying group gave way to general amazement and jubilation when Cameroon beat Argentina in the opening match of the tournament. The result was put down to the sort of fluke giant-killing that was always on the cards in Cup football, like Venables' defeat at the hands of Port Vale in the English FA Cup.

In England the *Sun* had used the result to indulge its favourite sport of Argie-bashing, berating Maradona's team for losing to a bunch of obscure blacks, and printing a map of Africa across most of the front page, with a giant arrow showing readers where Cameroon was. Now only the hopeless 'Cameroonie Loonies', as the paper called them, stood between England and a World Cup semi-final: the top four in the world and, even if the team lost, the best finishing position since 1966.

Another 20 million watched the Cameroon match. After 25 minutes the predictions of an easy English win seemed to be confirmed when Platt scored with a header. Gazza was going his own way more than ever. It was like Robson's complaint during the Albanian warm-up game: England needed two balls, one for Gazza and one for the rest of the team.

But as Cameroon got more and more of the play, Robson looked terrified on the bench and Gazza, riding one hard tackle after another, was starting to lose his temper. By half time he looked insane with frustration, itching to hit back. In the second half that is exactly what he did. Gascoigne fouled Roger Milla, Cameroon's bald 38-year-old striker, giving away a penalty. Soccer's Eddie the Eagle, talent or no talent, had struck again. Cameroon went level at 1−1. A few minutes later the Lions of Africa, as they were known, scored their second and looked like scoring more.

England had been eliminated from the last World Cup at this stage courtesy of the Hand of God; now it seemed that He was at last on the right side. The team got two penalties, Lineker scored both and after extra time England ended up 3–2 winners. The Cameroons had won a moral victory, and the pressure to include more African teams in the finals intensified. Until now Africa had been restricted to a maximum of two teams, compared with fourteen from Europe. The main African complaint was that Britain alone was able to enter four teams for the competition, and African soccer authorities were campaigning for a reduction to provide more places.

This demand had prompted a surprisingly racialist response from Brian Clough of Nottingham Forest who at one time, had run his own campaign to be manager of England. 'If the African nations ever succeeded in their plan for one British team in the World Cup, I'd vote Tory. I ask you – a load of spear-throwers trying to dictate our role in world football,' he said. Remarks like this had ruled him out of the England job and he instead applied to do the same job for the Republic of Ireland. 'It's easy enough to get to Ireland,' he said. 'Just a straight walk across the Irish Sea as far as I'm concerned.'

European talent scouts followed the Cameroon team back to Africa, but the 'massive potential of African soccer', the main new cliché of Italia 90, was soon forgotten in England as attention forcused on the next match: the semi-final against West Germany to be played in Turin. No neutral observer gave England a flicker of a chance.

The meaningless facts so beloved of soccer commentators provided an overwhelming weight of evidence. Since England's win in the 1966 final the two teams had played each other ten times: England had won only twice. The Germans had won the World Cup in 1974 and had been runners-up in 1982 and 1986; but England had never again got further than the quarter-finals. Even the 1966 win had been a fluke. From the safe historical distance of a quarter of a century, the Wembley win had been re-examined and it was now generally accepted that one of England's goals had not crossed the line and had been

176

awarded by mistake by a Russian linesman. If the goal had been disallowed the final might have taken a different course.

In terms of transfer-market value West Germany's players were in a different league. Within the past eighteen months their four strikers alone had changed hands for a total of £15 million and all of them now played for Italian clubs. More importantly, while England had struggled to get to the semi-final, the Germans had breezed through their games in the earlier rounds, living up to the national stereotype of ruthless robotic efficiency. It was Audi-VW versus Austin-Rover. *Vorsprung durch Technik.* No contest.

The result of the other semi-final, between Argentina and Italy, raised the stakes even more. According to the form book the hosts should have won, leading the two most fancied teams, Italy and West Germany, to the final, as intended by the seeding system. Instead the Argies had fouled and cheated their way to a draw after extra time. They then won the tie-breaker: a nerve-wracking penalty shoot-out in which the Argentinians excelled.

The penalty system was supposedly fairer than tossing a coin, but it had the same disadvantage of encouraging less talented teams to play for a draw. After that they would have a fifty-fifty chance of winning; maybe better if they had rehearsed and were psyched up for it. But the Argies' negative tactics had cost them dearly. On average the team had committed a foul every four minutes throughout the competition and, as a result, several important players had been banned from appearing in the final.

If England beat West Germany in the semi-final they would face a weakened Argentinian side in the final, which would be the ultimate opportunity to exact revenge for Maradona's handball in Mexico. As underdogs and good sports (England were about to win the play-fair award for committing the least number of fouls in the competition) everyone in the world outside Argentina and Scotland would be rooting for England. In this golden scenario Gascoigne was on course to lift the World Cup and become a planetary hero, the most famous man on earth.

But first England had to beat West Germany. On the afternoon of the match the country came to a standstill. The streets of every town and city were deserted as people laid in supplies of tinned lager, much of it, if the marketing connection with Gazza, Tottenham and soccer was working, Holsten Pils, and otherwise prepared for the big game. In London the rush hour did not take place for the first time since the Blitz. The British TV audience touched 25 million, by far the biggest figure for a televised sporting event.

The match itself was total drama. Gascoigne almost scored in the first minute and the first part of the game was all England. West Germany did not get in to the game until the second half and things were still fairly even when they scored a third of the way through the second half. The German goal was suitably sickening, a lucky deflection off England defender Paul Parker which ended up in the net through sheer luck.

Parker quickly made amends by passing the ball expertly to Lineker who beat two defenders and thumped it past the German goalie to even the score. The last twenty minutes of normal playing time were pure frenzy, a human pinball game, with both sides coming close to getting a goal. The general public was getting a rare glimpse of the real pleasure of watching soccer: the exhausting, emotional rollercoaster which switched from elation to tension and then to terror as the opposition came close to scoring.

The match finished as a 1–1 draw, which seemed like a victory for England, the underdogs. There followed half an hour of extra time when the premium would be on English stamina (a product of the exhausting 50-plus-match English League and Cup season) rather than German skill. Gascoigne pitched straight in, tackling hard and, after five minutes, fouled the German player Thomas Berthold by accident. The foul was not especially vicious, was mainly due to Gascoigne's overenthusiasm and was nowhere near as serious as the sort of stuff being dished out by the Argies in other matches. But Berthold dived, to use the technical term, and rolled around on the floor, making it look far worse. By chance the incident took place right in front of the bench where the German trainers were stationed. They jumped up and down and shouted at the ref, demanding retribution.

The theatricals had the desired effect. The cameras zoomed in on Gascoigne's face as the referee called him over to one side. He looked suitably contrite, eyebrows arched and obviously expecting a mild ticking off and a warning to calm down. Instead the ref pulled out a yellow card. A look of astonishment flashed across Gascoigne's face. This changed to pain as his shoulders dropped and he turned away staring in anguish and disbelief at the ground. It was Gascoigne's second booking of the tournament, which meant he would be automatically disqualified from the final against Argentina if England got through.

Lineker tried to talk to him but he seemed to be in a daze. The England captain had seen Gascoigne disappear into similar black moods during Tottenham games under far less pressure. The great danger now was that Gascoigne would vent his frustration by thumping the nearest German, risking a sending-off and leaving his team a player light.

'He's lost it,' Lineker mouthed to Robson on the bench, making a tapping gesture on his forehead. The moment of truth came almost at once when Gascoigne was subjected to a far worse tackle by a German player and went flying flat on his face. The England fans screamed abuse and Lineker and Robson held their breath. Instead of retaliating Gascoigne got up quickly and shook the offending player's hand.

The frenzy continued. Waddle hit the post and the Germans came close to scoring more than once. At the end of extra time it was still 1-1. The match would be decided on penalty kicks. As the players waited for the

179

ref to organise the shoot-out Gazza finally let go. Robson came over to congratulate and console him and he broke into tears. The cameras zoomed in again to record the scene which, for hundreds of millions around the world, would be the abiding image of Italia 90: the Tears of Turin.

England lost the shoot-out, leading to condemnation of penalties as a way of settling important matches (there had been no such complaints from Tottenham when they won the UEFA Cup by the same method in 1984). But there was no chance of the system being reformed, partly because it appealed to the TV networks which were beginning to dominate arrangements for the next World Cup finals in the USA in 1994. The American TV companies and audience had almost entirely ignored Italia 90 and only 'the PKs', as the US commentators called the penalty shoot-outs, had raised a flicker of interest. Beyond this, the *Louisville Courier* had remarked that soccer was 'about as exciting as *Tristan and Isolde*'. Now there were inconclusive demands to play World Cup games in four quarters instead of two halves, so that the whole spectacle would look more like basketball and more advertising breaks could be inserted.

Gascoigne left the Turin stadium with tears in full flood, collapsed in the arms of hard man Terry 'Butch' Butcher, one of the older troopers. Back in London Bryan Robson, unable to play because of a toe injury and doing a spot of TV punditry instead, had sympathised with Gascoigne, pleading for the TV cameras to stop showing his distress. Fortunately for Gascoigne they continued anyway, providing long, priceless minutes of personal exposure to a world TV audience measured in billions, and spreading Gazzamania, virus-like, from England to the rest of Europe and the world.

As Gazza wept, Irving Scholar, who had watched the match from the stands, had every reason to leave the ground with the broadest of smiles. Naturally he was upset at England's failure to get to the final, but he knew that the vast interest in soccer caused by England's creditable performance was bound to have a positive

180

impact at Tottenham. The PLC's share price had been firming up as England progressed through the competition and especially as Gascoigne and Lineker emerged as household names. It was estimated that the two players' up-front transfer value had increased to as much as £15 million now that Italian interest had been stimulated. A record £2.25 million worth of advance season tickets had been sold to fans eager to watch Gazza and Gary work the same magic for Tottenham in the League next season. It was not often that a company doubled its capital value on the back of 90 minutes' work by two employees.

Scholar stayed in Italy for the World Cup final. Germany beat Argentina 1−0 with a late penalty in an ugly, boring match studded with cynical fouls by both sides. Two Argie players were sent off, and Maradona nearly joined them after arrogantly pushing the referee in the chest. The consensus soon emerged that England's match against West Germany had been the 'real' final, and Gazza's personal drama the undisputed high point.

FIFA calculated that an implausible total of 31 billion worldwide had watched the competition on TV. In a last moneygrabbing move the organisers cut the pitch in the Olympic Stadium, Rome, into 306,000 pieces and sold the sods as souvenirs at £50 a go, and much more for important bits like the penalty spot. This was a case of life imitating art: Venables had described a similar scene in *They Used to Play on Grass*, his co-written novel.

Scholar returned to London, bubbling with talk of football's bright future. If only the financiers would hang on, ride out short-term debts and back dynamic chairmen like himself, huge profits were there for the taking. The awesome size of the World Cup's TV audience proved that there were tens of millions to be had from sponsorship and TV rights for big games. Things could only get better. The 1994 World Cup final was designed to rope in the USA. Where the Americans went the Japanese were sure to follow; as with golf. If soccer replaced its sterling and lira base with dollars and yen, additional zeros would suddenly appear all over the balance sheet.

Behind this cheerful talk, Scholar was facing his greatest crisis so far. The debt to the Midland had now climbed to over £15 million and interest charges were draining away almost £3 million a year. Scholar knew that there would be demands to sell Gascoigne and Lineker to reduce the debts. This made no sense. As expected, after the World Cup UEFA had lifted the ban on English clubs in European competitions. At the same time the structure of the European Cup had been changed to a mini-League system, similar to the World Cup.

This meant if Tottenham qualified by winning the English League, and got through the first qualifying rounds, they would be guaranteed five 'event-like' European games. Unlike the League matches, TV rights for European games were individually negotiated. That meant a guaranteed income of at least £2 million; maybe a lot more if Gazzamania continued. There was more sponsorship and ticket money to be had. Scholar had already told the *Sunday Express* he saw no reason why Tottenham should not charge £50 a ticket, instead of £15, for games like these.

If Gazza and Lineker went, all his work, and the big gamble of redeveloping the ground and spending on players at the same time, would be lost. Gazza was only 23 and just starting his international career: the best was yet to come. He was 'an appreciating asset', Scholar told the *Guardian*, who would reach the peak of his powers during the 1994 World Cup. Italia 90 had increased his value by a factor of five and USA 94 might push it much higher.

Lineker was another matter. Spurs could not sell him even if they wanted, to, for the very good reason that he did not yet fully belong to Tottenham. Because of its debts the PLC had paid Barcelona only the first £600,000 instalment on his £1.2 million transfer fee, negotiated eighteen months previously. Now Venables' old club was threatening to 'repossess' the England captain if they did not get their money immediately.

The problem was that neither the PLC, nor Scholar personally, had the money to make the final payments. There was no chance of the Midland extending the overdraft while Scholar and not their man on the board, Bobroff, was in charge of how it was spent. Tony Berry's sources of finance had dried up. Scholar had already put some of his own money into the club, but could not afford to gamble another million.

This was an especially knotty problem for Scholar. He had been able to explain away the loss of Waddle as the player's own desire to leave Spurs, but there could be no similar excuse if Lineker went back to Barcelona. So far he had managed to keep the true gravity of the position from the fans, shareholders and the press. The departure of Lineker was certain to create a huge public row, lighting up the real story of the PLC's finances in a blaze of publicity and causing a further loss of financial confidence and support.

Letting Lineker go was unthinkable, and selling Gascoigne had to be avoided at all costs. It was all so frustrating. For the want of a few million pounds, which was peanuts compared to the money he had seen changing hands during Italia 90, his beloved Tottenham might be forced to throw away its footballing and financial future.

But Scholar had been in tight corners before. From the original takeover to the flotation, appointment of Venables and TV negotiations the conventional thinkers had said it could not be done. Scholar knew that the board had more or less thrown in the towel, and would soon be demanding the sale of players. If he was again to save his beloved club, Scholar would have to look beyond the board to find a new financial supporter, a kindred spirit and fellow gambler prepared to ignore convention in the pursuit of football's bright future.

He was about to go out on a limb and make his most audacious move so far. A move that would leave the combined worlds of soccer, finance and the media reeling.

13: A FATE WORSE THAN DEBT

Italia 90 had a direct and positive impact on the finances of Robert Maxwell's Derby County. Mark Wright, the England central defender who had started his career with Maxwell's other club, Oxford United, had played well in Italy, pushing up his estimated transfer value to over £2 million. This had brought an instant capital gain of £1 million, more than Maxwell had paid to get control of the entire club in 1984.

The *Mirror* announced that Derby had rejected a £2.5 million bid for Wright from Liverpool with the news that Maxwell had walked out of a meeting of the International Monetary Fund to deal with it. The story predicted a bright future for the club and was illustrated with a huge picture of Maxwell embracing the beaming Wright.

On top of the revaluation of Wright, the League had negotiated a much better TV deal in the previous season. The humiliating 1986 contract had brought in only £6.2 million. This had been increased to £20 million over five years, mainly by exploiting competition between the existing networks and the new satellite stations. A Division One club like Derby could now expect to get at least £500,000 per season from the screening of League and domestic Cup games. At the same time attendances, season tickets and sponsorship money were all set to increase as the positive effects of Italia 90 hit home.

The real financial prize was still European competition, open again to English clubs for the first time in five years. TV rights to European games could be sold individually and were estimated to be worth up to £250,000 per game.

184

A run of matches leading to a European Cup final would bring in anything up to £6 million in TV rights alone, and probably £10 million when extra sponsorship and ticket sales were added to the total.

The problem for Maxwell was that neither Derby County nor, still less, Oxford United had any chance of getting into Europe; even though they had done quite well in their modest way since his last involvement with TV negotiations in 1984. Oxford had emerged as a good Cup team, winners of the Milk Cup in 1986. A series of good runs had brought matches against Manchester United, Everton and Arsenal, with Maxwell cashing in by auctioning tickets like a tout to the highest bidder.

The *Mirror* publisher got so excited about Oxford's Cup game against Arsenal, the team he purported to support, that he delayed the flight of a *Mirror* jumbo jet hired for a 'mercy mission' to Ethiopia so he could be at the kick-off. Arriving at Addis Ababa at 2 a.m. the next morning, journalists were astonished to find that Maxwell had arranged for the Arsenal game to be screened on Ethiopian TV, and even more amazed to find that Oxford won 3 – 2.

In 1985 Oxford won the Division Two championship, taking them into Division One for the first time in their history. Having updated his supporter equipment from rosette to the more modern beanie hat and souvenir scarf, Maxwell joined the team's lap of honour, jogging heavily round the pitch and taking his turn to wave the trophy around in front of the jubilant fans, revealing that he had been so confident of success that he had placed a personal bet of £8,000, at odds of 16 – 1, on the championship.

To celebrate Maxwell had a 64-page commemorative picture book called *Rags to Riches – The Rise and Rise of Oxford United* printed and sent to all 25,000 employees of his Empire as a Christmas present. The cover featured a picture of Maxwell, complete with his favourite red bow tie, fondling the Division Two trophy with Jim Smith, the Oxford team manager. John Ley, a soccer hack, was hoiked off the local Oxford paper to write it.

'Oxford United are a shining example to everybody of what can be achieved by determination, good management and good support,' Maxwell said, adding a poetic touch: 'We have turned an ugly duckling into a swan.' Ley commented, bizarrely, that these were 'typical romantic sentiments from a man whose hobbies, according to *Who's Who*, are chess and mountain climbing', before saying that Oxford were in 'the high country' and Maxwell planned to 'build up their strength and resources, and to lead them to even greater heights.'

The rest of the book consisted of a sycophantic account of the chairman's activities, illustrated with various smiling, sweaty and heroic poses. There were pictures of a pro-Maxwell demo by supporters, complete with small children carrying placards saying: 'OXFORD UNITED NEEDS YOU MR MAXWELL', backing the chairman's ceaseless demands for the local council to provide money for a new stadium. The whole production was finished off with a giant double-page picture of Maxwell, hands held high above his head, graciously accepting the cheers of the adoring Oxford crowd: just the sort of thing the surviving printers at the *Mirror*, where the workforce had been summarily reduced by half, wanted to look at over their Christmas pudding.

Derby, placed under the chairmanship of Maxwell's son Ian to get round the League Management Committee's rule on multiple ownership, had also done well. The club had shot up from Division Three to Division One in consecutive seasons. Derby was a much more famous club than Oxford and also had a better ground. So Maxwell took the strategic decision to bolster Derby at the expense of Oxford. Maxwell replaced Ian as Derby chairman as soon as they were promoted to Division One. Another son, Kevin, took over as chairman of Oxford, where Maxwell's daughter Ghislaine (described in *Rags to Riches* as 'the girl with the film star looks') was already on the board.

Over the next few seasons Oxford's best players had been steadily sold off or transferred to Derby. Mark

Wright, Oxford's only England international, was the first to go: transferred to Derby via Southampton. This was followed by the departure of John Aldridge, scorer of a record 30 goals in the promotion campaign, who went to Liverpool for £875,000. No players of comparable quality, or cost, were bought for Oxford. When the club inevitably dropped back into Division Two, Maxwell sold the team's two remaining stars. Ray Houghton was sold to Liverpool for £850,000 and Welsh striker Dean Saunders went directly to Derby.

Thus fortified, Derby finished fifteenth in Division One after the 1987–88 season, with an average gate of 17,300 compared with Tottenham's 26,000. The milking of Oxford to provide support for Derby was exactly the sort of activity the League Management Committee had feared. In the eyes of many people the transfer of Saunders to Derby was particularly worrying. Derby had gained an international class striker to bolster their attack on the Division One championship, but the £1 million transfer fee was purely a paper transaction. The money had gone straight back into Maxwell's coffers.

The Management Committee was powerless to stop this sort of thing, but it was able to veto Maxwell's next attempt to buy a Division One club: Elton John's Watford. The podgy piano wizard had bought a controlling block of Watford's shares in 1976 when they had been in Division Four. With his support the team reached Division One in a few seasons, proving once again that in the lower divisions a little bit of money went a long way. In 1983 the club had finished second to Liverpool in the League championship and in the following season were runners-up in the FA Cup, losing at Wembley to Everton.

But Elton John was in trouble and announced that he could no longer afford to finance the expansion of the club. Part of the reason was a monumental libel case Elton had begun against the *Sun*. In the summer of 1987 the paper had done to Elton what it had done in the previous year to David Pleat, publishing an outrageous front page story about his sex life. 'ELTON JOHN IN VICE BOYS SCANDAL – STAR'S LUST FOR BONDAGE', the *Sun*'s story, was based on the false and unsupported allegations of a rent boy who, after being paid by reporters, told how he had recruited tattooed skinhead rent boys for Elton John.

Unlike Pleat, the Watford chairman had refused to take the *Sun*'s attack lying down and announced he was going to sue for libel. 'They can say I'm a fat old sod, they can say I'm an untalented bastard, they can call me a poof, but they mustn't lie about me because then I'm going to fight. And I'm determined to be a winner,' he said. The first to run out of nerve or money would lose everything. Elton John's lawyers were already demanding damages of £50 million if he won when the case came to court. But even though right was on his side, Elton could not be certain of victory in the unpredictable world of the English law courts. To carry on Elton needed a fund of millions to withstand the pressure and cover the equally enormous court costs if he lost.

Maxwell, as owner of the *Daily Mirror*, had naturally taken a deep interest in the Elton John affair: the prospect of Elton placing a £50 million millstone round the neck of Rupert Murdoch, owner of the *Sun* and therefore his main publishing rival, was especially delicious.

The *Mirror* at once leapt to Elton's defence, ripping into the *Sun*'s story and tracking down the rent boy. Under the headline 'MY SEX LIES OVER ELTON JOHN', he revealed: 'I made it all up. I did it for money and the *Sun* was easy to con. I've never met Elton John.'

Things were going well for Elton but he still needed money to keep the legal action going and insure himself against the wrong result in the courtroom. An emergency sale of his collection of rock memorabilia had raised some money and now, coincidently, Maxwell offered him £2 million for control of Watford. This was not much for a club whose team boasted two £1 million-rated strikers: Luther Blissett and John Barnes, both England internationals.

188

After the Derby deal the League Management Committee had rewritten the ownership rule, extending it to close family members, and publicly regretted that the restriction could not be made retroactive. They soon made their opposition to his latest purchase clear. Maxwell fought back, pointing to a supposed connection between Watford and his printing company, the British Publishing and Communications Corporation, soon to become part of the Maxwell Communications Corporation, which was based in the town. He was now playing his favourite role, posing as the local Mr Bountiful, placing the BPCC at the disposal of the community, just as he had supposedly rescued Oxford because of the Pergamon connection.

Maxwell cleverly proposed that Watford would be controlled not directly by his family, but by the BPCC, with the Corporation's chief executive John Holloran installed as Watford's new chairman. The League stood firm, despite the flurry of noisy legal action that often attended Maxwell's business activities, backed by the full blast of propaganda on the back page of the *Mirror*. Maxwell lost interest in the club and Elton John, coincidentally, won a £1 million libel settlement from the *Sun*.

Maxwell's failure to gain control of Watford finally convinced him that the League Management Committee was serious. There was now no chance of buying another club, least of all one of the Big Five that had a chance of regularly playing in Europe. For now he was stuck with Derby where his plans for the big time had taken an unexpected turn. Maxwell suddenly announced that Johan Cruyff, a big cheese in European soccer, and lately manager of Ajax Amsterdam, was to be appointed as the club's technical director free to use his contacts and the Maxwell millions to bring the best players in Europe to Derby.

There was only one problem with this idea: the first Cruyff and Derby's existing manager, Arthur Cox, knew about it was when they read it on the back page of the

Daily Mirror. Cruyff had never expressed any interest in Derby County, a club of which he had scarcely heard. He had approached Maxwell with the idea of buying a small club in Holland. Maxwell had put the proposal to Harry Harris, the *Mirror*'s chief soccer writer, who said it was a waste of money, and came up with the idea of making Cruyff technical director of Derby instead. But the Flying Dutchman was not interested and when his club buying plan fell through he went off to manage Venables' old club, Barcelona.

The Cruyff saga showed Maxwell's frustration with Derby. He had provided the team with Shilton, Wright and Saunders but they had managed only fifth place in the League in the 1988–89 season, eighteen points adrift of the champions, Arsenal. Other clubs, such as Tottenham, where Gascoigne, Stewart and Lineker had just arrived, were spending heavily on new players. Maxwell gloomily realised that he would have to come up with millions just to keep Derby in the race. With Derby stuck in the doldrums and banned from buying another club, it was doubly frustrating for Maxwell to see the much bigger prize of Manchester United come back on the market in the autumn of 1989.

The prospective purchaser was Michael Knighton, a little-known property dealer from Derbyshire who had persuaded the club's owner, Martin Edwards, to sell his 51 per cent stake in the club for the bargain price of £10 million. Maxwell was furious. When he had tried to buy United five years previously, Edwards' asking price had been £15 million. Since then Maxwell had lumbered himself with Derby, making him unable to mount a counterbid and leaving him fuming on the sidelines. Why had Edwards cut the price?

Harry Harris, the *Mirror* sports hack behind the Cruyff idea, put together a team to investigate Knighton. Harris, a small but sprightly man, was one of the few *Mirror* journalists Maxwell trusted implicitly. He was a lifelong Spurs supporter who had started his reporting career on the local *Tottenham Herald* and graduated to the *Mirror* in 1986, two years after Maxwell bought the paper. From humble beginnings as the number two soccer writer on the sportsdesk, he had quickly risen to become Maxwell's unofficial adviser on everything to do with the game, including his own business dealings.

Harris' first major *Mirror* assignment had been to cover England's 1986 World Cup tour as a member of the travelling circus of soccer hacks. On the day before he was due to fly off to Mexico, Harris was at home in Croydon when he got a call from the *Mirror* newsdesk: Maxwell had just arrived back from Bulgaria and wanted to see him at Heathrow at once. The desk said it was about Bobby Robson, the England manager, but there were no other details. The boss was forever summoning people in this way.

Harris jumped into a taxi, wondering what it was all about. Maybe the boss had used his contacts to set up an exclusive interview with Robson. That would be handy. He needed to be well in with the England manager to ensure a good supply of exclusive material during the World Cup.

When Harris arrived at Heathrow he found that Maxwell had commandeered an entire floor of a Heathrow office block and was holding court, conducting half a dozen business negotiations at once, as normal, and flanked by yes-men and advisers. 'Ah Harry,' Maxwell had boomed across the room in the theatrically matey voice he often used when discussing soccer. 'You've got the front page; the whole of page two comment. You can run the story. Robson must go. *Mirror* readers want him out.'

Harris was dumbfounded. Robson at that time was doing reasonably well, as his own articles had been saying. 'Er, can I discuss this?' he asked with his habitual nervous giggle. 'I'm not sure I really agree.' The advisers fell silent and stared at their shoes, awaiting a Maxwell explosion.

This time Maxwell fell silent, prompting Harris to continue. 'It might be the wrong time to run the campaign,' he said, blinking behind his designer specs as he imagined what would happen when Robson read the demand for his sacking, sitting next to him on the plane the next morning. Harris later found out that Maxwell had read a small story in the *Sunday Express* that morning, mildly rubbishing the England manager for a cock-up during a game against Scotland. Robson, who had always had difficulty remembering names, held up the wrong number from the touchline during a substitution and brought off Spurs' Glenn Hoddle, the man who had scored the winning goal, by mistake. Maxwell thought it was typical of his old foes in the administration of English football that they had picked a man capable of making such an elementary error. 'How can men like these be trusted with soccer?' he had fumed.

Harris decided Maxwell was determined to run the story anyway, whatever he said. The priority was to limit the damage to himself and the *Mirror*. He agreed to write the article on condition that his name did not appear on it. The advisers relaxed, and resumed their background chatter as Maxwell began dictating. The diatribe was then read over the phone to the newsdesk so it could be put on page one as Maxwell intended.

With this service completed, Harris had offered to wheel his boss's luggage to his waiting limousine. Halfway across the concourse Maxwell tried to start up a conversation. 'You are very quiet. Is anything the matter?' Maxwell had croaked, peering down at his companion. Harris restrained himself. 'Of course there is,' he said, 'I'm worried about that front page.' Maxwell ordered him to stop, announcing magnanimously: 'I shall phone the editor and make sure that your name is not on it. Wait here.' Maxwell marched over to a payphone, eased himself in and made the call.

'Bad news, Harry,' Maxwell said on his return. 'They've already printed the front page. It's too late to change it.' Harris knew this was rubbish, there were hours to go before edition time and the change could be made in minutes. There was no point in protesting: the nervous strain of contradicting Maxwell twice on the same day was too much. Instead he waited until the proprietor had been packed into his waiting Roller, and phoned the newsdesk.

'What's going on?' Harris demanded. The desk sympathised but explained that the readers were sick of reading articles by Maxwell, and would not put up with another. The editor, Richard Stott, had decided that the demand for Robson's sacking would have looked absurd without the authority of the chief soccer writer's by-line. Basically he had been stitched up.

After that Harris had seamlessly adjusted to life under the Maxwell regime, helped by the fact that he genuinely admired his boss as a businessman with a genius touch for putting deals together. The admiration was mutual. Maxwell had worked with and trusted Harris even before he had bought the *Mirror*, when Harris was on the *Daily Mail*. Now he was at the *Mirror* rival sports hacks moaned about the way the boss showered Harris with favours. There was even an apocryphal story that Maxwell had given Harris two luxury BMW cars, even though Harris could not drive.

After the early shocks Harris was learning to deal with his boss's sudden brainwaves and constant interference with the paper's editorial coverage with remarkable tact and diplomacy. On the positive side, Maxwell's own soccer exploits were a constant source of great stories to which he naturally had automatic and exclusive access. And so he had no difficulty in getting Maxwell more interested in the plan to investigate Manchester United, centring on uncovering the business background of Michael Knighton.

Following up stories in the *Manchester Evening News*, Harris quickly found that Knighton simply did not have the money needed to buy Edwards' shares and then offer another £10 million to buy the club outright, as he had promised to do. On top of this Knighton had promised to invest another £10 million in the club to complete the redevelopment of the Old Trafford stadium; a total bill of around £35 million.

It turned out that Knighton's biggest single asset was a castle in Scotland worth about £2 million. His total property holdings added up to £13 million. To buy United Knighton would have to borrow heavily or find a backer. Harris decided that Knighton was either deluded: 'a Walter Mitty' as the *Mirror* later called him, a man high on all the ego-boosting publicity; or 'a chancer', as he put it, a get-rich-quick artist planning to buy United cheap and sell on quickly to a third party.

Maxwell's great fear was that United would end up in the hands of a powerful and capable businessman who would present a major challenge to his own soccer business plans. If this happened the option of buying United after getting rid of Derby, which he had never ruled out, would be gone for good.

One possibility was Rupert Murdoch, his deadly media rival, who had already put down his marker at United by investigating the possibility of screening the club's matches on his Sky TV channel. There was no evidence that Knighton was acting as a stalking horse for Murdoch, but the mere thought was enough to horrify Maxwell. Murdoch had outmanoeuvred Maxwell in the late 1960s to buy the *Sun* and *News of the World* from under his nose. The order from Maxwell to 'get Knighton' was never issued, as some later said, but it did not need to be. Harris set about his prey with relish; it was a great story in its own right. Under the headline 'UP FOR GRABS – KNIGHTON SEEKS A BACKER' Harris announced the start of a '*Mirror* probe' into the 'shenanigans, chaos and confusion surrounding the takeover of a soccer club that is an institution in this country'. The whole sports department was mobilised as Knighton was pilloried in the *Mirror* as 'a barrow boy' and 'a clown who has made United a laughing stock'. Harris filled up the back page of the *Mirror* every day for two weeks with the story.

United's chairman Martin Edwards was placed in the firing line for agreeing to deal with Knighton in the first place: 'KICK THEM OUT', the paper demanded, next to a picture of Knighton and Edwards smiling and shaking hands. The *Sun* weighed in on Knighton and Edwards' behalf, using its normal hyperbole to describe the saga as 'the takeover battle of the century', and fuelling Maxwell's suspicion that Murdoch was lurking in the background, ready to buy the club.

Murdoch's *Sun* matched the *Mirror* blow for blow, giving Maxwell's paranoia another twist. When the *Mirror* reported 'KNIGHTON'S A GONER', the *Sun* replied with 'KNIGHTON: UNITED'S ALL MINE'. The *Mirror*'s 'KNIGHTON IS OUT' was countered with 'KNIGHTON: I WON'T PULL OUT'.

The turning point came when Harris weighed in with the support of United hero Bobby Charlton, who was quoted in huge type saying that Knighton had 'cheapened the image of the greatest club in the world.' Nobody could survive an attack like that from the mild-mannered Charlton, respected as a man beyond reproach. That night the United board finally rejected Knighton's bid and the *Mirror* claimed the credit:

KNIGHTON DEAL COLLAPSES
A TRIUMPH FOR YOUR *DAILY MIRROR*
55 DAYS OF SHAME OVER AT UNITED
GOOD RIDDANCE TO WALTER MITTY!

'Michael Knighton's deal to buy Manchester United is finally and officially dead and buried,' Harris gloated, before turning his guns on Edwards: 'This sordid episode in Manchester United's history will never be finally laid to rest until Knighton, and indeed Edwards, are out of the door.'

Knighton disappeared from the scene, moaning about the way the *Mirror* had treated him, especially the more spiteful reports like 'KEEP OUT! – FANS WARN KNIGHTON', a story in which Harris reported: 'Michael Knighton has been warned that if he shows up at Manchester United tomorrow he will face the full fury of the Old Trafford fans.' A picture caption baldly stated:

'KNIGHTON – UNITED FANS HATE HIM'. 'They just savaged me like a piece of meat,' Knighton whinged.

Maxwell seemed to be proved right about Murdoch's interest in the club. Six weeks later the news broke that Murdoch had investigated buying Edwards' stake through an intermediary.

Two months later Maxwell was considering a new offer for United in the unlikely event of finding another loophole in the League's multiple ownership rule. Maxwell's financial analysts had put the value of the club at £33 million, but Edwards had again upped the price. After the *Mirror* vilification campaign he was not prepared to sell to Maxwell for less than £40 million. Edwards then announced that United would follow Tottenham on to the Stock Exchange with a flotation, ruling out the possibility of a private sale to Murdoch, Maxwell or anyone else.

Harry Harris had emerged from the United affair full of beans, praising himself for his fearless role in exposing Knighton. The final mop-up took in 'the lying *Sun*' under the crude but weak pun 'THE SUN SHINES OUT OF OUR HARRIS'. 'The fading *Sun* has become the laughing stock of soccer over the Knighton affair,' the *Mirror* said, adding: 'The paper has scored an own goal of humiliating proportions, so why not tell them so.' The *Sun* sportsdesk's phone number was then printed with an invitation to 'pick up the phone and blow them an enormous raspberry'. By midday the *Sun* was swamped with calls, paralysing the sportsdesk as intended. But the *Sun* hacks merely put a tape loop on the line, redirecting the calls to the *Mirror* which, in turn, received an avalanche of fart-like phone messages.

More importantly, Harris had risen enormously in the opinion of his boss, making him an important figure in English soccer, able to advise Maxwell on which players to buy and sell and on the soundness of proposals like the SuperLeague. He advised on new soccer business opportunities, influencing the future of Oxford, Derby and any of the other clubs Maxwell was interested in and,

196

when the right time came, wrote it all down on the back page in an endless series of ready-made 'Mirrorsport Exclusives'.

The savaging of the Manchester United board during the Knighton affair shut the door on a possible takeover of the club. After the horrors and humiliations of Harris' 'Kick Them Out' campaign, it was unthinkable that Martin Edwards would ever sell, though Maxwell still wanted one of the Big Five clubs.

Harris investigated Arsenal and Liverpool but found that there was no chance of getting a stake in either club. Both were stable and in profit and would not welcome outside involvement. Everton was slightly more vulnerable, but they were the smallest of the Big Five and scarcely a better bet than Derby. That left Tottenham.

When Harris returned from the World Cup Maxwell questioned him about Gascoigne, or 'Garzer' as the publisher pronounced the midfield ace's nickname. Harris confirmed the general chatter that Gascoigne was probably set to become one of the best English players of his generation. More importantly, he had picked up the story that Tottenham was in financial trouble and might have to sell him to the Italians after the next season.

Maxwell's latest populist soccer crusade took shape at once. He did not yet know how, or any of the details of the Spurs cash crisis, but he was already determined to become known and loved as the Man who Saved Gazza for England. He got his chance to save Gascoigne and keep Lineker in England within days of the end of the World Cup. Scholar, still desperate to find a new backer who could prevent the sale of Lineker and Gascoigne, called Harris to sound out Maxwell.

Scholar had known and trusted Harris for many years, both as a fellow Spurs supporter and, with Maxwell's support, a crusader against the Football League 'Mismanagement' Committee. Although Maxwell claimed he invented this stunningly obvious piece of word-play, the credit should really have gone to Scholar, who first started using it during the 1984 TV negotiations. By now

Harris had used the phrase so often that he got a Christmas card from Graham Kelly, then League secretary, with the message: 'Greetings from the Mismanagement Committee'.

Harris had originally introduced Scholar to Maxwell during the TV negotiations and the three-way relationship had got even closer when Scholar and Maxwell, whom the Tottenham chairman called Uncle Bob, without a hint of irony, hit it off. Maxwell gave Scholar patronising respect, and liked his approach, even though he sometimes forgot his name, spluttering at Harris: 'Get me that friend of yours at Tottenham.'

This time it was Scholar who wanted to speak to Maxwell. 'You know things are bad at Spurs,' he told Harris, taking him into his confidence, 'but I haven't told you how bad.' Scholar then explained that he needed money within days to pay off Barcelona and prevent the repossession of Lineker. 'Do you think Maxwell would be interested in helping?' he asked.

Harris told Scholar he was in luck. Gazza and the World Cup campaign had caught his imagination and he was sure that Maxwell would want to help keep him in England. There was at least a chance that he might want to get involved with turning the club around. Harris told him to ring Maxwell directly. Uncle Bob got moderately excited about the prospect, and came up with a secured £1.1 million loan to keep things going, enabling Scholar to pay off Barcelona and prevent the departure of Lineker.

The story of how Lineker had been only hours away from returning to Spain was kept secret and did not appear in the press until Harris broke the story as an Exclusive in the *Sunday Mirror* months later. But for the time being it remained a closely guarded secret; Maxwell did not want to be identified with Tottenham until he had looked at the club more closely. With the immediate crisis over Scholar and Maxwell began negotiating a package that would pay off the debts and put Tottenham back on course to become the most successful club in the country.

198

Maxwell and Scholar met to thrash out the general strategy, which was to be similar to the original stock market flotation. It involved a new rights issue of shares in the PLC that would again wipe off the club's debts. The problem was that nobody was likely to buy additional shares in the PLC. After the excitement of the World Cup Tottenham's share price had slumped to 90p, 10p less than the original issue price. The fans might buy some more, out of blind faith and loyalty, but that would not bring in much cash, especially as they had recently shelled out for higher priced season tickets. No serious outside investor would buy.

The main point was Maxwell's agreement to underwrite the issue, meaning that he would buy any unsold shares when the issue closed. In practice, this would mean more or less all of them, at a total cost of £12 million. From the start Maxwell insisted that he did not want a controlling stake in Tottenham, at least not for the moment. But he did have two demands: his dealings with Scholar, including the Lineker loan, had to be kept absolutely secret until both sides were ready to sign the deal and launch the rights issue, and the Tottenham board should unite unanimously around the plan when it was finalised.

Scholar turned up at the PLC's board meeting three days later with a glint in his eye. He explained that he had found a new source of cash, a 'benefactor' – no names – who had already provided him with the money to pay off Barcelona and was ready to help the club out of its difficulties, bridging the gap until Euromillions started to flow. The board was suspicious, but gave Scholar and Derek Peter, the PLC's finance director, permission to negotiate for a full-scale financial rescue package. At this point, with creditors beginning to ask awkward questions, they had no other option. Bobroff, significantly, was not present at the meeting.

Harris went off on holiday to Majorca. Scholar kept in touch by phoning him every morning and evening to let him know how things were going, asking for hints on how to handle Maxwell's famous ego and difficult mood changes. They never discussed board matters in detail, but Scholar seemed to need to get things off his chest. He had not discussed the deal with anyone else.

During a sticky moment Harris suggested giving Maxwell the largely ceremonial title of President, a position that did not mean very much in England, but which would appeal to Maxwell's vanity. The big names in European soccer were the club Presidents, including Maxwell's rival Silvio Berlusconi of AC Milan who had successfully woven his soccer interests into a ramified business empire based on television, computers, publishing, property and supermarkets. Harris knew that Maxwell saw himself as a British version of Berlusconi and was well aware of the kick Maxwell would get from describing himself as President of Tottenham Hotspur during his frequent business meetings with Berlusconi. But Scholar was worried about opposition to Maxwell's involvement in the club and insisted that he did not take a formal position. Instead he would be described only as a major shareholder and any statement would emphasise the fact that Maxwell would hold only a minority of shares in the refinanced company.

The deal which eventually emerged was relatively straightforward. Shares priced 130p each would be offered for sale, and Maxwell would have a 25.1 per cent stake. Scholar would probably remain the largest share-holder with about 26 per cent of the total and together the two men would control the club.

A comprehensive agreement was drawn up, including a clause specifiying that Gascoigne would not be sold, at least before the end of his contracted period with the club. The agreement also gave Maxwell the right to inspect the club's books in return for which Maxwell promised 'due diligence' in completing the deal.

Scholar was delighted. The rights issue would melt away the debt mountain, keep Gascoigne and Lineker at White Hart Lane and leave him in charge of the club, with Maxwell's support. Uncle Bob was likely to stump up some more money in future so that he could live up to the promises he had made to Venables when he had first arrived at the club. El Tel, Gazza and Gary would stay at Tottenham; the boardroom rift would be healed; the club would have cash to buy new players; and then: Glory, Glory Tottenham Hotspur.

Bobroff might attempt to oppose the deal, but he would be powerless. The board would be forced to accept the deal, simply because there was no alternative. If Bobroff did oppose the deal he would fall foul of Maxwell's insistence on board unity and would have to go. Scholar, for one, would shed no tears over that.

The deal was certain to go through now, Scholar decided. It was just a matter of choosing the right time to make the announcement. All that was needed was a few routine checks by Maxwell's lawyers and accountants. Nothing could go wrong now . . .?

14: A PLAN FOR GREATNESS

In the early hours of 2 August 1990, 30,000 Iraqi troops, supported by an advance column of 350 tanks and squadrons of jet fighters, crossed the border into Kuwait, overthrew the Sheikh and installed a pro-Iraqi puppet government.

Panic immediately gripped the world's financial markets. Memories flooded back to the Middle-Eastern war of the 1970s, which had put up the price of oil. That had caused rip-roaring inflation and recession throughout the western world. Share prices collapsed and were prevented from going into a tailspin only when it was realised that Iraq was not going to invade Saudi Arabia and that the American airforce would eventually arrive to destroy the Iraqi armed forces.

These events seemed destined to have only a slight effect on soccer. Jon Smith, the FIFA licensed football sponsorship agent who had done the Mars Bar and other deals during Italia 90, got to work organising a match between the Saudi Arabian national squad and a team recruited from the arriving allied army. The idea was partly designed to boost morale amongst the hordes of bored, alcohol-free GIs and British squaddies waiting for Saddam Hussein's Mother of Battles. It was also designed to exploit the massive prime time TV audience for the Desert Storm show and begin to whet American appetites for the all important 1994 World Cup. In the event, the match was overtaken by events and never took place.

The impact on the tangled financial affairs of Robert Maxwell was much more dramatic. Maxwell's empire had expanded rapidly throughout the 1980s, financed by heavy borrowing. It was known that the sky-high interest rates of the late 1980s had eaten heavily into profits, and had already hit the share price of his main company, Maxwell Communications Corporation. Far less well known was the way in which Maxwell had secured much of his borrowing on the share price of his own companies, arranged in a Byzantine structure of holding companies and subsidiaries underpinned by a mysterious charitable trust based in Liechtenstein.

As long as world share prices moved upwards, as they did for most of the 1980s, each part of the rickety structure supported the others. When interest rates were low the empire was able to record huge capital gains as the value of new acquisitions outstripped the cost of interest charges needed to buy them.

Maxwell's personal worth, measured in his family's shares in Maxwell companies, was correspondingly huge and he was rarely out of the lists of the 50 wealthiest people in the country. In reality the whole Maxwell operation was a gigantic house of cards. Once one part of it began to slip, weighed down by high interest rates and falling share prices, the whole lot might come crashing down. The position was in some ways similar to the problems faced by Tottenham Hotspur after the failure of its clothing acquisitions, Martex and Stumps, but on a much larger scale. The truth was that Maxwell was not rich at all. His companies were carrying debts of about £500 million, making him probably the poorest man in history.

Some people in the City began to fear that something like this was the case, but nobody could be really sure. The true worth of Maxwell's Liechtenstein linchpin company was impossible to estimate, as it was protected by the strictest banking secrecy laws in the world. One thing was certain: unless the trust had half a billion pounds at its disposal, Maxwell would never be able to pay off his creditors should they decide to come knocking on his door. He would go bust and the huge consortium of London-based banks would have to pick up the bill. There was no doubt that it could break some of them, threatening a collapse of part of the banking system.

This fact became the cornerstone of Maxwell's entire operation. It was a financial version of the Emperor's New Clothes. Nobody in the City dared suggest Maxwell did not have the money: the consequences were far too threatening. Maxwell also fully exploited the notoriously draconian British libel laws, issuing injunctions and writs against any journalist who dared to question the solidity of the empire or the ethics of his business practices. Maxwell had let it be known that he would issue a libel writ on the very mention of his name in connection with any financial impropriety and so not even the relatively simple matter of his looting of the Mirror Group's pension funds came to light until it was too late to do anything about it.

The world slump in share prices was a problem which not even Maxwell's army of lawyers could fend off. But as US forces began to arrive in the Gulf during the autumn of 1990, the threat to Saudi Arabian oil subsided and the immediate crisis passed. Eventually even the price of oil fell back to pre-invasion levels, helped by the extra production in the Gulf states demanded by the Americans as part of the price for sending troops. But the future still looked very threatening and Maxwell decided to batten down the hatches with a series of economy measures.

He at once put a freeze on further expansion in the empire, no matter how cheap in relative terms, causing him to pull out of the Tottenham share issue. Scholar was distraught and complained that having made the deal Maxwell was bound to carry it out with 'due diligence' as they had agreed. Maxwell's lawyers saw things differently.

'Due diligence' might have sounded like an obligation on Maxwell's part to go ahead, but the clause's effect was exactly the opposite. It was like the completion period in a house purchase. The Tottenham board might be in

204

a position to sue for some compensation, but the money available would not be great and Scholar would have to break the much clearer agreement to keep their talks secret and fall out with Uncle Bob if he wanted to get it. This, Scholar realised, was not a good idea, especially as Maxwell had said he might revive the deal if the economic scene improved later in the year.

Maxwell told Harry Harris, who did not let on that he had been kept fully informed of developments by Scholar, that he simply could not afford to buy into Tottenham: 'I'll do it later in the year,' he said. For now he could not risk anyone asking if he could really afford to spend another £12 million on soccer. It might prompt a broader investigation of his finances. Maxwell's next move was to put Oxford and Derby up for sale, along with his shareholdings in other clubs, including Manchester United, Oxford and Reading. As part of the Emperor's New Clothes approach it was vital that this should not be seen for what it was: a desperate scramble to prune losses and pull in every available penny from fringe activities such as soccer to keep up interest payments on the Empire's debts.

Instead Maxwell constructed an elaborate rationale, unveiled at a news conference for the financial press called to detail the progress of his new paper, the *European* which, he claimed, was well on course with a readership of 300,000. Market research conducted for the *European*, Maxwell revealed, showed that the population of Europe was becoming more spiritual in its outlook, moving away from sport towards the arts and high culture. There would be only a limited place in the new European order for soccer, he had decided.

Maxwell's advisers clenched their teeth. They had seen their boss in this sort of mood before. He was capable of drifting off, warming to his own theme and making wild pronouncements that he found difficult to back away from. This had happened a few years previously when, at a press conference to mark the launch of the *London Daily News*, Maxwell suddenly announced that the paper would produce editions round the clock. It was the first the editor had heard of the idea, but he was required to carry out the decision, later blaming it for the failure of the paper, which closed after a few months with losses of £60 million.

There was little chance of Maxwell making any rash or expensive promises in the current climate. Instead he launched into a lofty critique of the state of soccer, and its lack of spirituality. 'Football in Britain could not be in a sorrier state,' he boomed. 'It has been neglected for so long it is difficult to see how it can be retrieved without massive expenditure.' He then provided the main news point of the meeting: that he wanted to sell Derby, adding that all his football interests were for sale 'at the right price'.

The sale was confirmed for a wider audience in a Harry Harris exclusive which explained that his boss was 'disillusioned by the way the game is being run'. Maxwell's own statement was much more blunt and blamed the Derby supporters: 'Non-support is the reason for me saying enough is enough. They must realise I don't have a licence to print £50 notes.' The sale price of Derby, said by the *Mirror* to have made a £500,000 profit in the previous season, was put at £8 million. Maxwell was merely seeking a 'partner' for Oxford, which had been run down to the point of unsaleability and was losing £10,000 a week.

There was no mention of Maxwell's recent plan to buy into Spurs, or that he had already loaned Scholar £1.1 million to complete the purchase of Lineker. 'We are not washing our hands of British football,' he was quoted as saying, 'but it is time somebody else took on the responsibility of these two clubs.'

Maxwell's apparent decision to get out of football was greeted with ill-concealed glee by some of those associated with the League Management Committee. It seemed that their main foe had thrown in the towel and would trouble them no more. Seasoned Maxwell watchers were more suspicious. Could it be that he was merely clearing the decks, selling Derby to get round the League's multiple-ownership rule and getting ready to bid for another club? There were wild guesses that he had finally patched things up with Martin Edwards of Manchester United, and a new bid was confidently expected by some.

The suspicions were even greater, and far more accurate, on the Tottenham board. Maxwell's name had been bandied about in the Tottenham camp as a possible candidate for Scholar's mysterious 'benefactor', the 'un-named party' who he said would save the club. Scholar said nothing, but it was easy enough to read the signs: the chairman had always been close to Uncle Bob through the TV negotiations and his mentor was free to make a bid for Tottenham. The secrecy agreement was maintained, but the rumour mills were running at full belt and the Maxwell angle was starting to be picked up by journalists and pundits. The *Guardian* was the first to take a wild guess, suggesting in its soccer round-up column that the Derby sale was the first step in a takeover bid for Tottenham.

Harris, anxious both to help Scholar and get another exclusive, spotted the *Guardian* piece, cut it out of the paper and sent it up to Maxwell's office with a request for permission to run the story in the *Mirror*. Maxwell, horrified, sent back a stinging reply: 'Don't touch it'. Harris, now as frustrated as Scholar, backed off. But Maxwell's authority did not run inside his rival Rupert Murdoch's newspaper headquarters in Wapping. The *Sunday Times'* City editor, Jeff Randall, had reached the same conclusion as the *Guardian*, and, helped by contacts close to the Tottenham board, pounced and revealed full details:

MAXWELL'S £12m DEAL FOR SPURS
SCHOLAR HOLDS SECRET TALKS

The Randall story was devastatingly accurate, but left out one important fact: Maxwell had pulled out of the deal two weeks previously. The revelation caused mayhem in the Mirror Group's editorial offices where journalists thought they ought to share Harris' inside track on Maxwell stories. This was the first they had heard of the Tottenham deal. Apart from Harris, who had been told the details only indirectly and unofficially by Scholar, they were as much in the dark as the Tottenham board.

Journalists on the *Sunday Mirror* were the first to see Randall's story when the first edition of the *Sunday Times* arrived on Saturday night. They asked Maxwell for details and permission to run the full story and Maxwell's reaction. They got the same reply given to Harris earlier in the week: 'Don't touch it'. By lunchtime the story was all over the papers and was leading radio and TV news bulletins, but the *Mirror* boss was refusing to confirm or deny the story.

Harris rushed into the office, realising that he had to tread very carefully. He found Maxwell in a funk, demanding to know who had leaked the story, and realising that he had not only to confirm the story, but at least suggest he was ready to go ahead with the deal. Otherwise he would have to let the cat out of the bag by revealing that he could not afford a measly £12 million.

Scholar later denied that he was the source of the Randall story, even though Harris had told him that it would be in Tottenham's interest to leak the story and force Maxwell's hand. Now Harris finally got Maxwell's permission to run the story he had been sitting on uncomfortably for several months, carefully written to avoid saying that Maxwell would definitely go ahead with the deal:

EXCLUSIVE: MAXWELL INVITED TO INVEST IN TOTTENHAM

£12 MILLION TO MAKE SPURS KINGS OF EUROPE

A PLAN FOR GREATNESS

Harris explained that the money would be used to pay off Tottenham's debts, enabling Venables to buy the extra players he needed to 'take on AC Milan, Juventus and Marseille'. Scholar was quoted as saying: 'Mr Maxwell's record in football is exemplary,' adding: 'He's always been prepared to invest heavily in football – and at a time when many people turned their back on it.' Anticipating opposition, Scholar added, fatefully: 'Many people will have mixed feelings about Mr Maxwell, but they don't know the man.'

The Tottenham board was now well and truly split. Some approved of his plan, but others were in uproar, not only at the details of the deal but at the pre-emptive way it had been announced in the newspapers and the secrecy and stealth Scholar had apparently used to force their hand. Over the next few days a series of emergency board meetings was held at the West End offices of board member Douglas Alexiou.

Bobroff, as Scholar had anticipated, led the opposition. This was Scholar's chance for revenge. Tottenham had to accept the Maxwell offer, he said; there was no real alternative. Maxwell's conditions were fair, and they included a demand to deal with a united board. If Bobroff did not like it he should resign.

Bobroff refused, telling other directors that other bids, including one from a consortium led by the Baltic finance company were still on the table. There was no chance of him going quietly. As chairman of the PLC he was in a position to block the deal and he still controlled the all-important connection to the Midland Bank. By now Scholar and Bobroff were glaring at each other and at one meeting came close to exchanging blows. In an attempt to cool things down, one of the other directors joked that it was a good job that they were meeting at Alexiou's office – he was just the man to sort things out between the two men who had once been so close. Alexiou was, by profession, a divorce laywer.

Scholar eventually brought things to a head by proposing a motion of no confidence in Bobroff. It was passed by three votes against one: Bobroff's. This meant he was out of the chair of the PLC, soon to be replaced by Scholar, but he remained a member of the board. Scholar and his shareholder allies could almost certainly muster enough votes to get rid of him, but directors of any company can be voted off the board only at an AGM after the presentation of the annual report.

Scholar at once got support from Maxwell and Harris with more megaphone diplomacy on the back page of the *Mirror*. 'I'm flashing the yellow card at those involved in squabbles,' Maxwell was quoted as saying. 'It is inconceivable that I or anybody else would entertain having discussions about rights issues or become involved in any way with a club where some of the board are behaving like children.' To make things perfectly clear Harris said that Maxwell's statement could be 'interpreted as a "yellow card" for Bobroff'. Privately Maxwell was much more direct. 'I want Bobroff to accept me, or I want him out of the way,' Maxwell told Harris.

The attack on Bobroff was supported by *Mirror* broadsides backing the Maxwell offer, and aimed squarely at the Tottenham fans. Since the Tears of Turin there had been repeated rumours that Gascoigne would be sold to an Italian club to help pay off Tottenham's debts. The *Mirror* now stressed that Maxwell's Plan for Greatness included a contractual clause that would keep Gazza at White Hart Lane.

Harris then revealed the details of Maxwell's loan to Tottenham which had been used to complete the Lineker transfer. The article said that the England captain had been only five hours away from forced return to Spain and that without Maxwell's largesse Spurs would have lost him for good. 'It was only chairman Irving Scholar's personal loan from Robert Maxwell that kept Lineker at White Hart Lane,' Harris said. To complete the propaganda pincer movement this was followed by articles suggesting that Chris Waddle was 'likely' to be bought back from Marseille to play alongside Lineker and Gascoigne at Spurs 'as soon as they sort out their financial crisis'.

But the Lineker loan revelations in the *Sunday Mirror* inevitably attracted the attention of the League Management Committee, which was now demanding to know the conditions under which Maxwell had loaned money to Scholar. This was especially worrying for the League, as it was a possible breach of their rule number 86, which banned direct financial dealings between chairmen. Since the rule had been framed to prevent club chairmen fixing games in return for money, Maxwell took offence at the implied slur against his reputation.

Members of 'football's mismanagement committee,' Maxwell raged in the *Mirror* 'are shooting their mouths off, yet here is a game totally mismanaged, totally destroyed by their incompetence. They have been making all sorts of innuendos. It is disgraceful.'

In the City Maxwell's involvement was immediately seen as the first step towards a full takeover bid. As a result Tottenham shares had leapt upwards as quickly as the board's jaws had dropped, increasing the club's quoted value by 16 per cent to £11.5 million virtually overnight, forcing the Stock Exchange authorities to act. Tottenham's shares were suspended at 91p until Maxwell's position was clarified. At the same time, the Exchange censured Scholar for negotiating with a prospective purchaser without telling shareholders, a possible breach of the Companies Act.

Scholar had not anticipated the Exchange's action against him, and he was totally unprepared for it. The move instantly changed the balance of power on the board. After being isolated at first, Bobroff was now making all the running. Scholar hit back with a new £4 million shirt deal with Umbro. The money would, with the Midland's support, allow the PLC to continue trading until the difficulties with the Stock Exchange and League could be sorted out, allowing the Maxwell plan to go ahead. After the Stock Exchange censure, Scholar resigned as chairman of the PLC, though he did remain on the board as chairman of the football club which, as a subsidiary, was far less financially sensitive.

Bobroff had won the first round and was more determined than ever that Maxwell should not gain control of Tottenham. Bobroff's position was still far from secure. The Umbro deal had eased the immediate cash flow problem, but the PLC was sailing very close to insolvency. Interest payments were pushing the PLC's debts up from the £12 million revealed in the latest accounts towards £15 million and, according to some press reports, the club was £20 million in the red.

The Midland Bank had the right to call in the overdraft at any time and the only thing preventing this, financial observers believed, was the dire PR consequences for the Listening Bank. If Tottenham Hotspur PLC had been a small engineering company that nobody had heard of, instead of a national institution, few doubted that the bank would have closed it on the spot.

Instead the PLC had been placed under the supervision of the Midland's Intensive Care Unit, which looked after terminally ill companies, and was living from day to day. Fully appraised of Tottenham's critical financial condition, and in no hurry to part with the money needed to refinance the club, Maxwell could afford to wait, piling on the pressure on behalf of Scholar, and keeping up a ceaseless propaganda campaign through the *Mirror*. If Spurs did not accept his offer soon he might walk away, he warned, leaving the club to go to the wall. This would have suited Maxwell anyway, since he knew the Midland would not allow this to happen, the effect of this brinksmanship was to leave things frozen.

To clarify his position on Spurs in person, Maxwell attended the annual meeting of the Fleet Street soccer writers' association. 'If push comes to shove and the banks act,' he grunted, 'then Tottenham would have to sell Gazza and Lineker. The banks will not increase overdraft facilities. They are looking to reduce them.' Flanked by Harris, Maxwell broadened out his talk into another attack on the administration of British soccer. According to one reporter Maxwell used his little joke

212

about the League Mismanagement Committee 27 times during his talk, pausing a little each time to allow the assembled hacks to appreciate the quality of his wit.

By this time the Mismanagement Committee had cleared Maxwell of any offence resulting from the Lineker loan. He was still not satisfied. Calling members of the Committee 'stupid idiots', he claimed their statement that the loan was not a breach of their rules 'as they stood', was a slight, and demanded a full apology. Asked if the Lineker loan had been repaid Maxwell looked offended: 'I don't keep track of the petty cash,' he snorted.

The League refused to apologise, matching his wit by accusing him of being a financial hooligan: 'Robert Maxwell mirrors one of the unfortunate traits of the modern game. He can afford the entrance fee but he doesn't appreciate the value of decorum.' The League then demanded to see a video tape of an over-the-top Maxwell performance on TV am, warning that they might fine him for bringing the game into disrepute. More importantly, the League said they were still not happy about Maxwell's efforts to get rid of Derby and Oxford and emphasised they would veto his involvement in Spurs if the clubs remained in his ownership.

With the Maxwell deal looking less and less likely, Tottenham's financial position was getting more desperate by the day. Creditors, alerted by all the publicity, were demanding immediate payment, making the crisis even worse. The debt was now estimated as £18 million, with interest payments of £40,000 per week entirely wiping out the additional TV revenue Scholar had fought so hard to secure.

The great fear was that unpaid creditors would obtain a winding-up order, forcing the club to be closed and its assets sold so they could be paid. Chelsea, Crystal Palace and Queen's Park Rangers had to ask the League to intervene to get gate money they were owed, and Tottenham had to face the humiliation of paying £500 compensation to Tranmere Rovers after failing to hand over on time a share of gate receipts for a League Cup game.

In an attempt to restore confidence the board appointed the neutral figure of Nat Solomon as chairman, in place of Douglas Alexiou who had been trying to steer the rudderless ship since the resignation of Scholar. Solomon was no stranger to boardroom strife. His last job had been with the Pleasurama casino group where he had been chairman for five years before organising the sale of the company to Mecca for £700 million in 1988. Aged 65, he might have considered retiring but was instead pointed in the direction of Spurs, which he claimed to have supported since childhood, by the PLC's financial advisers, Shipley Brown.

Solomon was now facing one of the toughest jobs in his career. On the day he was appointed, the PLC's auditors published delayed financial results for the previous year, showing losses of over £2 million. The accountants had said they were not even sure the company had enough money to have a chance of paying its creditors and, therefore, legally continue in business. Worse than this, as the auditors pointed out, as things stood the Midland would have to be ready to extend the overdraft even more if the PLC was to continue trading. Solomon's brief, agreed with the Midland Bank, was to reduce debts through 'asset disposals', which was interpreted as the code for selling off Gascoigne, at least, and possibly Lineker and most of the rest of the team as well. Harris helpfully printed a list of the Spurs squad, estimating what each one would fetch on the transfer market.

The prospect of Spurs having to sell off Gascoigne gave the initiative back to Scholar. He was now able to say what a good deal the Maxwell offer had been, and how the PLC had missed a marvellous opportunity by turning it down. Once again, as Scholar saw it, this was all Bobroff's fault. Perhaps the board and shareholders, especially the fan shareholders, would now realise that the Maxwell deal was the only way forward, at least if Spurs wanted to hang on to its star players and its chances of reaping European riches. To make the point, Scholar's corporate Christmas card that December featured a picture of Gazza above the teasing legend: 'When you wish upon a star...'

Things were thus finely balanced when Scholar was interviewed on TV soon afterwards, during Tottenham's televised match with Manchester United on New Year's Day 1991. Asked by commentator Gary Newbon if Tottenham would have to sell Gascoigne and Lineker to pay off its debts, Scholar chose his words with care, saying that 'from a personal point of view, I wouldn't agree with that under any circumstances'.

When asked if the club would sell them over his head, Scholar, aware that every Tottenham fan in the country would be watching, came close to openly criticising the board. 'It certainly wouldn't have my backing, under any circumstances whatsoever,' he said.

Newbon then asked who would own the club in future. Would it be Robert Maxwell? 'I can't answer that at the moment,' he said, nervously. 'The shareholders will, er, will have a proposal, hopefully, over the next couple of months, erm, when they will decide the future owner-ship, if you like, as you put it, er, of the company.'

Newbon had a final question. Would Scholar still be involved in running Spurs?

'Er, I sincerely hope so,' he said.

15: THE MANAGER: CAN YOU TAKE THE PRESSURE?

Terry Venables had maintained a diplomatic silence about the financial crisis at Tottenham, taking refuge in his role of protecting the morale of the team which, despite all the fuss, was at last beginning to click.

Gary and Gazza scored all the goals in an emphatic 3 – 1 tonking of Manchester City in the first game of the 1990 – 91 season. After that the lads had a run of ten League games without defeat: the best start to a season by any Spurs team since 1960, when the Glory, Glory boys did the Double.

It was another false dawn. A 2 – 0 defeat away at Coventry in December was the start of three sucessive defeats, and started a slide down the table which went on for the rest of the season. Venables' explanation for the change was quite simple: the team was knackered and he did not have players to replace them when they needed a rest.

Four months into the season Gascoigne had torn a stomach muscle, Lineker was often well below par and there were no players of remotely comparable quality to replace them in the forward line and midfield. The defence was just as weak. Fenwick was out with injury, replaced by the lacklustre Icelandic international Gudni Bergsson, imported cheaply from Valur FC, Reykjavik.

By February the injury problem had reached crisis proportions. Five first-team players, including Gascoigne and his replacement, Vinny Samways, were left out of a team for a League match against Wimbledon. The team was so patched up that Gascoigne's position was taken by Mitchell Thomas, normally a full back, and Nayim, the Moroccan who had arrived from Barcelona as part of the Lineker deal, and was normally a midfielder, played in defence. Lineker played, but only just. 'Gary has had a few knocks,' Venables explained forlornly. 'He could do with a break, but I couldn't afford to leave him out as well.' Tottenham were beaten 5 – 1 by Wimbledon, the team's worst League result for five years.

The thrashing was made all the worse by the fact that it had been dished out by a team which Venables held beneath contempt for playing a brand of dogged (the soccer euphemism for dirty) and skill-free football normally associated with the lower divisions. Venables had sniffily observed in 1988 that Wimbledon were 'killing the dreams that made football the world's greatest game' and that he could take any non-League player and make him into a Wimbledon player in a matter of weeks.

(A similar remark about Watford who, Venables said, had 'put-back football by ten years', brought a stinging reply from Danny Blanchflower, the captain and great hero of the Spurs Double team. If Watford had really taken football back to the 1970s they would be doing everyone a favour, Blanchflower said. There would be no million-pound salaries, no millions of pounds of debt and ten times as many people would be going to watch much better quality football.)

The main complaint about Wimbledon, as far as soccer connoisseurs were concerned, was their addiction to the 'long ball game', as the old kick-and-rush formula was now called, and which meant kicking the ball up the field for the forwards to chase. The rest of the game was usually a matter of physically confronting opposition players, leading to a long string of fouls and free kicks. At Liverpool, Bill 'Shanks' Shankly had famously placed a plaque, reading 'THIS IS ANFIELD' above the players' entrance on to the pitch in an attempt to intimidate visiting players. At Wimbledon the psychological warfare had been updated by the players yelling 'Let's get the bastards' as they embarked for another 90 minutes of 'welly', in front of a regular home crowd of less than 5,000, the lowest by far in Division One. After a Wimbledon game, it was said, the ball was left screaming for mercy.

Wimbledon shrugged off the insults, claiming they played 'power football' and if soccer brains did not like it that was too bad. Manager Dave Bassett proudly described his team as 'the borstal of football'. The club had joined the League only in 1977 and shot up from Division Four to Division One between 1983 and 1986. The standard terrace joke was that Wimbledon's progress up the League had been like a fairytale: Grimm.

There was more bad luck, this time off the pitch, before a game against Chelsea. Venables and the players had been enjoying their customary pre-match lunch at the Royal Lancaster Hotel when the doorman told them that the team coach had been towed away by the police. Venables at first thought this was a wind-up organised by Jeremy Beadle: exactly the sort of stunt Gascoigne might get involved in. But it was true, and a club official had to be despatched to the pound to rescue the players' kit, as Venables and the players set off for the game in a fleet of taxis.

When the club was criticised by the League for arriving late at Chelsea, Venables complained: 'I think it's incredible the police didn't come and ask us to move the coach. It could have been an old ladies' outing or something.' Tottenham lost the match and, with so many injuries racking up, there were those who said that the team had played like a bunch of old ladies.

The run of bad results emphasised Venables' utter dependency on Gascoigne and Lineker. When they were both in the team and fit, Tottenham were championship contenders. Without them, or the money to replace them, the team would have trouble staying in Division One.

In the second half of the season Tottenham won only two of their twenty League games, one of them against Derby, who had the same problem of player shortages as a result of Maxwell's own transfer freeze.

Although the club still had classy players such as Saunders, Wright and Shilton, the only new Derby player was Ian Wilson, who had arrived on loan from the Turkish club Besiktas. Maxwell did not attend Derby's televised game against Tottenham. He spent precisely 63 minutes at the ground during the entire season, turning up to watch Arsenal, but leaving early after being booed by the fans.

Maxwell-baiting had become a popular pastime on the dilapidated Derby terraces, and it was certainly more fun than watching the team, which was sinking to the bottom of Division One with the lowest number of points in all four divisions of the League. 'He's fat, he's round, he's never at the ground – Uncle Bob, Uncle Bob' had become the regular chant when an opposing side scored, pointing up their team's lack of fresh blood. Taking advantage of the TV cameras at the Tottenham match a group of Derby fans organised a demo with placards and banners that read:

> GIVE SPURS OUR CZECH
> GIVE TOTTENHAM A BOB
> WE WANT MAXWELL OUT!

Most of the Derby crowd wanted the club to be taken over by Lionel Pickering, a local businessman who had offered Maxwell £3 million, £5 million short of the asking price. Maxwell's rejection of the bid had come in the form of simultaneous articles on the back page of his newspaper and in the Derby programme, published on the day of the Spurs match.

'The Derby chairman has been the subject of a relentless and vicious campaign to sell to Pickering,' Harry Harris wrote in the *Mirror*, describing his boss as 'the man who rescued Derby from oblivion'. The rest of Harris's exclusive consisted of four solid columns quoting Maxwell, who denounced Pickering as not a 'fit and proper person' to run a football club and who was trying to take over the club 'on the cheap'. *Mirror* readers were

219

then treated to Maxwell boasting about his service to the club. 'Under my chairmanship and that of my son, and with millions of pounds provided, a brilliant manager took the club back into the second division and then into the first,' Maxwell said, conveniently forgetting that he had recently tried to replace Derby's 'brilliant manager', Arthur Cox, with Johan Cruyff without telling him. 'No one else stepped forward when times were bad', Maxwell continued. 'Not Mr Pickering, nor any other local businessman. The choice was between me and extinction.'

According to Maxwell the protestors were being put up to it by Pickering and the local media. The *Mirror* announced that Pickering and Graham Richards, a hapless local radio sports reporter who had the temerity to criticise Maxwell during a Radio Derby phone-in, were banned from Derby's ground 'because of their offensive conduct against the club'. With a final conspiratorial touch Maxwell added darkly: 'I believe that Mr Richards is a Nottingham Forest supporter.' Derby supporters thought this was a bit thick coming from a man who unashamedly supported Arsenal and changed his football clubs for business reasons as easily as his rival Rupert Murdoch changed nationality.

The second leg of the attack was published as an 'open letter' in the club programme. Maxwell explained that 'the reason why we have not maintained our progress over the last two years is that we have not had matching support from enough fans'. Derby lost the game 1–0 and the immediate reason the team 'failed to progress' that afternoon was a goal by Gary Lineker, the player whom, as Derby fans by now knew, Maxwell had effectively bought for Tottenham.

This was the last straw. The fans remained in the ground after the match and held a demo, which went on long after the TV cameras had been switched off. Most stayed on the terraces but about two hundred invaded the pitch, chanting 'Maxwell out!' and demanding to hear from Arthur Cox, the manager. Cox did finally address the crowd, in tones as sympathetic as the tannoy and his relationship with Maxwell would allow. 'Please, lads and ladies,' he said, 'please leave the pitch and conduct yourself with dignity as you have over the last six and a half years.' When this had no effect Brian Clough who, unbeknown to the fans, was present at the ground in his role of TV pundit, got on the mike. Cloughie, manager of Derby when they won the League in the happier days of the 1970s and still a Derby hero, was more blunt. 'It's, er, Brian Clough here,' he barked in the famous nasal monotone. 'Go home.'

The demonstrators gathered their banners and trooped off to the main gate where they sat down and blocked the way of the Tottenham coach, Greenham Common style. The focus of the demo was now Gary Lineker, with the muddled thought that his goal should have been disallowed because Maxwell had paid for him, and the match ought therefore to be declared a draw. But Lineker, the player with the cleanest and most wholesome image since Bobby Charlton, was a hard man to hate. All the fans wanted to do was make their point and incon-venience him a bit by making him late for supper. The fans thought they had been thwarted again: a rumour spread that Lineker had been whisked off in Maxwell's private helicopter so he could attend a soccer junket in London.

There was great trepidation when Clough himself appeared at the gates to break up the demo. He was known to take a very dim view of anything which smacked of football hooliganism and was famous for having thumped a fan who had run on to the pitch at Nottingham Forest. This time he was more restrained and the fans, overawed by his presence, soon trickled away. The *Sun* gleefully reported the demo under the headline 'GET OUT MAXWELL' with a picture of Maxwell looking remarkably toad-like. 'The 1–0 defeat leaves Maxwell's Derby looking certain to join their chairman's newspaper, the *Daily Mirror*, in the second division,' the paper gloated.

Maxwell made no reply and the *Mirror* did not even mention the Derby demo on its back page. Maxwell had anyway lost any remaining interest in the club and allowed it to slip down the table to face certain relegation. When the season ended Maxwell liquidated the club's human assets, just as he had previously done at Oxford. The promise he made at the start of the season to keep Mark Wright at the club was broken when the England hero was sold, along with Welsh international Dean Saunders, to Liverpool for a total of £5.1 million as part of the process of selling the club. The deal took the total transfer income from the sale of Derby and Oxford stars to almost £10 million in three years.

The fate of Oxford had been even more dramatic. The club had been thrown to the wolves and was about to record a loss of £1 million for the year. All Oxford's valuable players had been sold. The hunt to replace them led the club's scout to Aylesbury prison, where they expressed interest in signing Paul Reynolds from the convicts' team as soon as he finished his sentence for armed robbery.

The fate of Derby and Oxford was enough to ensure that the Tottenham fans did not share Scholar's enthusiasm for 'Uncle Bob' Maxwell. More to the point, he was a self-confessed Arsenal fan. Some of the more activist fans had organised themselves into the Tottenham Independent Supporters Association with the aim of welding together small shareholders into a 20 per cent voting block at the PLC's AGM in February. The Association, known as TISA, had been established in the unlikely setting of the basement of the University of London Students Union in November 1990, after the publicity surrounding the Maxwell bid revealed the full scale of the financial crisis.

TISA members nursed various grievances, including the recent increase in the price of season tickets by 40 per cent to £360; the abolition of the Shelf and even the sale of Waddle, which they quixotically hoped to put right. The immediate focus of the campaign was simply to find

222

out what was going on at the club and who was to blame. Seven hundred fan shareholders turned up for the AGM, held in the Chanticleer club at the back of White Hart Lane. TISA members turned up in force, picketing the entrance with placards saying:

£22m DEBT – IT'S HUMMEL-IATING
WHERE'S THE MONEY GONE?
BOARD OUT!

One poster showed pictures of Gascoigne and Scholar, asking: 'Should Tottenham dispose of its assets or its liabilities?' There was not much doubt in their minds about which was which. Inside the room there was a mood of suppressed hysteria as fans wearing scarves and supporter gear crushed up against pin-striped investment brokers. So many people turned up that the meeting started twenty minutes late, after Nat Solomon imposed some order on events. He was joined on the platform by Venables and what seemed to the fans to be a huge number of anonymous Men in Suits who nervously shuffled their papers.

Solomon tried to defuse things by explaining how the board had been thoroughly honest. There were genuine reasons, he said, for the lack of information given to shareholders and fans. The board cared about Tottenham as much as anyone. He even said that all board members were prepared to resign if it would help the club. But it would not help, so they were staying.

In the meantime the important thing, Solomon said, was not to have too many arguments in public: that would only damage the club and its reputation. 'Send him off!' shouted a fan in reply. 'We're a laughing stock!' yelled another. 'What about Gascoigne?' Solomon persevered, delivering the main bombshell of the day: rumours about the sale of Gazza were true. 'We have had serious indications of interest in Mr Gascoigne. I would not want to help would-be buyers by putting a price on him, but if someone came in we would obviously have to think about it,' he said.

A shudder ran round the room. There were audible yelps of pain. But instead of pushing ahead and changing the subject, Solomon tried to solicit sympathy, badly misjudging the mood of the meeting. 'We will only sell if the price is right,' he ventured, 'but if we get an offer which is so much we can't refuse...'

A fan raised his voice above the hubbub and interrupted: 'There is no right price for Paul Gascoigne. Sell the other companies,' he begged: 'Ask the fans for help. Do anything before you sell him. We come to watch eleven players, not subsidiary companies.' There was a storm of applause. Solomon fiddled with his glasses and looked helplessly at the other board members. The fans now had the initiative.

Next into the fray was Steve Davies, a lawyer and one of the organisers of TISA. Contradicting the normal football-fan stereotype, Davies was a quiet, logical and unflappable person who had pulled together the fans' general grumbles into a list of twenty questions about the club which he put to Solomon, one by one. When Davies asked about the amount of interest being paid on the debts, Solomon wearily turned to Ian Gray, the PLC's new chief executive and said:

'Er, perhaps you would like to answer that one, Ian?'

Gray blurted out that the figure was '£40,000' causing another roar of protest. He was less specific about the total size of the PLC's debts. The annual report put the total at £22 million; but that figure was already nine months out of date. The fans knew from press reports that Hummel had been a financial disaster. But what about Martex and Stumps, the other clothing subsidiaries? Were they making any money?

'They were successful when we acquired them,' said Gray. The room burst into laughter as he added, 'But they, er, are not profit-makers any more.' The lighter note introduced by Gray's gaffe did not last long. The next item on the agenda was the re-election of the board. Another of the more articulate fans took the floor. 'I see

224

no proposal in the report and accounts for the resignation of directors,' he said, angrily. 'Who is carrying the can for this total disaster that you present to the shareholders today?'

For a moment Solomon seemed to lose his cool. 'The directors recognise their responsibilities,' he snapped back. 'They are all fired with a determination to see things through.' The chairman then put forward the names of Tony Berry and Ian Gray for election. The meeting voted against them, almost unanimously. The votes did not carry much weight: TISA had been successful in mounting a media campaign against the board, but the aim of putting together a substantial voting block had not worked, as they had only about 1,000 organised supporters. The old board was re-elected with a huge majority of the proxy votes held by board members and their allies.

In a final outburst of emotion a fan grabbed the mike and said he had been sitting next to Bill Nicholson throughout the meeting. The mention of the man who had done the Double for Spurs with a fraction of the money spent by Scholar and Venables brought a reverential hush to the hall. 'If anyone should be on the board,' he said, 'it should be Bill.' Nicholson was asked to stand up and he got a standing ovation.

As finance gave way to football the pressure lifted from the platform and Solomon introduced Venables for the now traditional tactical team discussion. The time wasters who at the previous AGM had wanted to know why the manager fielded left-footed players in right-footed positions now distinguished themselves by asking if Gascoigne would be fit for next week's game against Chelsea, and what Venables thought of Spurs' departed Belgian striker Nico Claesen.

Dealing with broader questions about the team's lack of success in recent matches, Venables could only point to lack of players. This infuriated Scholar, who had provided £8 million for sixteen new signings, but went down well with the fans. When the session ended, a small group of fans marched gingerly up to Venables and handed him a TISA independent supporters' badge. 'Thanks,' said Tel. 'And don't forget to bring your boots on Saturday.'

Outside the hall Steve Davies of TISA was being interviewed by the waiting pack of journalists, sounding very much like the manager of a defeated team slagging off the referee during a post-match analysis session. 'We are very disappointed,' he said. 'The board has not explained why the company is in such a mess, and has offered no plans for solving the crisis.'

As far as TISA was concerned, the only glimmer of hope to emerge from the meeting was an announcement from Venables that as part of a consortium of sports-related businessmen, he was seriously interested in buying Tottenham. This idea had first emerged in November when Venables' thoughts on the future were revealed in a suitably adulatory biography written by his father Fred. 'I'm getting to the time in my life when I want to be my own boss,' he had said, remembering how much he had enjoyed 'the financial side of the game' when he had been on the board at Queen's Park Rangers in the early 1980s.

'I would also like to think that I could be a better chairman than most,' he continued. 'For a start I'm good at football, not developing property or selling pork sausages like some other chairmen – I know every job there is to be done at a club.' This was a direct swipe at Scholar, the property developer, and Manchester United's Martin Edwards who started out in the wholesale meat business (given United's ferocious buying and selling of players on the transfer market, people could have been forgiven for thinking he was still in it).

Venables had not expressed a specific interest in buying Spurs, only in boardroom activity in general. He was merely 'setting out his stall', the soccerspeak term for showing what he had to offer. 'I suppose to run my own football club from top to bottom would qualify as my last great ambition in the game,' he said. 'I've got one year left on my contract at Tottenham, and then maybe I'll have to sit down and do some serious thinking.'

The *Sun*, keen to compete with Harry Harris's endless Maxwell-generated Spurs exclusives, pounced. The paper rewrote the passages and splashed the resulting rehash all over the back page:

I'LL BUY MY OWN CLUB
I'M NO SAUSAGE SALESMAN
SUN WORLD EXCLUSIVE
BY TERRY VENABLES

The report was a classic example of the venerable art of 'lifting', Fleet Street jargon for taking excerpts from sources like books and old interviews and passing off the results as news. The article was illustrated by a manic-looking Tel playing his board game called 'The Manager', which he was trying to hype at the time as a useful side-line. The fans noted gloomily that people won the game not by winning trophies, but by making maximum profits on the transfer market.

There were rumours that Venables had been preparing to buy the club since the new year, but he had always refused to discuss plans in public. By the time of the AGM all Venables was prepared to say was that he was 'trying to get something in place'. Two weeks later Tottenham's accountants, acting for the Stock Exchange because of the continuing suspension of the PLC's shares, announced the receipt of a formal bid from Venables.

The offer did not get a good reception from the board. Scholar, still the largest shareholder, was the most hostile. By now Venables and Scholar had fallen out badly, due to Venables' belief that he should have been able to spend more on new players. This had been followed by a public row over the manager's £200,000 basic salary, which Scholar wanted reduced and replaced with performance-related bonuses.

Scholar did not reject the Venables bid out of hand, but demanded a minimum sale price of £1 per share, valuing the club at about £12 million, and his own 26 per cent share at over £3 million. In return for selling, Scholar also wanted a contractual assurance that Venables would pay off the Midland and, most importantly, keep Gascoigne and Lineker at White Hart Lane. These conditions pushed up the effective total purchase price to almost £30 million. It seemed unlikely that any financier would come up with that sort of money when the much more profitable Manchester United, which was at the time preparing for a Stock Market flotation, could be had for half the price.

Bobroff and Alexiou, two of the other major shareholding directors, were almost as unenthusiastic, not least because Venables was demanding their removal from the board as part of his bid. As supporters of the new Solomon regime they were prepared to see Gascoigne go to reduce the debts, or to allow a purchaser to sell him off to get some of their money back. Their main concern was that Venables simply did not have the cash to buy the club. The danger was that he would simply bid down the sale price, losing millions for the shareholders when the club was eventually sold.

They were more interested in an offer from Baltic which, as Solomon had revealed at the AGM, had proposed a rights issue similar to the Maxwell offer, but on far less favourable terms. Tony Berry was the only board member to back Venables' offer with any enthusiasm, even though he had previously been one of Scholar's closest boardroom allies and had backed the former chairman's campaign to get rid of Bobroff at the time of the Maxwell offer.

Since then, like Venables, Berry had deserted Scholar, leaving him more isolated than ever. Berry's main concern now was to stay on the Tottenham board, which, after the collapse of his Blue Arrow empire, was all he had left to maintain his status as a high-profile entrepreneur. Like Scholar, Berry loved the glamour that went with being associated with Tottenham Hotspur. Even when his Blue Arrow empire had been roaring in the mid-1980s, making him the darling of the City and the financial pages of the papers, Berry had always maintained he got the most excitement and satisfaction from his involvement with Spurs.

At the height of his financial powers Berry had been able to raise enormous loans on the strength of his reputation. For now all he could do was offer Venables invaluable advice on how to approach City institutions and then cheer him on from the sidelines. Most of the financial running on Venables' behalf was being made by the unlikely figure of Frank Warren, the Islington boxing promoter who, at the time, was recovering from the professional hazard of being shot in the chest. Warren was on his uppers after the shooting and the failure of the London Arena, his main business venture, and was not prepared to put any money into the consortium. He was merely acting as an intermediary, introducing Venables to Larry Gillick, a 44-year-old Scottish property developer. He was not a well known figure in the worlds of either finance or soccer, though his father Torry had once played for Everton and Glasgow Rangers.

Gillick claimed to have funds of £40 million ready, but the only track record the board could find was his involvement in a 1980 proposal to redevelop a greyhound-racing stadium in Ayr. The scheme had not worked out and the development company involved was reported to have lost almost half a million pounds. The board opened negotiations with Gillick anyway, based on an offer price of 91p per share, and undertakings both to repay £11 million to the Midland and to keep Gascoigne at the club. The total purchase price was £20 million. But the new owners would still be saddled with debts of £10 million, and Venables might soon have to spend as much again on new players to patch the holes in the team and complete the final phase of developing White Hart Lane.

Berry had been keen to accept the bid from the start, and at the end of March he was joined by the rest of the board. The reason was the collapse of the Baltic bid, favoured by Solomon and Bobroff. The finance company had offered to back a rights issue similar in some ways to the Maxwell offer but, humiliatingly for Bobroff, the terms were far worse. Baltic offered only 40p for the new shares, a third of the value Maxwell had been prepared to underwrite. The company also wanted assurances that people owed money by the PLC would wait for up to four years before being repaid out of new profits.

The board knew this would be unacceptable to Tottenham's creditors and the deal collapsed, again enabling Scholar smugly to point out what a marvellous opportunity the Maxwell offer had been, and how wrong Bobroff had been to reject it. Other potential rescue packages, including one from Hambros bank, melted away just as quickly. In a bizarre twist, Isadore Brown, the American millionaire who had tried to buy his way on to the board when the Tottenham share price had slumped to 52p in 1986, turned up at the last minute. Brown seemed to be interested mainly in venting his spleen on Scholar and Bobroff who, he said, had 'acted like they were living in a dream castle,' since they had rejected his previous and more serious bid for a place on the board.

With no other players in the field the Midland Bank was urging the board to give serious consideration to the Venables – Gillick bid, despite all the doubts. After nine days of talks, the board had satisfied itself that Gillick and Venables would be able to come up with the £20 million they said they had on call, even though Gillick was as yet unwilling to reveal who his ultimate backers were. This was not very promising, but things were getting desperate. The Midland was starting to demand the immediate sale of Gascoigne to the Italian club Lazio which, following Solomon's green light at the AGM, had made a firm offer of £8.5 million to buy the player.

At White Hart Lane, faxes bearing speculative bids from top Italian clubs were piling up almost by the hour. Until the Lazio deal, Scholar had been holding all the aces in the long-running poker game being played in the board-room. The thousands of fans who held small blocks of shares could be relied upon never to sell to anyone, and so any takeover consortium would need all of his own 26 per cent share in the PLC to be sure of control. This fact had always been central to Scholar's thinking, and had made him invulnerable to takeovers in the past, no matter how big the PLC's losses had been in any particular year.

The Midland had been more of a constraint and threat than an external takeover. But the bank's power to make him sell out depended on their willingness to close down the club. This, he calculated, they would never do. But now that Solomon was in the chair in his place, the banks could at least sell Gascoigne. The only alternative was to take the Venables bid seriously. This he now did, but made things as difficult as possible by adding further conditions to the deal. Scholar stuck to his demand for a contractual agreement that Gascoigne would not be sold, that Venables would give a commitment to invest in the club and buy the additional players needed and, more vaguely, demanded an assurance that the interests of small shareholders would be looked after. Venables agreed.

The last formal hurdle was a reference to the Stock Exchange's Takeover Panel, which would examine Gillick's financial credentials and make sure he had the money. The City was now taking a close interest in takeover bids by less well-known financiers after the enormous brouhaha caused by the sale of Harrods to the Fayed brothers after stiff competition from Tiny Rowland's multinational Lonrho. The brothers had passed themselves off as stereotypical Middle-Eastern plutocrats in order to clinch the deal, but had turned out to have been very modestly-off bazaar merchants from Cairo.

Closer to home, in the world of soccer, Michael Knighton's 'Walter Mitty' bid for Manchester United was still fresh in the memory of everyone on the business side of soccer. The *Mirror's* Harry Harris went into action at once, rubbishing Gillick and his previous business dealings.

Within weeks the Venables – Gillick deal was off. The board issued a statement through its financial advisers saying, in suitably ponderous terms, that it had 'not received the detailed assurances and information' it required about the background of everyone involved in the deal and 'the funds available to them and their source'. The statement concluded: 'The most recent indication as to the terms of the proposed offer would not be acceptable to the board.'

All board members except Scholar had placed their eggs in the Gillick basket and, with no other bid in sight, they were now pushed to one side as Scholar again moved centre stage. The Lazio deal was still up in the air and the Midland had been routed as comprehensively as the board. To complete the mop-up, Scholar tried to patch things up with Venables, offering him a £100,000 pay increase if he stayed with the club when his contract ran out at the end of the season.

But Venables was not interested and announced that he still wanted to take over the club, and was looking for another backer. If not, he implied, he would leave Tottenham along with Gascoigne when the season ended in June. The question was, where would he go? None of the Big Five had a managerial vacancy, and Bobby Robson had been replaced after Italia 90 by Graham Taylor of Aston Villa. Venables, who had always expressed interest in being a national team manager one day, said that he had been 'hurt and amazed' not to have been on the shortlist alongside Taylor, adding that the authorities had not approached him because he was not an 'FA type'. 'Fair enough,' he said. 'I'm no longer interested in managing England. Sod 'em; forget it, I'll do something else.'

But apart from a rumour that he had been approached by the US national squad in time for the next World Cup, it was not clear what the next step up the ladder would be, apart from owning as well as managing Tottenham.

The battle lines were now drawn: Scholar and Maxwell versus Venables. Most of the fans, and the independent supporters' association, were loudly backing Venables, who was still a hero with the White Hart Lane crowd despite his failure to win a single trophy during his three years as manager. Scholar was seen by the fans as a much more distant figure, vaguely held responsible for getting the club into trouble in the first place and almost handing it over to Maxwell, who was feared both at Tottenham and throughout soccer. 'The role of manager in the English League is being diminished by amateur directors who want to play at professional football,' Venables had complained soon after the original offer by the *Mirror* publisher. 'If we get Maxwell as well as Scholar then we all move one step nearer the bootroom, myself included.'

But, as the AGM had shown, the opinion of the fans counted for little in the boardroom where, ironically, Scholar had more sympathy for them than most. All the fans could do was provide moral support for Venables, feed the media's obsession for Tottenham stories, and provide a running commentary on boardroom developments from the terraces, where they now chanted 'We all agree, Terry is better than Scholar'. (The fact that Warren, who had helped Venables put his bid together, was, like Maxwell, a devoted Arsenal fan was quietly overlooked.)

The new wave of fan warmth towards Venables was partly due to Tottenham's good run in the FA Cup. The team's performance in the League continued to be dire and there was now no chance of winning the championship. The team was heading for a finishing position of tenth place in Division One. Spurs fared better in the Cup where, through the luck of the draw, they came up against a series of weak teams from the lower divisions. Blackpool had been disposed of in the third round by the narrow margin of one goal in a game of stunning mediocrity played in a bracing seaside gale. Maxwell's decimated Oxford United were tonked 4−2 in the next round, as expected, with Gascoigne getting two goals despite not being fully fit. He had strained a stomach muscle in January and Venables had not regularly

233

included him in the team for League matches for months, allowing him to rest, and deploying him only in the vital Cup matches. After the win against Oxford he played occasionally in the League, but was included for the next Cup match against lowly Portsmouth. The game was another dreadful team performance, and there was little doubt that Tottenham would have lost were it not for Gascoigne who, despite his injury, scored both goals in a narrow 2−1 win.

Gascoigne's injury had horrified the bankers. If he did not fully recover, his value on the transfer market would drop, destroying Tottenham's only mortgageable asset. Ideally the money men would have liked to play safe, allowing Gascoigne to play the minimum of games needed to keep him match fit and locking him in a padded cell between training sessions to make sure he did not injure himself.

The need to avoid injury between games was a major headache for top footballers, especially players such as Gascoigne who had few interests outside the game. The 1970s saw a trend for footballers taking university degrees (Tony Galvin, one of the old-stagers axed by Venables when he arrived at Spurs, had a degree in Russian studies), but the fad had passed. Insurance contracts often excluded exciting hobbies because of the risk of injury, and so pastimes such as parachuting, water-skiing or motorised skateboarding, which might have appealed to Gascoigne, were definitely out. The intense boredom between games was one of the reasons so many turned to golf or drink, or both. Gascoigne's own choice was fly-fishing. There was not much chance of even Gazza doing himself in with a fishing rod, but he was always going to be a target for the game's professional 'hard men' when he was obliged to play a game of football.

Gascoigne had already been through a celebrated series of battles with Vinny Jones, the skinhead defender who had made his name in 'the borstal of football', Wimbledon. Jones was the latest character in a long and honourable hard-man tradition, stretching back through

234

Leeds United's Norman 'Bite Yer Legs' Hunter in the 1970s to the violent nineteenth-century origins of the game. Nat Lofthouse, the leading star of the 1950s, popped up to explain how things had changed over the past forty years. 'There were plenty of fellas who'd kick your bollocks off,' Lofthouse said. 'The difference was that at the end they'd shake your hand and help you look for them.'

Jones was most famous for the way in which he had tried to take out Gascoigne during a match between Newcastle and Wimbledon. He followed Gascoigne around the pitch, winding him up about his weight problem, never straying more than a few feet from his target until he was asked to take a free kick. 'Stay there, fatty,' Jones had then told Gascoigne. 'I'll be back in a minute.' Jones returned and, when the ref was not watching, backed into his target and grabbed him by the balls, causing him to crease with agony. After the match Don Howe, the Wimbledon coach, said that the incident had shown that Jones was 'a very disciplined lad. We asked him to do a job on Gazza and he was first class.' Jones himself said: 'I don't know what all the fuss is about. I wasn't even booked.'

The needle match had continued with Jones sending Gascoigne a single red rose before their next match, saying how much he was looking forward to meeting him again. Gascoigne treated it as a joke and sent Jones a toilet brush in response. But incidents like this could have a serious side. It was said that South American clubs hired private detectives to discover the phobias, superstitions and family illnesses of star opponents so that man-markers could spend the game upsetting them.

After his two goals against Portsmouth in the fifth round, Gascoigne was again included in the team to play in the sixth, the quarter-finals, against Division Two Notts County. The man assigned by County to 'do a job' on him was Paul Harding, a rugged defender, who followed the Tottenham star round the pitch, constantly niggling him. After one Harding foul, the much-vaunted maturity

Gascoigne had shown in similar circumstances during the 'Tears of Turin' episode evaporated and he elbowed Harding in the face. There was some sympathy from the pundits for the provocation Gascoigne was increasingly having to put up with, but it was agreed that he had been lucky not to get a red card.

Spurs had to struggle to beat County. At half time the team was losing 1–0 and looked set to go out of the Cup. Venables dispensed with the normal half-time exhortations and told the team the whole future of the club was riding on the result: 'You haven't got much choice,' he said wearily, 'you really have to go for it. It's 45 minutes and if you don't do it that's the end of it.'

Venables' board game, 'The Manager' had not been subtitled 'Can You Take The Pressure?' for nothing. Kenny Dalglish had just resigned as manager of Liverpool, complaining that the strain was too much, and in the past other managers had suffered even more severely. Wilf McGuinness, who had taken over from Matt Busby at Manchester United in 1969 but failed to live up to expectations, was the most famous victim. He went after just a few months, but not before anxiety caused all his hair to drop out, leaving him as bald as a billiard ball.

Venables was never affected as badly as this, and could always call upon hidden reserves of character. But the fate of Tottenham and his own bleak future, combined with the death of his mother Myrtle, which hit him hard, were starting to get to him and the cheery Cockney mask were sometimes slip.

The players got the message. A trip to Wembley was now the club's only hope. It would prevent the bank taking direct action, at least until the FA Cup final itself was played in May, giving Venables time to put together another bid for control of the club. Otherwise Gascoigne would have to go; Lineker would probably leave as well, and Venables would follow them. Most of the other players had little chance of transferring to another top club and they would be stuck in a team almost certain to sink, like Derby, into Division Two. They had 45 minutes in which to save their professional careers.

This dire threat seemed to do the trick; the team picked themselves up and Spurs won the match 2 – 1. The winning goal came from Gascoigne, taking his total in the FA Cup to five of the eight scored by the team since the Blackpool match, winning each game in turn. Spurs' name now went into the draw for the semi-final, to be broadcast live on TV straight after the Notts County game.

Cup draws are low-key, but nevertheless exciting, TV rituals, often more gripping than the matches that take place as a result of the activity. In time-honoured fashion, distinctly doddery looking FA officials dip their hands into a velvet bag, which is arthritically shaken, producing a faint clicking noise which is one of most exciting sounds in soccer. The balls are examined, sometimes with difficulty, and the numbers and team names read out in suitably ponderous tones. It is all very different from the showbiz-led Italian approach where the draw for the World Cup had been turned into an open-air TV extravaganza, complete with laser beams, dancing girls, celebrity ball-drawers and arias from grand opera.

The British version resembled bingo as played in a northern working-men's club, complete with elderly members of t'committee, trousers up to their armpits, presiding. The velvet bag for the semi-final draw contained four numbers corresponding to Arsenal, Nottingham Forest, Tottenham and West Ham United. Tottenham were drawn against Arsenal, who were having one of their best seasons for years. The way to the final now looked well and truly blocked.

The Arsenal – Tottenham semi-final was at once renamed 'the real FA Cup final' by the papers, and as though the FA wanted to prove it, the two clubs agreed to play the match at Wembley (mainly to avoid using Hillsborough, the only suitable neutral ground big enough to deal with anticipated ticket demand, but still haunted by the 1989 semi-final disaster). The game was set to be the latest instalment of the long-running needle match between the clubs and their fans. The Spurs crowd called Arsenal fans 'the Gooners', or most simply, 'Arse', and their general attitude was summed up by one of their favourite terrace chants:

> We hate Arsenal
> And we hate Arsenal
> We hate Arsenal
> And we hate Arsenal
> We hate Arsenal
> And we hate Arsenal
> We are the Arsenal haters.

According to the form book Tottenham had no chance of winning. Arsenal were in pole position to win the League, full of confidence and eager to do the Double by winning the League and FA Cup in the same season. In 1961 Spurs had been the first modern team to achieve the Double, but Arsenal matched them by repeating the feat exactly ten years later. Now they were ready to leave Spurs behind by becoming the first team to do the Double twice: logically the Double – Double or the Quadruple. Not even Liverpool, who in 1986 had achieved the third and most recent Double, had managed that.

Venables had been at Wembley as a team manager three years previously as part of the Football League's shambolic centenary celebrations. The occasion was a match between England and the Rest of the World, a celebrity team composed of foreign internationals including Maradona and Michel Platini of France. Venables, put in charge of the World team, had been amazed to find the dressing room completely unequipped and had to shell out £80 of his own money to buy a first-aid kit and magic sponge. After the game League officials refused to pay up until Venables threatened them with an instant press conference.

This time Venables and his team arrived in the luxury Spurs coach, the main discomfort being caused by

Gascoigne, hyperactive as ever, bouncing up and down the aisles, winding everyone up or, as Venables put it, 'oozing the will to win'. Gascoigne took over the pre-match pep talk, showing no signs of worry over his stomach injury, or after effects from the knock-out injection needed to get him to sleep the previous evening, stealing the scene from Venables and urging the team to give, in the standard cliché, '200 per cent'.

Gazza came out on to the pitch in the same mood and was soon at the centre of events. After five minutes Spurs won a free kick near the Arsenal penalty area and Gazza smacked it straight into the net. The Tottenham fans went wild and Gazza did a one-man, high-speed lap of honour, arms spread wide and head back like an opera diva. Venables later described the goal as one of the best free kicks seen at Wembley since the war. For once the standard hyperbole was justified. Then Gascoigne dribbled past the Arsenal defence, put together a couple of good one-two passes, sending the ball towards the Arsenal goalmouth. A half cross bounced off a defender into the path of Lineker, who coolly tapped it into the net. Pandemonium. Tottenham were 2–0 up only twenty minutes into the first half. Against Arsenal. At Wember-lee.

The fans went mental. At this rate, in line with the wildly optimistic thinking of the soccer fan, there was no reason why the team should not keep it up, scoring one goal every ten minutes, producing an expected 9–0 win. Tottenham, led by Gascoigne and Lineker, were playing like England at their best in Italia 90: fast, ball on the ground, and with a lot of skill.

But Arsenal got back into the game. Just before half time Spurs' reserve defender Justin Edinburgh (who in desperation was nearly sold to Plymouth Argyle earlier in the season as part of the cash crisis) miskicked in front of goal and allowed Arsenal to get one back. The pressure was now on Tottenham and Gascoigne was at it again during the half-time break, babbling away in a sweaty repeat performance of his warm-up talk before the game.

The second half was all Arsenal, with more and more frantic attempts to get an equaliser. Kevin Campbell almost managed it, but hit the post causing the 40,000 Tottenham fans in the ground to have a near-heart attack. But the Arsenal pressure gave Spurs the chance to score by counterattacking 'on the break' in soccerspeak. Lineker duly went past the thinned-out Arsenal defence on a solo run and shot weakly from an unlikely angle. The Arsenal goalkeeper David Seaman let the ball slip through his fingers: 3 – 1. There was now no chance of Arsenal winning and Tottenham fans spent the rest of the match celebrating.

Gascoigne led the team sing-song on the coach on the way home and the celebrations continued at a party thrown by Venables for club officials at Scribes West, the nightclub-cum-dining establishment in Kensington which he co-owned. Venables was the star of the show and treated the revellers to his Frank Sinatra act, singing 'My Way'.

Arsenal at least had the satisfaction of winning the League, booking them a place in the European Cup which had been reorganised into a World Cup-style event with a mini-League system, guaranteeing a run of lucrative matches if Arsenal could get past the first qualifying round (which, in the event, they failed to do). It was an open secret that this was a trial run for a future European SuperLeague.

Tottenham minds were soon refocused on the final which was to be played against Nottingham Forest or, according to the papers, against the single-minded personality of Brian Clough, the Forest manager. The contrast between tough, no-nonsense northern Cloughie, and the flash, Cockney Venables, and their supposed enmity, was a favourite tabloid soccer sideshow which was now flogged to death in preparation for the big match.

Another trip to Wembley would at least bring in some more money, whatever the result, and winning the Cup would put Spurs into the European Cup Winners' Cup, which Manchester United were about to win, bringing them an estimated extra £3 million in ticket sales and TV money. That sort of money would only make only the smallest dent in the debt mountain. But it was a start, and Venables started working round the clock to prepare his team for the clash with Clough, while putting together another bid for control of Tottenham Hotspur PLC.

As Venables, more than most, had reason to know, football is a game of ups and downs, where strong personalities are heroes one minute and villains the next, and then heroes again. There was solace to found in the blindingly obvious, but somehow deep and soulful, words of premier footie philosopher Bill Shankly: 'Football is a game of 90 minutes and it's not over until the final whistle is blown.'

16: THE BATTLE OF WOUNDED KNEE

Five days after Tottenham's FA Cup semi-final win Nat
Solomon sent a secret letter to Robert Maxwell asking
him to make a fresh bid for the club. 'If you think that
this possibility is worth exploring,' he wrote, 'I and the
company's advisers would be willing to meet to enter into
immediate talks with you and your advisers with the aim
of reaching early agreement.' Solomon stressed that his
approach had the full backing of the Tottenham board,
which meant that Bobroff had been persuaded to drop
his objection to Uncle Bob's involvement in the club.
Bobroff's change of heart had not come easily: it meant
giving in to Scholar.

Maxwell did not reply to Solomon's letter; for the very
good reason that he had no money. The finances of his
empire had improved slightly since he pulled out of the
original Plan for Greatness, helped by a mini-boom on
the Stock Market after the American victory in the Gulf.
But he was still far from secure and could not afford to
tie up money urgently needed to meet interest payments
on his empire's debt mountain.

His official line was that he was waiting for a formal
apology for the mild criticism the Committee had handed
out when his secret loan to Scholar had come to light,
and that he would not even consider 'saving' Spurs until
the League had publicly grovelled in the approved
fashion. Maxwell had described them as 'stupid idiots'
unable to 'collectively pump up a football'; and since an
apology would anyway involve the League denouncing
its own rules, he knew that it would not be forthcoming.

242

The ball was firmly in his court, ready for a magnanimous lifting of the apology demand when he was ready to make his move for Spurs.

Maxwell knew Solomon was desperate anyway, and decided to let him stew in his own juice. After the collapse of the Venables – Gillick bid, helped by Harry Harris's investigative reporting in the *Mirror*, there were no other potential backers in sight. That meant the asking price was certain to continue to fall.

The right time to buy Spurs would be in July or August. By then the empire would have been reorganised to prevent immediate collapse, and might even begin to expand again on the back of the predicted end to the recession. Money from the sale of Derby would be available later in the year and could go straight into Spurs. Maxwell's overall investment in soccer would then remain about the same; but the value and potential of his football assets would have increased considerably.

Back in the Spurs' boardroom Maxwell's silence was deafening. The Wembley Cup final, and possible entry into Europe, would bring in some immediate cash, but not enough to make a real dent in the debt mountain. One City analyst described the financial effect of winning the Cup as being like 'giving a starving man half a sandwich'. Cup glory presented the Midland Bank with a definite downside: the ultimate deterrent of closing down the business unless they got on with selling Gascoigne was now an empty threat, at least until the Cup final was over. It would be easier to shut down the Republic of Mexico, which also owed them rather a lot of money, than pull the rug from under the English FA Cup finalists.

With no reply from Maxwell, and no other rescuer on the horizon, the bank was pushing for the immediate sale of Gascoigne. So far this had been blocked by Scholar, still on the board as the largest shareholder. Solomon moved to remove Scholar's veto by threatening to put the PLC into administration, which meant effectively handing control to the creditors. To avoid administration

243

the board agreed to speed up the sale of Gascoigne to Lazio, the Roman club sounded out by Solomon and soccer agent Denis Roach earlier in the year.

Solomon and Denis Roach secretly flew out to Rome at the end of April, just three weeks before the FA Cup final, to finalise the deal. They found Gian Marco Calleri, the Lazio President, more keen than ever to buy the 'dog of war with the face of a child' who, by now, had been hyped to godlike status by the Italian media. Gazza's deification had been helped by the downfall of Maradona, who played for Napoli and had just been voted Most Hated Person by Italians, beating Saddam Hussein and even Madonna. He was then revealed to be a cocaine addict, giving a new meaning to blow football and partly explaining his extraordinarily aggressive performance during Italia 90.

More directly, Lazio had suffered a run of poor results in the Italian league, leaving them near the bottom of the table. They had already missed the chance of getting into any of the European competitions next season and Calleri badly needed Gazza to cheer up his fans, who were being asked to fork out £5,000 each for 'debentures', which would give them the right to buy season tickets. (A similar scheme was later offered in Britain by Arsenal where, despite the lower price of £1,500 per fan, it was denounced as an outrageous rip-off.)

After meeting Solomon, Calleri believed Gascoigne was his at the bargain price of £7.9 million, half a million less than the sum agreed in principle back in March, and payable when Gascoigne was safely delivered to Italy after the FA Cup final. Calleri and Solomon tried to keep the meeting secret, but the details inevitably leaked, causing predictable outrage. 'SOLD DOWN THE RIVER' shrieked Maxwell's *Sunday People*, saying that all the talk of keeping Gascoigne at White Hart Lane since the rejection of Maxwell's bid for the club had been 'hot air'.

Venables spoke out at once, saying that Gascoigne had signed nothing personally and still had the right to refuse to go if he did not want to. He pleaded with Gascoigne to stay at Spurs and bombarded him with advice. Gazza would be wasting his time with Lazio: 'It's like signing for Norwich,' he said. The club was one of the weaker and less glamorous ones in the Italian league, best remembered in Britain for a 1971 street fight between the team, led by their club-wielding manager, and rioting Arsenal fans.

Lazio's recent form showed they needed Gazza more than he needed them, and the pressure would be on him to perform. He was only 23, still improving and needed a lot of coaching. The right time for an Italian move would be after the next World Cup in three years' time. He was likely to get far more money then by signing for a top-line club such as Barcelona or Juventus. 'Wait for one of the big boys,' was how Venables put it, 'and don't take second best.'

Support for Venables' argument came from an analysis of the fate of British players who had gone for Italian gold. Those who went towards the end of their careers and made the effort to learn the language and appreciate Italian culture had settled and done well. Gazza was thinking of commuting back to Geordieland during the week, and his quip, 'I won't have any problem with the language, I can't even speak English yet,' did not show much sign of the required attitude.

Gazza was much more like Ian Rush, the Liverpool striker who had spent a year with Juventus at the height of his powers, complaining that 'it was like being in another country'. Other footballers had found the greasy Italian food a problem. 'No matter how much money you've got,' Luther Blissett of Watford had moaned when he was at AC Milan, 'you just can't seem to get any Rice Krispies.'

There was an additional problem for Gascoigne. Winding up temperamental players like him with constant fouling was a standard tactic in Italian soccer. As Bobby Robson's reservations during Italia 90, and the more recent elbowing incident during the Notts County game, when he nearly knocked out Paul Harding, seemed to show, he would have difficulty in keeping his composure.

Gascoigne wavered slightly. His lawyer and official spokesman Mel Stein pointed out that the player had not even been to Rome or seen the club yet. He was still willing to go, unless a severe problem cropped up. He wanted the money. It was all very well for Venables to say that he would get more in the future, but that was jam tomorrow. The Lazio deal would bring him about £2 million immediately, with a salary of up to £1 million a year, plus fringe benefits such as cars and villas and his share of the inevitable marketing spin-offs.

Gascoigne's friend Chris Waddle had explained that it was not too bad living on the Continent. The important thing was to grab what was on offer now. Anything could happen in the future. He could lose the knack, crack up or develop a drink problem like George Best had done; or simply fall out of favour with the fans and the England selectors. He might even break his leg and have to retire. The money he had amassed so far would soon go and his three CSEs in English, Maths and Environmental Studies were not much to fall back on. Gascoigne had gone straight from school into football. But Waddle had at first worked in a Tyneside sausage factory. It had not been much fun.

Similar advice had come, in a backhand way, from George 'Georgie' Best, still regarded by soccer sages as the greatest-ever British player, who said on a TV chat show that Gascoigne's value and abilities had been wildly exaggerated. The number eight on Gazza's shirt, he said, referred not to his position on the field, but to his IQ. Best said he had seen plenty of young players like Gascoigne who operated on pure boyish enthusiasm. Few of them gained the maturity required to become a really great player. Best reckoned that Gascoigne would be finished within two or three seasons, when age slowed him down a bit. He should therefore grab the money and run. The *Sun*, working up a Best versus Gazza feud, reported Gazza as replying charmlessly that Best was a 'scum bastard' and 'a drunken fat man'.

When Gascoigne refused to rule out the move to Lazio, Venables began to rattle the chains of legal action. He claimed that his own manager's contract gave him the final say over transfers, a clause that he might now use to keep Gascoigne at Spurs. Calleri hit back angrily by saying that a deal was a deal and Gascoigne would be playing for him next season. 'If Mr Venables is so interested in rescues,' Calleri added, showing a slightly muddled understanding of British institutions, 'he should join the Lifeguards.'

Far from giving up, Venables immediately announced a new bid for the PLC, which met Scholar's demand that Gascoigne should stay at Spurs. The new bid was more complicated than the first, and was so beset with technical and legal problems that many dismissed it as a simple delaying tactic. For a start he was offering only £3.25 million, in return for which he wanted a controlling 35 per cent stake in the refinanced club. The calculations were based on a share price of 60p, less than half what Maxwell had offered, and the same price offered by the Baltic consortium and rejected as too low a few weeks previously.

Instead of trying to pay off the Midland in full, Venables was prepared only to guarantee interest payments on the overdraft, paying off the debt in instalments. The total value of the offer was hard to estimate, but it would have meant Venables finding something under £10 million in the first year of his control of the club, compared with the £30 million on offer during his first bid. Venables claimed the more 'realistic' sums involved would make it easier for him to come up with the money and complete the deal, thus removing the problem that had sunk the bid he had made with the backing of Gillick.

The Midland Bank was sceptical. Venables was unable to say who his new financial backer was, and the bank feared a time-wasting repeat of the Gillick affair. It could not prevent negotiations with Venables being reopened, but it insisted that the Gascoigne sale went ahead.

There were other, more technical, problems with the

bid. If Venables became the largest shareholder, the Stock Exchange would have to waive its rule requiring shareholders with a controlling stake in a company to offer to buy it outright. Venables could not afford that. The Exchange, which had already censured Scholar and was almost as exasperated with the PLC as the Midland, might not play ball. Another worrying aspect was Venables' intention to sell off White Hart Lane to finance the deal and then rent the ground for matches. Scholar and others were opposed to this, even if it meant keeping Gascoigne at Spurs. There was the further disadvantage of losing money for ground improvements made available by the Football Trust after the Taylor report on ground safety. Clubs qualified for Trust money only if they owned their grounds outright.

Maxwell had been watching these events with intermittent intensity, kept up to date by Harry Harris. Football was important to him, but played only a small role on his business agenda. He would concentrate on it for a few minutes each day. But he was still working towards his mid-summer deadline for a new offer to buy the club. He had made little progress on the sale of Derby, which was now becoming more urgent, but confidently expected another begging letter from the PLC board the moment he got rid of the club. It was vital in the meantime that Venables did not become a stalking horse for Murdoch, buying a controlling stake in the club with his arch rival's backing.

There were some worrying signs that this might be about to happen. Venables wrote regularly for Murdoch's main paper, the *Sun*, which had unsuccessfully defended Venables and Gillick against the vilification dished out by the *Mirror*, just as it had defended Michael Knighton's attempt to buy Manchester United, with Murdoch hovering in the background, two years previously.

Since then the recession and high interest rates had hit Murdoch's empire almost as hard as Maxwell's. Discreet probing revealed no signs that Murdoch was limbering up for a bid, or that he was willing to borrow the necessary money. The problem for Murdoch was Sky television, which at the time was in trouble after a disastrous launch. The service was being run on a shoestring, but was still racking up potentially ruinous debts. Murdoch had announced that he would close the operation if it did not come solidly into profit by 1993 and as yet there were few signs of that happening. Since Murdoch's sole reason for buying into soccer was to put it exclusively on Sky, a bid for Tottenham did not seem likely when Sky might not even exist.

The Tottenham board finally rejected Venables' second bid on 29 April. The bid had collapsed after what was described as 'hours of hard talking' in various London hotels. Venables cancelled a press conference due to be held at Scribes West to celebrate the deal, but announced that he was not beaten yet and claimed still to be looking for new backers.

Venables could at least claim the support of the fans, through the Tottenham Independent Supporters Association. TISA staged a pro-Venables demonstration at White Hart Lane, four days after the collapse of his second bid. There had been demonstrations at soccer games before but, like the protests against Maxwell at Oxford and Derby, they had tended to be *ad hoc* affairs, organised on the spur of the moment and haunted by the possibility of hooliganism. The late 1980s saw a growth in organised Fan Power, centred on the national Football Supporters' Association, set up to oppose the government's ill-fated national registration scheme.

Fan Power had found its voice in a new rash of fanzines produced by supporters in opposition to official match programmes, which had always been banal and, as Hunter Davies had complained, had mostly been turned into advertising brochures for rubbishy club merchandise. By now most groups of supporters in the country had a fanzine, using the new weapon of irony to become the scourge of their particular club's management. The fanzines had titles like Brighton's *There is a Rat in the Camp*, based on their manager's reaction to the club's relegation to Division Two: 'There is a rat in the camp trying to throw a spanner in the works.' There was great admiration for titles like Luton's *D-Pleated*, celebrating ex-Tottenham manager David Pleat's return from disgrace, and the frankness of Division Four Darlington's *Mission Impossible*.

Tottenham's fanzine, *The Spur*, was one of the slicker productions, printed on glossy paper with a cover price of £1. It was put together by a professional editor, Stuart Mutler, working from a flat in Portobello Road, west London. In line with the enterprise culture surrounding the club, the fanzine offered its own range of merchandise, including a rubberised Gazza mask, which it urged fans to wear at the Cup final, and designer T-shirts featuring a picture of a fresh-faced Lineker with a halo above it.

The Spur kept up a running commentary on both the team's performance and the boardroom struggle, cheering up the fans with a fictional series called 'Minion to Misery' which ridiculed 'Irving Gentleman' as a power- and money-mad Lothario, playing up to his reputation as a ladies' man. Scholar, in contrast to the more mean-spirited Gascoigne, who had threatened to sue *The Spur*, sportingly said he enjoyed reading it, and that it made him laugh. Less amusingly for the board, the magazine also provided a platform for the TISA, whose pro-Venables demonstration was organised to take place during the last home League match of the season against Nottingham Forest. The demo had been organised weeks previously with the aim of persuading the board to accept Venables' bid, when it had still been a live proposition. Now the board had shown Venables the door it seemed like a fundamentally quixotic gesture, but it went ahead anyway, fuelled by the new sense of crisis.

The Association circulated a leaflet asking fans to remain behind after the match and 'sit down in support of Terry Venables' who, the organisers belatedly asserted, had 'put forward proposals to the board to rescue the club, which represent the last chance to keep Gazza and prosper. The board must accept them.' Club officials seemed unusually co-operative and even allowed selected agitators into the ground with three-foot placards bearing the letters 'S-C-H-O-L-A-R O-U-T' on one side and 'V-E-N-A-B-L-E-S I-N' on the other. The signs were flipped back and forth during dull intervals in the game, getting a round of applause every time.

The game itself ended as a 1–1 draw. Both teams were in the middle of the table and so there was very little at stake, and neither side wanted to give too much away in terms of tactics before the main event of the FA Cup final, now just two weeks away. After the game there was a cheerful atmosphere as the fans sat down and the police, who had been kept well informed, were happy enough. The presiding officer, Chief Inspector Barry Keenan, even told the organisers that he sympathised with the protest. He had wanted to buy his daughter a season ticket but, after the price increases, had decided he could not afford it.

After ten minutes Venables came on the pitch and the crowd cheered again, though at this point it seemed to be more about encouraging him to win the FA Cup than anything to do with finance and takeover bids; the details of which were still a mystery to most fans. Venables waved and clapped back, which seemed to satisfy most people.

The whole event was judged a huge PR success, even though the fans discovered to their mild irritation that Scholar had not been present to see his name dragged through the proverbial mud, just as Maxwell had failed to turn up to receive similar treatment at the hands of the Derby crowd earlier in the season. But the rumour later circulated that Scholar had seen the protest when he watched a video of the Forest game in his Monte Carlo apartment.

The demo certainly hurt Scholar, the board member who cared most about what the fans thought. Scholar would have been justified in seeing himself more and more as the Hamlet figure of the drama, assailed by outrageous fortune and deserted by the board and now even his fellow fans. The moneymen were just not interested. The fans' main argument, that they paid for the club with their ticket money and therefore had a right to be consulted about its business dealings, was seen as patently absurd. Football was a product like any other. The fans were the consumers. Like all consumers they wanted something for nothing, and would take it if anyone let them. Giving football supporters a say in the running of football would be like giving shoppers in a supermarket the right to dictate how the food industry was run, and what prices should be charged.

And so Tottenham Hotspur lumbered towards the FA Cup final, billed as the most important match in the club's 109-year history. The team was knackered and patched up, half of them faced the prospect of being summarily sold off, and the other half would remain in a denuded team destined, in all probability, to sink down the divisions like Maxwell's Derby. The board were at each other's throats; sundry bankers, financial administrators and Maxwell himself were hovering in the wings, with the liquidators not far behind them. They were not even sure they would be paid if the PLC went bust. They had won only two League games in the last five months, and had been hammered 5 – 1 by Wimbledon.

Their one moment of glory had been the semi-final against Arsenal, but apart from that they had scraped through to the final by narrowly beating a string of no-hope Division Two and Three teams. They had been hounded, pilloried and humiliated by the press all season. Gascoigne, the star of the show, and Venables, the manager they respected and liked, were on course to leave the club.

Now they had to play Nottingham Forest, trained to perfection and brimming with a mixure of justified self-confidence and fear of displeasing the ferocious father figure of Brian Clough. The Mighty Brian had already described Tottenham, in their current plight, as football's version of Hell, and he could always threaten to transfer insufficiently zealous Forest players to White Hart Lane as the ultimate professional punishment.

Clough's young team, featuring his own son Nigel as centre forward, had hammered their semi-final opponents West Ham 4−0, and were playing the sort of fast, ball-on-the-ground 'passing game', which was supposedly Spurs' forte. Stuart 'Psycho' Pearce, the team's England international defender, was holding the line at the back and, in contrast to Tottenham's dismal League performance, the Forest attack had started to click. The team had recently put four goals past Leeds, five past Norwich and beaten Chelsea 7−0 in the League.

There was great delight in pointing out that Venables, for all his free spending on players and talk of one day managing England, had so far won only the Division Two championship and the Spanish League. In contrast, Clough had won the European Cup twice, the League Championship three times (twice with Derby) and had spent only a fraction of Venables' transfer total in the process. Clough recruited his players locally, put the fear of God into them and concentrated on solid teamwork rather than individual brilliance and fancy flicks.

Off the field, the main drama was provided by the continuing boardroom struggle and the proposed sale of Gascoigne, which was now being reported as an established fact. The prospect of Gascoigne either failing to win a trophy before his transfer out of English soccer, maybe for good, or winning the Cup for Spurs and then being whisked off by the moneybags Italians, was certain to strain even football's rich vocabulary of melodramatic cliché. Either scenario would allow the soccer hacks to tap out the dream sentence: 'Heartbroken Gazza fought to hold back the tears...'

As the media got ready for the anticipated repeat performance of the Tears of Turin, and Cloughie concentrated on getting his team ready for the match, Venables was forced to divide his time between coaching and trying to revive his takeover bid for the PLC. His latest plan involved direct negotiations with Scholar to buy his stake in the company.

He might then be able to find his own version of Maxwell: a friendly millionaire ready to work on a new 'Plan for Greatness'. Venables' negotiations went on through Cup final week, late into the night of Friday 17 May, the day before he was due to lead the team out on to the turf at Wembley. Scholar's asking price was too high.

By now Scholar was reconciled to leaving the Tottenham board. There was talk of a renewed Maxwell bid in the wings, but he was sick of the whole business and wanted out. His only condition was that he take back from new investors the money he had originally invested in 1982. Taking inflation into account, this meant about £2 million. This, he thought, was only fair. His boast was that during nine years at the helm he had not taken a single penny out of the club in terms of salary and expenses, and had even refused to cash his dividend cheques when, in the early days, these had existed, and been worth hundreds of thousands.

Venables could come up with only £3.25 million to buy the club which was not enough to meet Scholar's £2 million personal target. Scholar dropped his price by £250,000 on condition that Gascoigne would not be sold, which was a reverse of the true market position (Tottenham shares were worth more, not less, if Gascoigne stayed). This seemed like the act of a genuine fan, ready to leave a quarter of a million pounds in the club if he bowed out of the financial side, just for the thrill of watching Gascoigne play in Spurs' colours.

Having failed to reach agreement, the two men made their separate ways to Wembley. Venables met the players for the traditional pre-match hotel breakfast and then travelled in the luxury coach to Wembley. Scholar made his way directly to the stadium along with about 40,000 Tottenham fans, some of whom had paid up to £200 on the black market for a ticket in the new all-seater stands. Scholar was to have the honour of watching the game with the Quality in the Royal box. He sat within chatting distance of John Major. As a sports fan the new

Prime Minister shared few of the anti-football prejudices of his predecessor, Margaret Thatcher. Maggie was blamed by fans and officials alike for inventing the unworkable national football supporters registration scheme. The idea had been about as popular as the poll tax and Major now allowed it to disappear from the agenda.

Mrs Thatcher had zero interest in football and had even failed to capitalise on Italia 90 when she had the chance. Politicians from other countries flocked to be associated with their teams. President Menem of Argentina duly turned up in his team's dressing room to take part in a press conference, genuflecting before Maradona who, prior to the drugs-and-sex scandal, was elevated to the official position of Special Ambassador for the occasion. Maggie, in contrast, had ignored the whole event, though she did later meet Gascoigne for a photo opportunity at the height of Gazzamania. 'She's just like me,' Gascoigne had said about the Iron Lady, 'nice and cuddly.'

The new Prime Minister was a Chelsea fan, but not in quite the same way as Mrs Thatcher. He was knowledg-able about football and would discuss the merits of various players and teams in his peculiar Dalekspeak. 'Arsenal,' he said, commenting on the club's champion-ship win, 'are, I must say, a super team; in fact a very good team indeed.' The change of Prime Minister had at least avoided an embarrassing confrontation between Thatcher and Clough, a supporter of the 1984 miners' strike and other socialist causes. 'I hope she is not going to be two-faced enough to turn up in the Royal Box at the next FA Cup final,' he had said when the registration scheme had first been proposed, 'because she hasn't been football's friend.' With politics taken care of Scholar manoeuvred himself into the best position of all, sitting right next to Princess Di. The chairman was looking tanned and fit after a break in Monte Carlo and was behaving as though he did not have a care in the world.

Having made the momentous decision to leave the board as soon as Venables scraped the money together, he had the look of a man out to enjoy himself with a clear conscience. He was leaving the club much as he found it. At 1982 prices the accumulated debt was about the same as he inherited from Richardson. The FA Cup had been in the trophy cupboard when he arrived and, if the team won that afternoon, it would be there when he left. His legacy to the club, he reckoned, was almost entirely positive. He had brought in one of the greatest managers in Europe, who was at last about to prove his worth. He had transformed White Hart Lane into one of the best stadiums in the country and provided the fans with players like Waddle, Lineker and Gascoigne.

He had to take the blame as chairman of the football club, but it was Berry's diversification plans and Bobroff's underestimates of the cost of construction that had forced him to sell. Even that would not have been necessary if the board had backed him and allowed Uncle Bob to come to the rescue. Some of them were already starting to regret that. History would be his judge. One day he might be remembered in the same reverential tones as Bill Nicholson: a Tottenham Hotspur great. The important thing was that the Lillywhites should win the Cup and crown the end of his reign in a blaze of glory. And here he was seated next to the future Queen of England. Not bad for a grammar-school lad from Hendon.

The assorted moneymen assembled in the box were rather less relaxed. The representative of the Midland Bank's Intensive Care Unit was particularly uncomfortable, as he was whenever Gascoigne ventured on to the field. The club's principal asset had now recovered from the stomach-muscle problem which had kept him out of League matches for part of the season. Serious injury was always a possibility, especially with such a reckless player as Gazza. For those in the know the presence of Clough was a constant reminder of the precarious life led by professional footballers. As a young Sunderland player Clough had been the Gazza of his day, a soccer genius who lived only for football and scored an average of a goal per game. But on Boxing Day 1962 he slipped on a frozen pitch, smashed his knee and was forced to retire soon afterwards. His next job was as an unpaid managerial assistant at Hartlepool United, and his fight back to the top had been a long, hard slog. Those who knew him well said the solution to the riddle of Clough's complex personality was a streak of twisted fate and a constant nagging twinge in his kneecap. He would still talk darkly about the Curse of Clough when things went wrong.

In 1962 the financial consequences of Clough's accident for Sunderland had been slight. But Gascoigne was written down in the Tottenham accounts as an amortised asset. Looked at financially, sending him out to play in the rough and tumble of English League matches was an enormous gamble, like entering a Rolls-Royce in a stock-car race. The moneymen had to wait only another 90 minutes and it would all be over. Gascoigne would have played his last match for Tottenham and would be safely packed off to Rome where Lazio had announced he would be shown to the crowd during their last match of the Italian season.

Venables and Clough led their respective teams out on to the pitch, creating the first stir of the afternoon. Tottenham were decked out in a bizzare new Umbro strip, consisting of wing-collared shirts and long, baggy draw-string black and white shorts, which came down to just above the players' knees. This was the latest offering from the shirt designers who, in their quest to stay one step ahead of the pirates who produced non-copyright versions of team strips, were providing wilder and wilder designs, especially for away change strips. Some teams were decked out in hideous clashing combinations of luminous mauve, lime green and yellow, making the TV soccer supporters' sets look like tanks full of tropical fish. At the same time the range of replica goods had been extended from the first and reserve strip: Manchester United were already offering a supporters' 'package' which included everything from replica socks to the manager's dug-out jacket.

From the kick-off everyone in the Royal Box was

watching Gascoigne who was in full whirling dervish mode, excitedly chasing the ball to no apparent effect and plunging into kamikaze tackles. There were a few gulps when, after three minutes, Gascoigne badly mishandled a tackle on a Forest defender and kicked him squarely in the chest. This was a potential red card offence, but the referee merely shrugged and did not even book him.

Scholar relaxed and was seen animatedly discussing the merits of Gazza with Princess Diana. Ever the flirt, he seemed to be blatantly trying to chat her up. 'Please, Your Highness,' he was heard to say at one point, 'call me Irving,' before turning, grinning like a Cheshire cat, to wink at the other Spurs VIPs.

Gascoigne's brush with the red card had done nothing to blunt his enthusiasm. Fifteen minutes into the game he went flying into Forest full back Gary Charles on the edge of the Spurs penalty box, with an even more recklessly late tackle. Charles fell heavily on Gascoigne, who lay on the grass rolling in agony and nursing his knee. The referee awarded a free kick to Forest. Tottenham formed the standard defensive wall, with Gary Mabbutt at its centre. Stuart Pearce ran up to take the kick and a Forest player pushed Mabbutt out of the way, allowing the ball to fly through the gap, straight into the net. Erik the Viking had no chance.

We woz robbed, the Tottenham fans complained loudly to the referee about the off-the-ball foul on Mabbutt which, they firmly believed, meant the goal should have been disallowed. In the Royal Box Gascoigne's mishap was creating far more interest than the goal. When Gazza got back on his feet and limped back into position for the kick-off to a round of sympathetic applause, Scholar relaxed a little and nervously resumed his chat-up routine, dividing his attention between the princess and worried glances at the pitch. Then Gascoigne slumped to the ground, showing that something was seriously wrong. Scholar's jaw dropped and the royal personage was ignored and virtually pushed to one side as he leapt to his feet.

258

The same reaction spread amongst the moneymen and VIPs as play was stopped to allow Gascoigne to be carried off the pitch on a stretcher. The men from the Midland turned as white as a Tottenham shirt. If Gascoigne was as badly hurt as it seemed, the deal with Lazio was now almost certainly off. 'What price Scholar's shares now?' one of the financiers asked, reckoning that the injury could wipe millions off the value of Scholar's personal holding in the PLC. With twenty minutes gone, the moneymen reckoned that the match was costing Scholar £100,000 a minute.

When the stretcher reached the touchline, the entire media pack swooped on Gazza's prone body, shoving cameras and microphones in his face in the hope of getting a tear or sob as he was carried off down the tunnel towards the dressing rooms. But he had covered his face with his forearm, and all they got were shots of his elbow and the tightly clenched line of his mouth as his head rolled in agony. Live coverage of the game was interrupted to show meaningless pictures of the back of an ambulance taking Gascoigne to hospital. Was it serious? Yes, it was. Early reports said he had broken his leg.

Surely Tottenham had no chance of winning the Cup now. Gascoigne had won the semi-final against Arsenal more or less single-handedly and without his individualistic goals the team would have lost to Portsmouth and Notts County in earlier rounds. Venables was leaping around, barking out orders and tactical instructions as he reorganised the team to plug the gap left by Gascoigne. Paul Stewart was moved to the midfield to take Gascoigne's place and Nayim came on as a substitute.

Surprisingly, Tottenham got back on top of the game. Lineker scored an equaliser, but it was declared offside by the referee and disallowed. The instant video replay showed that the ref was wrong and that the goal should have been allowed to stand. In an age of shirt advertising the fans demanded to know why the FA had not done a sponsorship with Optrex. Spurs were then awarded a penalty which Lineker took hurriedly and Mark Crossley, the Forest keeper, saved.

At half time, with Spurs still 1-0 down, the TV coverage was dominated by Gascoigne's injury. The earlier muddled reports had given way to more accurate information: he had twisted and snapped the ligaments in his leg and was being operated on immediately. There was no chance of him playing again for six months at least.

Ten minutes into the second half Allen and Nayim put together a fast one-two and set Paul Stewart free to score the equaliser. Clough sat Sphinx-like in his dug out, arms crossed, bolt upright, motionlessly exuding the Curse. After that it was all Tottenham, but the game was heading towards a draw and extra time which would favour Clough's younger, fitter team. But Tottenham tore into the game from the restart. After three minutes Paul Stewart flicked a Nayim corner in front of the Forest goal and into the path of defender Des Walker who inadvertently headed the ball into his own net.

Twenty minutes later Gary Mabbutt, the Spurs captain, was holding up the silverware. Tottenham, against all odds, had won the FA Cup for a record eighth time. For Scholar it was a personal triumph. He would be leaving the club a winner. He celebrated by phoning a financial journalist who had been giving him a hard time and yelled on to his Ansaphone: 'We have won the Cup. All I want to say to you is *Bollocks*. That's with a capital B. Goodbye.'

With the Cup safely in the trophy room, and Scholar ready to sell out, the two financial teams fighting for control of the PLC lined up for the boardroom equivalent of the Wembley final. Maxwell activated the letter he had received six weeks earlier from Solomon, claiming that the Tottenham board had unanimously asked him to put together a rescue plan. Maxwell had not wanted to make his move so soon, but his hand had been forced by alarming news from the Venables camp.

Two weeks before the Wembley final Harris had picked up rumours that Tel had been contacted by Alan Sugar, the electronics entrepreneur who had recently cashed in £35 million worth of shares in his Amstrad electronics business, taking his personal worth to well over £130 million in real money, not faked Maxwell-style share pyramids and bogus securities. Sugar had announced at the time that he was going to reinvest in cheap commercial property, exploiting the depressed London market for long-term profits. White Hart Lane, which was close to Sugar's birthplace and original operating base in Hackney, might fall into that category. But Maxwell was convinced that Sugar might be acting in concert in some way with Murdoch or, at the very least, that the two men were co-ordinating their activities around football and its potential value to Sky TV.

Since the summer of 1988 Sugar had been the main producer of dishes for Rupert Murdoch's Sky TV, and the partnership was one of the closest and most sensitive business relationships in the country. At the joint press conference called to mark the launch of the service Murdoch had described Sugar as 'probably Britain's greatest entrepreneur'. Everyone who observed the working relationship knew that the compliment was both sincere and mutual.

Murdoch had built his multinational News Corporation from a chain of inherited newspapers in Australia, expanding into Britain in the 1970s with a combination of ferocious hard work and a ruthlessly unsentimental eye for the reading tastes of the mass market. Sugar's start in life had been much more humble. All Sugar had inherited was East End chutzpah and a feeling that the world did not owe him, or anyone else, a living. Now, at the age of 42, the bearded electronics wizard had risen to live in Chigwell, part of Essex settled by East Enders who, like Venables, had Done Good. Sugar's higher profile in recent years had brought him to the attention of *Arena* magazine, which had patronisingly voted him a Noovo of Note (meaning *nouveau riche*) with Jonathan Ross, Nick Logan and, co-incidently, Venables, as capturing the very essence of the self-made eighties man.

Sugar had started out selling discarded television sets from his council-flat bedroom as a teenager in the 1950s, graduating to a Hackney market stall selling car radios before making it big by inventing the 'tower system', the first mass-market hi-fi, just in time to catch the consumer boom of the 1970s. The Amstrad Tower was a large, impressive-looking box covered in important-looking dials, lights and switches, containing some cheap but clever electronics to make it function. Sugar cheerfully described his invention as 'a mug's eyeful'. It sold at half the price of traditional stereos, enabling his target audience, which he described as the 'truck driver and his wife', to have at least the feeling of joining in the trendy middle-class good life. The people loved their Eyeful Towers and the system took the market by storm, much as Murdoch's *Sun* had done with its daily eyeful of Page 3.

After that, the rumour spread that Sugar was a man with the Midas touch and more millions flowed as he led each new consumer electronics fad, from videos to home computers. Summing up Amstrad's approach to business, Sugar had said: 'We're interested in the mass-merchandising of anything. If there was a market in mass-produced nuclear weapons, we'd market them too.' Moving in more elevated circles, Murdoch tended to wrap up the same moneymaking formula in the language of free markets, consumer choice and personal political freedom. The basic thought was the same, and satellite TV, the latest mug's eyeful, was perfect for them both.

For months the Maxwell camp had been scanning the radar for signs of a Murdoch move on Tottenham. The motive was obvious enough. Murdoch had failed to get Disney Channel for Sky at a price he could afford, denying him what was known in the trade as a 'dish driver': a unique reason to buy the otherwise mediocre service. The idea was that heavy advertising of an especially appealing, and preferably exclusive, Disney offering would recruit the nation's children as a salesforce who would pester their parents to hire the dish as a one-off in an operation similar to the replica soccer strip business. Once the dish was bolted to the side of the house, inertia would take over and there it would remain.

Football was an obvious substitute, the pulling power of selected games demonstrated again by Italia 90. Murdoch had already expressed an interest in Manchester United, the club which, together with Tottenham, had always led the commercial policy of the Big Five. If he was able to influence the commercial policy of either club, he might eventually have the inside track on negotiations for TV rights for the Premier League.

English football delivered a baseline audience of about five or six million, which was not huge for ITV or the BBC, but which would be like the second coming for struggling Sky. Audiences would be consistently higher for Premier matches, rising to ten million or more for the Saatchi-style 'event matches' which would settle the newly simplified championship race towards the end of each season.

Ominously for Maxwell, Sky had already started advertising its soccer coverage on normal telly, half teasing and half threatening football fans with exciting snippets of commentary played over a blanked out ITV screen. The ads concluded with the Sky logo and, ironically, a version of Arsenal secretary Bob Wall's famous epithet about the soullessness of televised games played in front of small crowds: 'Football is like religion. It must be witnessed in a place of worship.'

Maxwell's contacts in the business world were confirming that Murdoch had considered making a bid for the TV rights for the Premier League, within a few years if not immediately, and the idea had been openly discussed at management meetings. The rumour was soon circulating of how Murdoch had phoned Sugar about Maxwell and told him: 'Don't let the fat cunt get Tottenham.'

Venables had yet to announce the backing of Sugar, or the details of his new bid, and had gone on holiday in Sardinia, telling peopole as he left: 'I'm still in there, seeking to do a deal.' Maxwell decided to act while

Venables was away. Using his normal pre-emptive public diplomacy Uncle Bob appeared on Central Television to announce he had 'slashed' the asking price for Derby County from £8 million to £4 million and invited immediate offers. This was his overt signal to the Tottenham board that, under the terms of Solomon's letter, he was ready to inject money into the PLC. The demand for an apology from the Mismanagement Committee was quietly dropped, as planned.

Maxwell did not get the reply he wanted. Instead Solomon told the press: 'Neither Robert Maxwell nor anyone else will be invited to rescue Spurs, because no rescue is required. The whole climate has changed dramatically for us in the last few days. There is no financial crisis here.'

Solomon's new confidence was based on the completion of the Gascoigne sale to Lazio which, paradoxically, had been sealed by his knee injury. The important new factor was Gascoigne's own attitude, the deciding factor Venables had always stressed. Until the accident he had been lukewarm about the offer, but Gascoigne's brush with early, enforced retirement had finally removed any doubt in his mind. Gascoigne kept up his unnaturally cheerful persona for PR reasons, posing on his bed playing space invaders and beaming with confidence for an exclusive picture in the *Sun*. But in reality the injury had terrified him. He decided he had to grab the money while he still could.

The minute the FA Cup final was over Solomon had invited Lazio's officials to London so that the future of Gascoigne could be discussed. To both his and Gascoigne's immense relief they were still keen to buy, though they were not now prepared to pay the full £7.9 million agreed in April, and there would have to be exhaustive medical checks before the eventual transfer. Solomon insisted that if the Romans wanted to go ahead they should pay a large slice of the expected transfer fee, which had now been built in to the PLC's business plan, at once. Calleri, the Lazio President, came up with £4 million at once, with the remainder of the total, now rumoured to be down to £5 million, payable when it was established that Gascoigne could still kick a football without keeling over in agony. Alongside the Lazio money Solomon could report that advance sales of season tickets had gone well, bringing in £1.5 million; there was the new Umbro shirt deal worth £4 million; and up to £3 million was likely to be available from the sale of TV rights to next season's European Cup Winners' Cup matches.

Like any good chairman, Solomon was talking up the prospects of his company. The new money coming in to the company might ease the immediate problem, but a major cash injection was still needed to pay off the accumulated debt. Privately, board members rubbished Solomon's public display of confidence and knew that the PLC would have to find a new backer, and that now meant either Venables or Maxwell.

Venables was the first into the ring, flying back from Sardinia to hold secret talks with the PLC board with Sugar present. Venables picked up where he had left his negotiations with Scholar, beefing them up to anticipate a counterbid from Maxwell. Before the Cup final Venables had offered Scholar £3.25 million for a controlling block of shares, based on a share price of about 60p. With Sugar's support this was increased to 70p, giving Scholar his target £2 million. There was another condition.

Venables and Sugar wanted Bobroff's 11 per cent block as well, giving them a 37 per cent stake for which they were prepared to pay a total of £7 million. Venables and Sugar would then replace Scholar and Bobroff on the board. Tony Berry, who had been encouraging Venables all along, would stay on the board with an 8 per cent stake. With the backing, or inertia, of the fan shareholders the new regime of Venables, Sugar and Berry would have an absolute majority on the board, which Sugar felt was essential if they were to withstand a determined takeover bid from Maxwell. With the Maxwell threat finally buried, the final stage of the takeover would take the form of a full bid for the company, backed by a rights issue which would bring in the money to pay off the Midland and allow Venables to start buying players again.

After their meetings Sugar and Venables were under the definite impression that the deal was in the bag, and everyone swore themselves to secrecy as usual. Scholar and Bobroff still had not formally committed themselves and now, in this last act of the drama, further meetings were arranged to agree a final price and tie up loose ends.

The next day full details of the bid, and the first public confirmation of Sugar's involvement in Spurs, were published in the *Sunday Times*, the Murdoch paper which had been extraordinarily well informed about the internal dealings of Spurs since the start of the crisis. All the papers and news bulletins followed up the story, reporting the Sugar takeover as an established fact. For the second time in a year the full Tottenham board and the fans learned about the future of their club in the newspapers and an angry emergency meeting of the board was held, dominated by an inconclusive mole hunt and an explanation from Scholar, representing Bobroff, that the deal had not gone through yet.

One effect of the leak was to prompt Maxwell to make an immediate, secret counteroffer to Scholar. When the news dropped, Maxwell was in Wyoming attending his son Ian's wedding, and he at once realised that this was his last chance to get control of Spurs, or at least prevent complete control passing to Sugar, with Murdoch and Sky lurking in the background. He was soon in telephone contact with Scholar, agreeing a better price for his and Bobroff's shares. Scholar then called Harry Harris, who was in Malaysia covering the England national team's summer international tour. The chief soccer writer was in the shower when the call came in at 7 p.m., local time, getting ready to host a dinner party in a Japanese restaurant for a bunch of Brit soccer hacks. Scholar gabbled the details of the latest twist in the drama, saying that he and Bobroff were ready to sell out to Uncle Bob, and telling him to stand by for an important call.

The phone rang again. It was Maxwell, his voice booming three-quarters of the way round the planet from the American midwest: 'Harry, come back immediately. I want to see you in the office at 9 a.m. tomorrow morning.' The phone went dead and Harris rushed off to the airport, toothbrush in hand, leaving the hacks to pay for their own slivers of raw squid.

17: GENEROUS IN VICTORY, MAGNANIMOUS IN DEFEAT

Harris had plenty of time on the plane back to London to ponder the cliché 'football's a funny old game'. It was hard to imagine anything else that would engage one of the richest men in the world intermittently phoning between a Kuala Lumpur sushi bar and a Jewish wedding in Wyoming, to heatedly discuss the fate of a small company in North London with a turnover not much bigger than a local builders' yard.

More importantly, he wondered what the *Mirror* finance department would make of his expenses, which now included a £2,500 one-way first-class ticket from Malaysia to Heathrow. There had been an endless debate in the office about whether the sports department could afford to send a reporter on the tour at all, which was widely seen in the football world as an insane waste of time and money. (*When Saturday Comes*, the leading national soccer fanzine, ran a cover claiming that the idea for the tour had come from David Icke, the former Coventry City goalkeeper who had recently revealed himself to be a prophet, driven by the energy patterns of his turquoise tracksuit.)

Harris arrived in the office on time the next morning, but he need not have bothered; Maxwell was a day late for the meeting. But when he did arrive he had some important news. The takeover of Spurs was going ahead. Maxwell had met Bobroff and believed he had a deal to buy his and Scholar's controlling stake for £9 million, £2 million more than what they had been offered by Venables and Sugar. The deal would be confirmed at a special meeting of the PLC board in two days' time.

The chief soccer writer splashed the story in the *Mirror*, downplaying the precise details of the deal and concentrating on something the fans would understand: Maxwell's promise to keep Gascoigne at Tottenham. This was the line which Harris had flogged to death all year. Starting long before the Lazio deal, Harris had kept up the pressure on the PLC, announcing a series of 'swoops' for Gascoigne, Lineker or both by AC Milan, Napoli, Juventus, Marseille and Real Madrid. Without the Maxwell millions Spurs would have no choice but to sell. 'The vultures are gathering on the financial corpse of Spurs, hoping they will give in under pressure so that the World Cup pair will have to be sold off,' he had written just after Maxwell's original Plan for Greatness. Since then every trick known to tabloid journalism had been thrown into the campaign.

The paper's traditional New Year horoscope predictions had been headlined 'SPURS WILL HAVE TO SELL GAZZA'. Mystic Queen Paula Paradaemus, '42 years a clairvoyant', revealed that Gascoigne would be 'tempted to change clubs in June or July'. The crystal ball had been more cloudy when it came to Lineker. 'There is a lot of rumour and gossip around him in February and March,' she had said, 'and he could plunge into a new situation in July or August.' Ramming home the point the *Mirror* had made, she added: 'That spells another departure from White Hart Lane.' The same line was now revived under the headline 'BOB'S YOUR UNCLE' to announce the new Maxwell takeover bid, and win the support of the fans. 'Robert Maxwell has emerged as the key figure to keep Paul Gascoigne in English soccer,' Harris wrote, adding: 'Only the dramatic intervention of the millionaire publisher can prevent the player's move to the Italian club Lazio.'

By now Gazzamania had gone off the boil, just like Teenage Mutant Ninja Turtles, the media craze that had preceded him. After the FA Cup final, which had been won without his help, the TISA fans no longer saw him as the only hope for the future. They were much more concerned that Venables should stay at the club. Europe's Biggest Soccer Brain had made it clear that he would leave within a few weeks if he did not get control of the PLC. Even if Maxwell could persuade Gascoigne to stay, if it came to a choice between Maxwell and Gazza or Venables and no Gazza, the fans were now certain to choose Venables.

The *Sun*, entering the fray as a counterweight to the *Mirror* in the propaganda stakes, confirmed this with a 'YOU, THE JURY' telephone-voting slot asking fans to back either Tel or Maxwell. Overdoing things as usual, the result was 5,205 for Venables against 236 for Uncle Bob. The joke was circulated that Harry Harris had been very busy on the phone that day. The reaction of the League Mismanagement Committee was just as negative. Maxwell had quietly dropped his demand for an apology from the Committee before he would put any money into Tottenham. The League had served its function as a fig leaf to cover his financial embarrassment. But the 'stupid idiots', as he had called the Committee and its members, were much less inclined to forget the public feud.

They said tersely that he would need to end his involvement with Derby, Reading and Oxford before they would even consider giving him the 'prior written consent' needed for a takeover at Spurs. Maxwell answered them in the usual way on the back page of the *Mirror*. 'DERBY ARE SOLD – NEXT STOP SPURS', Harris wrote, revealing that Derby was in the process of being sold to a consortium of existing directors backed by a midlands property tycoon. The price was £5 million, which was £3 million less than Maxwell had asked when he put the club up for sale nine months ago. But it was still six times what he had paid for it.

The next step was the special Tottenham board meeting called to discuss the rival bids for the company. Maxwell did not see this as an obstacle. Bobroff and Scholar had already agreed to sell to him and the meeting would have no choice other than to rubber stamp the deal. But Tony

Berry had lobbied effectively on behalf of Venables, convincing Solomon and the rest of the board that the manager must stay at all costs.

If Venables left, Berry argued, the team's morale, already strained by the drawn out crisis, would collapse. There would not be much money for new players, but the team had to do well in the European Cup Winners' Cup if the PLC was to have any chance of continuing its modest financial recovery. Rudderless and demoralised, there was every chance of the team dropping into Division Two, just as it had done soon after Bill Nicholson had left. That would be a disaster at any time, but if it happened at the end of next season it would be a catastrophe: Tottenham would fail to qualify for the Premier League.

In the background there was another consideration: a version of the 'stink factor' which had worried Bobroff when Maxwell first approached the club. Despite the best efforts of his lawyers, and a wall of gagging injunctions placed on the financial press, rumours about the rickety state of Maxwell's finances were beginning to circulate. The BBC's *Panorama* programme had a team investigating the labyrinth of holding companies and cross-ownership arrangements on which Maxwell had erected his financial façade, and the word was that they had some devastating allegations to make. Getting into bed with Maxwell might involve waking up to a nasty shock one day.

On the positive side, Venables and Sugar, still unaware that Scholar and Bobroff had agreed to sell to Maxwell, upped their bid by half a million to £7.5 million so the two men would have at least something extra to show for rejecting the Maxwell bid. Scholar began to crumble. The extra money now on offer did not sway him much. Sugar's bid had already covered his bottom line, which was his aim of walking away from the club with as much money in real terms as he put in.

The great attraction was the simplicity of Sugar and Venables' offer. The cheque was practically there on the table before him and all he had to do was accept it. As he had discovered when Maxwell had pulled out of the Plan for Greatness, things were rarely this simple when dealing with Uncle Bob. Maxwell had still not cleared things up with the League Mismanagement Committee. Who was to say that he would not go into one of his famous rages and provoke another row with them, ensnaring Scholar in more months of hell?

On top of this Berry's carefully worked out argument in favour of keeping Venables had put Scholar on the spot, as intended. Scholar had always said that football success was all that mattered to him and he now found it hard to deny that the team would be badly damaged if Venables left. Although they had fallen out over the past twelve months it was Scholar who had brought Venables to the club in the first place. When Venables' promises of instant success failed to materialise, Scholar had fought against the rest of the board to keep him. It was now hard for him to back down.

Not for the first time Scholar allowed his emotional attachment to football to outweigh hard-headed financial thinking. He joined the unanimous vote in favour of accepting the Sugar – Venables bid. All that remained was the legal formality of signing over the shares which, it was decided, would take place in a low key fashion in the City offices of Sugar's merchant bank, Ansbacher, the next day. There was a great sigh of relief followed by much smiling and back-slapping as it was realised that the nerve-wracking brinksmanship of the last twelve months was now at an end. Only Scholar seemed tense as he secretly wondered how Maxwell would react. Not that it mattered. He was thoroughly sick of the drama and decided that he would not even attend the formal signing-over session. Instead he would be quietly ensconced in his Monte Carlo apartment, surrounded by his Jimmy Greaves videos and Spurs memorabilia, leaving Bobroff to sign for them both.

The deal was announced by Sugar's PR man Nick Hewer and was at once reported in all the papers as a triumph for football over finance, with endless weak

'Sweet Victory' puns based on Sugar's name. Maxwell was derided as a megalomaniac who had got involved with the club only on a whim. *The Times* had even been moved to run an editorial about 'vanity capitalism', praising the super-rich for throwing money at various white elephants and entertainingly madcap schemes which would not otherwise get off the ground. The fact that Maxwell was fighting for his financial life and that Tottenham was the latest front to open up in his deadly war with Murdoch was overlooked.

The late editions of the papers carrying the 'Sweet Victory' story were still circulating when the parties gathered at Ansbacher's for the 5 p.m. deadline to complete the formalities. A relaxed-looking Nat Solomon presided, exuding businesslike bonhomie. Bobroff was there in person, flanked by advisers and looking much more uncomfortable. Venables and Sugar sent their lawyers to sign for them. In a mood of quiet efficiency, the Men in Suits carefully inspected the papers and documents, declaring that each point was in order and producing executive fountain pens, ready to sign.

But with minutes to go a call was routed through to Solomon. 'This is Robert Maxwell,' boomed the voice on the other end of the phone. Solomon's smooth countenance changed at once. The blood drained from his face as Maxwell told him that he was making a last-minute bid for Scholar's shares, and some of Bobroff's. Solomon said that was impossible. He said Scholar had already agreed to sell to Sugar and Venables. A look of horror crept round his face as Maxwell disabused him. He had just spoken to Mr Scholar who had changed his mind. There was no need for any further discussion. Maxwell said his lawyers were on their way to sign the necessary papers. The call was terminated.

Solomon replaced the receiver slowly and the assembled lawyers and bankers listened wide-eyed as Solomon told them what Maxwell had said. The stunned silence was broken by Bernard Jolles, the Ansbacher director looking after Sugar's side of the deal, who rushed out of the room to call his client on the hotline. The whole room exploded into uproar. What was going on? How had this happened? Did Bobroff know anything about it? The questions were pointless. The answer lay in a series of phone calls between Maxwell, Harris and Scholar, which had taken place that morning. Harris had got to work the moment Scholar arrived in Monte Carlo, asking him to reconsider and deal with Maxwell as he had always said he would. At first Scholar would not budge. He explained that he was fed up with the whole saga and just wanted out.

Scholar reminded Harris that it was Maxwell who had pulled out of the original rights issue, using the 'due diligence' loophole and leaving him in the lurch. Harris had sympathised. He liked Scholar personally and believed that he had done all the right things at Tottenham, out of pure devotion to the cause. Harris believed that the villain of the piece, so far as there was one, was Berry, who Scholar had allowed to lead the disastrous charge into diversification. It was ironic — no, it was just plain wrong — that the deal Scholar had just done would keep Berry on the board while he was humiliated and forced to skulk away from the club he loved.

As the two men looked back on the saga, Harris sensed that Scholar was changing his mind. He made a final plea on behalf of Uncle Bob. 'Give him one more chance,' Harris said. 'There were reasons why he had to pull out in August. He won't do it again.' Scholar gave in. 'If Maxwell buys my shares today the club will be his,' he said. But, Scholar warned, his voice quickening, there must be no strings attached and no more 'due diligence'. He would accept Maxwell's price so long as it was absolutely unconditional. Harris reported the news to his boss at about mid-day. Maxwell ordered him to go to his desk on the newsroom floor, stay there until midnight and get ready to clear the front page. He was about to get the biggest story of his career. Harris duly scurried off, savouring the reaction of the Murdoch press, which had been personally deriding him almost as much as his

274

boss, when they were made to eat their words.

Maxwell's lawyers and a team from his own merchant bank, Hill Samuel, swept up to Ansbacher in a small fleet of shiny black Ford Scorpios, clunking the doors as they jumped out on to the pavement, marched determinedly up to the front door and elbowed their way past the security guards who were reluctant to let them in. The guards at last relented, on instructions from Bernard Jolles, who realised that it was not a good idea to upset Robert Maxwell too much. In they strode, clutching the briefcase containing Maxwell's instructions and a cheque for £9 million.

Over in Monte Carlo, Scholar was keeping an open line to the *Mirror* building, talking alternately to Maxwell and to Harris, keeping him up to date. A separate line linked him to Ansbacher where he was filling Bobroff in on developments and trying to calm down Solomon, explaining the reason for his change of mind. Maxwell had said that he wanted to be a 'passive, long-term investor' and had no intrest in running the club. There was therefore no need for Venables to go. There would be no need for a collapse of morale and no rudderless ship figuratively marooned on the football field. Venables could still run the club as chief executive, or chairman, as he wished.

'Spurs will have two sugar daddies,' was how Maxwell put it. The maximum stake he wanted was 29.9 per cent which would include all Scholar's shares and another 3 per cent from other sources, probably from Bobroff. This would give him enough clout on the board to prevent Sugar doing anything he disagreed with, such as signing an exclusive TV deal with Sky, for instance. As Solomon realised, Maxwell was mounting a spoiling operation. His objective was to stop Sugar and Venables taking control.

Maxwell's lawyers were already finalising the new transfer documents which Scholar would use to sign over his shares to Maxwell and, at the same time, were negotiating to buy part of Bobroff's stake. Other than physically throwing them out of the building, there was

275

nothing Solomon could do to stop them.

Sugar took a much more robust line. He had reacted to Jolles' warning phone call by jumping straight into his car and driving to the City as fast as the rush-hour traffic would allow, arriving a few minutes after the Maxwell team. 'What the fuck's going on?' he raged at Bobroff. 'I thought we had a fucking deal.' The abuse was then directed at the Hill Samuel team. If Maxwell wanted to buy some shares, he told them, he should wait until the PLC got its Stock Exchange listing back.

The shouting match went on for hours, with more and more Men in Suits turning up. Specialist contract lawyers tried to prove that Scholar had given up the right to change his mind, and might even be sued if he did not go ahead with the sale. Others argued the exact opposite: that it was wrong for Sugar to try and prevent Maxwell from having a fair crack of the whip.

Additional legal experts and financial advisers appeared all evening, together with smaller investors alerted by Ansbacher's inability to confirm that Venables and Sugar had bought their way on to the board. Sugar personally shepherded them into a room so that his people could keep an eye on them and make sure they did not sell their shares to Maxwell. By 11 p.m. there were at least fifty people in the building, many of them shouting at each other, and wading through greasy Kentucky Fried Chicken wrappers. The greatest pressure was on Bobroff, who had told Sugar that Maxwell had made him a better offer and wanted to know if he could match it. The answer was a high-decibel 'no'. They had negotiated a price, Sugar insisted, and they were going to stick to it. Bobroff phoned Scholar to say that he was going ahead with the sale at the price agreed at the special board meeting. 'It's all right for you,' he added wimpishly, when Scholar tried to talk him out of it. 'Over here they're all shouting at me.'

Over at the *Daily Mirror* newsroom, Harry Harris waited patiently for confirmation of the scoop of a life-time. Harris had been at the centre of three-way phone traffic all day, and was beginning to feel like the ball in a game of ping-pong. As the evening wore on he noticed Scholar was getting less and less inclined to sell to Maxwell. The midnight deadline which Maxwell had mentioned to Harris came and went. Finally, at half past midnight, Maxwell called Harris up to his office and told him that the deal with Scholar had fallen through. At the last minute the League Management Committee had made it clear that they would not allow Maxwell to take over the club. He thought that his lawyers could reverse the decision, or work some way round it, but that would take time. He had offered Scholar more money, but payment had to be conditional on the sale of Derby County and approval of his involvement with Spurs by the League. Scholar remained adamant: no conditions. In the end he had sold his shares to Venables and Sugar.

When Maxwell received the news he became tremendously depressed and complained bitterly that Scholar had sold him out. Senior journalists at the *Mirror*, including Harris, gathered to decide what headline to put on the story, like a scene from Citizen Kane. The triumphant 'BOB'S YOUR UNCLE – MAXWELL SAVES SPURS' was mournfully dumped in favour of 'EXCLUSIVE: £9 MILLION SPURS DEAL IS OFF, SAYS MAXWELL. I'M PULLING OUT.'

Harris had written the story of his boss's defeat as positively as possible. He asked if the publisher wanted to read his article. But Maxwell was too tired and depressed to read it in detail. Instead he gave the chief soccer writer some advice. Maxwell slumped into his giant thronelike chair and turned up the palms of his hands. 'Remember, Harry,' he said in his deepest Churchillian growl, 'always be magnanimous in defeat.'

Five months later Robert Maxwell was dead.

POSTSCRIPT

On Thursday 20 June 1991, Alan Sugar and Terry Venables turned up at White Hart Lane, to the cheers of Tottenham supporters, to hold a press conference. Having gained control, Sugar took the position of chairman of a newly formed board that included Venables in his dual capacity as a major shareholder and salaried chief executive of the PLC and group. Tony Berry, Venables' main supporter during the old regime, stayed on the board and, in addition, took the prized position of chairman of the football club. Nat Solomon stayed on, with much thanks, as deputy chairman of the PLC.

Sugar could not help but look a little lost, marching around the Tottenham pitch with an amused and slightly surprised look on his face. As he waved about the recently won FA Cup, he cheerfully confessed he knew very little about the game. Instead he was going to look after the finances. 'I will leave the football to Terry,' he explained. With Sugar in charge of making money, the combination was inevitably described as 'a winning team'.

The sale of Irving Scholar's shares to Sugar and Venables' company Edennote had gone through at a price of 75p per share. With shares bought from Bobroff, Sugar and Venables had taken a 36 per cent interest in the PLC for a total cost of about £1.5 million each. This was hardly a strain on Sugar; his personal worth was at least £130 million.

The £1.5 million was always going to be harder for Venables to find. The source turned out to be a finance company called Norfina, which had given him a £2 million 'hot' loan to be repaid within a year at a high rate of interest. The loan was insured and the insurance arrangement secured, in turn, on Venables' own holding in Tottenham. To some this arrangement seemed less than stable. But Venables was adamant that he could meet the steep repayments from his own resources: a task that would be made easier by his new £255,000 (plus bonuses) chief executive's salary. The deal made him one of the most highly paid employees in the country, and represented a 40 per cent increase on the £175,000 he had received as team manager under the Scholar regime. The manager's job went to Peter Shreeves, who would handle the day-to-day coaching of the team, with Venables taking overall responsibility in a more strategic role.

The PLC they had bought was still saddled with enormous debts. The main item was the money owed to Midland. Mightily relieved that Sugar was now running the show, the bank was happy to convert £11 million worth of the overdraft into an agreed loan facility that could be paid off in instalments out of anticipated profits. But there was an important condition: the facility was to be reduced by the value of any asset disposals, which meant that the money from the delayed sale of Gascoigne would go straight to the bank. Working on a sale price of £5 million for the injured player, the Midland expected the size of the loan to be down to £6 million by the end of the year.

Other financial debris remained to be swept up. The £1.1 million loan made by Scholar to finish the purchase of Lineker, and financed by Maxwell, was still out-standing. The original plan was to pay back Scholar, and therefore Maxwell, from the proceeds of Uncle Bob's abortive Plan for Greatness rights issue. Instead, the loan period was extended, with liability assigned to Sugar, increasing the true size of his initial personal investment to £3 million. An undischarged £1 million loan note, given as part payment to the previous owners of Martex and Stumps, was renegotiated. The note, which gave its owners the right to close down Tottenham and demand the sale of White Hart Lane to realise their money, had been the bane of Scholar's life during the last few months of his regime. Now it was renegotiated, and was to be paid off in instalments finishing in April 1993.

With the debts brought under control in this way, the next financial chore facing Sugar and Venables was the mandatory legal requirement to make the same offer of 75p a share, given to Scholar and Bobroff, to the remaining shareholders.

This was a tricky and potentially expensive business. If all the shareholders took up the offer, it would cost Sugar and Venables another £5 million, on top of the £3 million they had spent to buy out the old regime. The only winners would be grateful shareholders happy to cut their losses and, like Scholar, to have done with the whole affair. Sugar and Venables stood to gain a bigger stake in the company, but this was hardly worth paying for: their 36 per cent stake had already guaranteed them effective control.

Venables and Sugar therefore pleaded with shareholders not to take up the offer. They got an undertaking from Berry and others on the board, with a total of about 11 per cent of the shares between them, not to sell. But institutional and speculative investors, trapped by the October suspension of shares, grabbed the money and ran. The mandatory offer cost Venables and Sugar another £1.5 million each, taking their joint stake to 65 per cent.

The rest of the shares remained in the hands of Berry and other boardroom allies, with about 20 per cent scattered amongst the fan shareholders who, as expected, loyally agreed not to cash in.

Sugar and Venables' total investment now stood at £3 million each and, once again, Venables must have found the process of raising of the extra £1.5 million much less comfortable than his partner had. Venables used the remaining half million of the £2 million loan agreed with Norfina, supplementing it with £750,000 from his own

280

pocket and £250,000 borrowed from Igal Yawetz, an architect.

Secure in their control of the company, and sitting at the head of a united board, Venables thanked the Tottenham Independent Supporters' Association and the fans in general for the 'tremendous support' they had given to his takeover bid. In return, he promised that the PLC would in future 'concentrate on football and closely related activities to ensure that Tottenham Hotspur FC takes full advantage of the opportunities which your board believes will be open to the major clubs over the next few years'. This was a reference to the old Super-League idea, and associated sale of TV rights, which had finally come into being as the Premier League.

At the end of the season all Division One clubs had announced their intention to resign from the Football League, establishing a new Premier League that would be linked to the Football Association but which would be organised by its own managing body. Venables at once joined the Premier League Committee, joining fellow Tottenham supporter Sir John Quinton, of Barclays Bank, who became chairman. The committee was immediately plunged into a wrangle over the number of clubs to be relegated and promoted between the Premier League and the Football League. The Premier League replaced the old Division One and the bottom clubs were to be relegated to the Football League's new Division One which, in effect, was the old Division Two.

As the new season, destined to be the last for the Football League Division One, began, the Premier League began limbering up for another of the financial 'opportunities' mentioned by Venables: the new deal with the TV companies. Informed comment soon put the value of Premier TV rights at £20 million per year, to be shared by Premier clubs only and not by all 92 League clubs as previously. This would guarantee at least £1 million for each premier club; plus the separately negotiated fees for European games.

By December 1991, six months after their takeover,

Venables and Sugar felt sufficiently confident to make a rights issue of Tottenham shares, bringing in money to pay off some more of the debts. The issue took place on the same day as half-year figures were published showing no real improvement in the company's trading position.

The PLC had projected losses of £3 million for the year, almost double the figure for the previous year. Despite this the offer was a success, but mainly because Sugar bought most of the new shares on offer to him. He had already made an unsecured £7 million loan to the club and he used the offer to convert the loan into equity at the premium price of 110p per share. This left him with about half the total shares in the company.

The PLC announced its intention to make another rights offer in the future; and this left Sugar in a strong position. If and when Tottenham came strongly into profit, investors would be again queuing up for shares in a rights issue. This would bring a lot of new capital in to the company but, since his personal holding was so large, Sugar would always remain in control. There were now no doubts that he was calling the shots.

But by the time of the rights issue the Sugar – Venables takeover was more popular than ever. The main reason was the death of Robert Maxwell in November and the threatened collapse of his empire. More marginal parts of the Maxwell operation, like his *European* newspaper, collapsed at once (though the *European* was immediately bought by a consortium of property developers) and others were sold off.

Sugar had meanwhile personally underwritten the sale of Gascoigne at the price of £5 million, kindling the quixotic hope that he might pay the money to Midland himself and keep Gascoigne at the club. Events on the field showed how desperately the team needed Gascoigne, or an extra player of his class and price tag. Venables had caused gasps at the start of the season when he bought striker Gordon Durie from Chelsea for £2.2 million. But Durie did not settle in well and the team had to rely on an endless stream of goals from Lineker.

But not even Lineker could prevent Tottenham's early exit from the Cup Winners' Cup. In the new year Lineker's performance seemed to be threatened by personal tragedy: his baby son George had contracted a rare form of leukaemia and was said to be close to death. With the full and generous support of Venables, Lineker missed a few games so he could concentrate on his family. Early in the new year, George's health improved and Lineker returned to the team. He continued to score goals, but the team was knocked out of the FA Cup in the third round by Aston Villa, and a string of losses in the League took Tottenham dangerously close to the relegation zone. Harry Harris and others in the fraternity of soccer hacks sharpened their pens, savouring the huge irony of Spurs' relegation which, in this season, would mean failure to qualify for the Premier Division.

It was not to be. In April Lineker scored two goals in a win over relegation rivals Luton, virtually guaranteeing Tottenham's place in the Premier. The revival in Tottenham's fortunes had been almost entirely due to Lineker, who had scored seven goals in four matches. By then it was known that Lineker himself would not be playing in the new League, having signed for the improbably named Japanese club Grampus Eight of Nagoya for an equally improbable fee, said to be in the region of £10 million.

The last week of the season left Tottenham with nothing to play for, but it did see the return of Gascoigne to football in a Spurs shirt – even if he was playing for the reserves in a friendly against the Tottenham youth team. This sort of fixture would not normally attract much press interest, but the presence of Gazza ensured that there were more tabloid cameramen present than at the average Division One match. Gascoigne duly scored a brilliant goal and then went into Gazza mode diving into a puddle on the pitch and splashing about: 'SPLISH, SPLOSH, LOTSA DOSH'. After passing final medical tests, he was transferred to Lazio.

Tottenham was safe, for the time being at least. But the

redistribution of TV wealth implied by the Premier League pushed the poorer clubs of the lower divisions even further into crisis and one, Aldershot, promptly went out of business before the end of the season. It also led to demands for a bigger slice of TV money to go to the players. Late in the season, with Cup finals and crucial League games pending, the Professional Footballers' Association threatened to strike unless the Premier League agreed to pay it a guaranteed £1.5 million share of any TV money, mainly to pay for insurance and medical fees for players. When the League refused to pay up, the PFA balloted its members and received the support of 90 per cent of Division One players. The League gave in and the PFA won the £1.5 million, plus a further 5 per cent of any earnings from TV rights over £10 million.

The TV bombshell that dropped turned out to be worth far more. In May 1992 the Premier League signed a deal with Sky TV (just as Maxwell feared) and the BBC, worth £304 million over five years, but with Sky contibuting most of the money and getting the lion's share of the coverage. Alan Sugar's role in the deal was controversial. After declaring his interest as the manufacturer of Sky's dishes, he lobbied hard for the rejection of a rival bid from ITV. The other clubs from the Big Five opposed him, claiming that whilst ITV was offering less money, Sky wanted to screen far more live matches. Overexposure, they said, would damage the game by reducing attendances. Both Sugar and Sky had no such doubts; their financial strategy overrode any other consideration. Once again, the question of football's future was raised with increasing urgency: would soccer continue as a live spectator sport, or simply become a TV experience, scheduled for the benefit of armchair viewers?

CHRONOLOGY

TOTTENHAM HOTSPUR

1981 AND BEFORE

1882: Hotspur club formed by boys from local cricket club and grammar school.

1908: Enter Football League Division Two, and are promoted to Division One at first attempt.

1936: East Stand built on uncovered side of ground.

1938: Record crowd of 75,038 established for sixth round FA Cup match against Sunderland. Still unbeaten.

1951: Football League champions.

1961: Spurs Glory, Glory team do the Double.

1963: Spurs win European Cup Winners' Cup and become the first British club to win a European tournament.

1969: For the first time in a decade Spurs finish lower in the League than Arsenal. Arsenal finish higher than Spurs in sixteen out of the next twenty seasons.

1971: Arsenal do the Double.

1974: Bill Nicholson resigns as team manager, and is replaced by Keith Burkinshaw.

1978: Ricky Villa and Ossie Ardiles bought from Racing Club, Argentina for £700,000.

1979: Decision taken to rebuild the West Stand.

1981: According to legend, Scholar has 'road to Damascus' idea to buy club on M1 *en route* to watch Spurs at Leeds United.

1981: Domestic transfer market peaks with Manchester United buying Bryan Robson from WBA for £1.5 million. Market does not recover until 1987.

1982

January: Robert Maxwell injects £128,000 into Oxford United two weeks before closure. Elected chairman of club at emergency board meeting.

February: Spurs' West Stand opens, with 72 executive boxes, described as 'a luxury hotel with seats on top'.

December: Scholar and Paul Bobroff take over effective control of Spurs after Arthur Richardson resigns. Douglas Alexiou becomes club chairman.

1983

May: Saatchi and Saatchi appointed as Spurs' advertising agency and marketing consultants.

August: First-ever live League matches on TV. Spurs advertise on TV.

October: Maxwell puts Oxford United up for sale, saying he is a Division One chairman and Oxford are not a Division One club.

October: Tottenham Hotspur PLC floated. Bobroff chairman of PLC. Scholar chairman of club with 26 per cent block of shares.

1984

February: Maxwell bids £10 million to buy Manchester

United, but pulls out when price is increased to £15 million. Buys Derby County instead.

May: Spurs win UEFA Cup final on penalties at White Hart Lane.

July: Maxwell buys the Mirror Group.

August: Keith Burkinshaw resigns as team manager, complaining that Tottenham has become a business rather than a football club. Peter Shreeves becomes manager.

1985

March: Millwall fans riot in Luton, injuring 47. Start of series of soccer riots and disasters, culminating in Bradford fire and Heysel tragedies.

May: Maxwell's Oxford United are promoted to Division One for the first time, and win Milk Cup.

June: English teams indefinitely banned from European competitions.

July: Spurs set up Hummel UK franchising operation.

August: New season starts with no TV coverage for the first time since 1964. Attendance at soccer matches collapses.

October: Saatchi-inspired SuperLeague plan leaked to the papers.

December: Humiliating TV rights deal – only £1.5 million for rest of season.

1986

January: Spurs shares at all-time low of 52p (half issue price).

June: Team finishes tenth in Division One. Shreeves sacked as manager and replaced by David Pleat from Luton.

July: Spurs sell Cheshunt training ground to help cover losses.

1987

March: Tony Berry of Blue Arrow, financial Golden Boy, joins the board. Spurs shares soon reach all-time high of more than 250p despite poor trading figures.

June: Pleat 'monstered' by the *Sun* after allegedly associating with prostitutes. Resigns and is replaced as manager by Terry 'El Tel' Venables in November.

August: Berry's Blue Arrow pulls off £800 million takeover of the US Manpower Corporation. City takeover mania peaks.

November: Maxwell in failed £2 million bid to get control of Elton John's Watford. Club interests now include Derby, Oxford, Reading, Manchester United and Watford.

December: Venables announces aim of winning Division One within a few seasons: 'We have not got time to fanny around'. Loses first home match to Charlton Athletic.

1988

May: Spurs finish thirteenth in League: worst season for many years.

June: New League television deal brings in £11 million after a bidding war between ITV and new satellite stations.

July: During close season Venables goes on transfer spending spree. Signings include Paul 'Gazza' Gascoigne, bought for £2 million from Newcastle United: a new British record.

August: First home game of the season (against Coventry City) called off because of ground developments. Two

League points deducted. Players 'gutted'.

1989

March: Bob Holt of Blue Arrow appointed chief executive, to supervise acquisition of further leisure subsidiaries.

May: Half-million trading loss recorded by Hummel subsidiary. Board decides to try to expand its way out of trouble.

May: Arsenal win League championship; Spurs finish sixth. Intense pressure on Venables to improve Spurs' performance.

June: Venables buys Lineker from Barcelona for £1.2 million.

July: Chris Waddle sold to Marseille for £4.25 million at start of season. Outcry from fans.

September: Paul Bobroff resigns as chairman of the PLC and then is reinstated. First public sign of serious splits on the board over commercial policy.

1990

March: Maxwell again involved in attempts to buy Manchester United. He is rejected and considers buying first Arsenal and then Tottenham.

June: Spurs losses for year are £2.6 million. Trading profit of £1.3 million wiped out by interest charges and cost of winding up trading agreement with Hummel UK, which has gone bust. Debt of £12 million to Midland Bank caused mainly by East Stand cost overruns. Figures not published until January 1991.

Summer: Bobroff preoccupied with defending his company, Markheath Securities, against a hostile takeover.

July: Gascoigne 'Tears of Turin' during Italia 90 World Cup. *Sunday Times* estimates his transfer value has increased to £15 million and has driven up Spurs' share price.

July: Ban on English clubs lifted, increasing the importance of immediate success in the League.

July: Maxwell secretly loans £1.1 million to Scholar's private company to prevent the 'repossession' of Lineker by Barcelona. Then agrees to underwrite £12 million rights issue at 130p for maximum 25.1 per cent of shares.

August: Iraqi invasion of Kuwait. World share prices plunge, causing a cash crisis for Maxwell, who pulls out of the Tottenham deal and puts all his football interests up for sale.

September: Maxwell is bounced into going ahead with the Tottenham deal after his involvement is leaked to the press.

October: Bobroff, opposed to the Maxwell plan, is ousted from the chair by Scholar. Tottenham shares suspended at 91p until Maxwell's role is clarified. Scholar then forced to resign as PLC chairman after Stock Exchange censure over Maxwell dealings.

November: Venables announces intention to buy Tottenham.

1991

March: Nat Solomon, under pressure from the Midland Bank, accepts Lazio's offer of £7.9 million for Gascoigne. Spurs liabilities reported to be in region of £22 million. Scholar announces Gascoigne and Lineker will not be sold while he still has an effective controlling interest in the club. Venables' first bid to buy the company is rejected.

April: Second Venables bid rejected. Team doing very badly in the League because of lack of money to replace injured players.

May: Spurs win FA Cup final against Nottingham Forest. Gascoigne seriously injures his leg, placing Lazio transfer in doubt.

June: Maxwell's last-minute bid to buy the club defeated when Scholar sells his stake to Terry Venables and Alan Sugar.

November: Maxwell dies.

1992

May: Premier League signs five-year exclusive live deal with Sky TV worth £304 million. Sugar is instrumental in clinching deal against 'Big Five' opposition.

BIBLIOGRAPHY

Ball, Peter and Shaw, Phil, *The Book of Football Quotations*. Stanley Paul, London, 1990.

Bateson, Bill and Sewell, Albert (eds.), *News of the World Football Annual, 1991–92*. Invincible Press, 1991.

Crick, Michael and Smith, David, *Manchester United: the Betrayal of a Legend*. Pan Books, London, 1990.

Davies, Hunter, *The Glory Game*. Mainstream, Edinburgh, 1990.

Davies, Pete, *All Played Out: The Full Story of Italia '90*. Mandarin, London, 1990.

Docherty, Tommy, *Call the Doc*. Hamlyn, London, 1981.

Fenwick, Terry, *Earning My Spurs*. Mainstream, Edinburgh, 1989.

Fynn, Alex and Guest, Lynton, *The Secret Life of Football*. Queen Anne Press, London, 1989.

Fynn, Alex and Guest, Lynton, *Heroes and Villians: The Inside Story of the 1990 Season at Arsenal and Tottenham Hotspur*. Penguin, London, 1991.

Goodwin, Bob, *Spurs: a Complete Record, 1882–1991*. Breedon Books, Derby, 1991.

Greaves, Jimmy, *Taking Sides*. Sidgwick and Jackson, London, 1984.

Green, Geoffrey, *Encyclopedia of Association Football*, Caxton, London, 1960.

Harris, Harry, *Tottenham Hotspur Greats*. Sportsprint, Edinburgh, 1990.

Inglis, Simon, *League Football and the Men Who Made It*. Collins, London, 1983.

Inglis, Simon, *The Football Grounds of Great Britain*. Willow Books, London, 1987.

Ley, John, *Rags to Riches: The Rise and Rise of Oxford United*. Queen Anne Press, London, 1985.

McGibbon, Robin, *Gazza!: A Biography*. Penguin, London, 1990.

Neill, Terry, *Revelations of a Football Manager*. Sidgwick and Jackson, London, 1985.

Rothmans Football Yearbook (1972–1992). Queen Anne Press, London.

Soar, Phil, *Encyclopedia of British Football*. Willow Books, 1988.

The Spur (various editions).

Thomas, David, *Alan Sugar: The Amstrad Story*. Century, London, 1990.

Tottenham Hotspur, *Official Handbook (various years)*.

Venables, Fred, *Terry Venables, Son of Fred*. Weidenfield and Nicholson, London, 1990.

Wall, Bob, *Arsenal from the Heart*. Souvenir Press, London, 1969.

Wilson, Neil, *The Sports Business*. Piatkus, London, 1988.